To Ela[...], a dear friend, Thank you for your interest

Generations

[signature] Sept 05, 20[..]

Generations

A Commentary on the History of the African
Immigrants and their American Descendents

Les Washington

Writers Club Press
New York Lincoln Shanghai

Generations
A Commentary on the History of the African Immigrants and their
American Descendents

Writers Club Press
an imprint of iUniverse, Inc.

For information address:
iUniverse
2021 Pine Lake Road, Suite 100
Lincoln, NE 68512
www.iuniverse.com

ISBN: 0-595-25386-5 (Pbk)
ISBN: 0-595-65141-0 (Cloth)

Printed in the United States of America

DEDICATION

This effort is dedicated to the members of the nineteenth (1966–1995) and twentieth generations (1986–2015) of black Americans to whom the torch is passed. For they are the generations whose academic, entrepreneurial, and moral successes will plot the course of the black American community for the next century.

It is also dedicated to my parents. It is, after all, only a composite of my heritage. They were the ones who taught me that self-esteem and self-confidence are products of the correct mixture of arrogance and humility. Also, I thank them for the notions of refined parental responsibility they, who were of the sixteenth generation (1906–1935), instilled within each of their seventeenth generation (1926–1955) children as we were growing up.

CONTENTS

LIST OF TABLES

PREFACE

When water molecules are cooled to a very low temperature, they form ice. When heated to a very hot temperature, they become steam vapor. At a point between these two extremes, the H_2O molecules form a liquid, their fittest state. Similarly then, the fittest state for the black American community exist somewhere between being the perennial victim and exceeding to ethnic arrogance. It is this fittest state lying between these two extremes that the black American community will attain socioeconomic resonance. And with socioeconomic resonance will come the self-esteem and self-confidence that will motivate them to achieve socioeconomic parity in the market places of America. It is the goal and objective of this commentary to alert the black American community of the urgency of applying an internal affirmative action program to launch a much-needed re-invention of it self. The success, or failure, of this work, rest quite literally upon its ability to convey certain assertions; some tradi-tional, and others more innovative. For that to work it must become a suc-cessful *town crier*. Each assertion, the traditional and the more innovative, must be convincingly relayed to all living generations of the black American community. The black American community, or BAC, consists of the five, and sometime six generations of children, parents, grandpar-ents, great-grandparents, great great grandparents, and even great-great-great-grandparents. Therefore, it is imperative that this commentary establishes itself as a medium akin to the historical town crier of the pre-mass-communication era. Through it, members of the "parents" genera-tion will have ready access to the cultural and moral estate of the four senior generations of their generational heritage.

As stated, this commentary is as the voice of the town crier. And as the town crier's voice is not modulated in the smooth tones of the music scale, neither are the words of this commentary necessarily compliant with the tone and writing style of classic literary form. I therefore plead your tolerance in areas where the concepts may not be as defined as they ought, nor the skills of grammar as polished as becomes a professional writer. I am after all, as a town crier, a novice. I know only that I must callout at the top of my voice in an effort to draw attention to a situation that I think warrants concern.

ACKNOWLEDGEMENTS

It is not possible to acknowledge all the support and encouragement that I have received during the course of this work. However, I would like to take this opportunity to pay tribute to some.

However, I do wish to acknowledge the motivation and source of encouragement that I received from my eleventh grade homeroom teacher back during high school. Her inspirational counseling—seemingly a thousand years ago now—provided a solid anchor for my inspiration.

To my family, I owe a corner slice of gratitude. To my daughters Jacquelyn and Theresa, thank you for your tolerance and patience. To my grand daughters Briana and Taylor, I love you both very much. Briana, forgive me for all the times that Grandpa might have been "to busy."

Thanks to all of my family for allowing me to be so self-indulgent with my time—time that rightfully belonged to them.

Lastly, to the many friends and well-wishers, especially those of SBC, and to co-workers who, knowing of my aspirations, became a constant source of support and encouragement.

Introduction

AN OVERVIEW: IN THE LEGACY OF THE 1619 AFRICANS

In 1619, twenty men and women, citizens of an African country arrived in Jamestown, Virginia, aboard a "man o' warre" ship. Certain historical facts tend to suggest that the ship flew the flag of Holland.

This commentary looks at the circumstances surrounding the arrival of those twenty Africans and seeks to establish continuity between them and the thirty-five million black Americans who live, work, play, and have their being in America today. In this attempt to establish continuity between the generations of the black American community, certain traditional approaches will be challenged. As one reads through this commentary, he or she will undoubtedly notice that the term "black Americans" is used throughout, rather than the current, and perhaps more politically correct term "African-Americans. It employs the term "black American" because it is considered by the author to be a more generic definition of the black American community's American nationalism. The truest characterization of the black Americans' nationalism is of course, simply "Americans." However, since the focuses of this commentary addresses both black and white Americans, "black Americans" is used to differentiate between them. "Black Americans" will be utilized when referring to the descendents of the African immigrants and the term "white Americans" will be used when referring to the descendents of the European immigrants.

What makes the term "black American" more generic one might ask? It's certainly not because all descendents of the African immigrants have black skin. We know that since being brought to America, the gene pool of the original African immigrants has been expanded considerably. It now includes descendents from a wide range, or assortment of other racial groups; consequently, the range of skin color variation among the black American community varies considerably. Therefore, the use of the modifier in "black Americans" does not intend to suggest that the descendents of the African immigrants all have black skin. It simply aligns itself with one of the more common features consistent among members of the black American community. For if one's African hood is not sustained by the compound term "black American," then neither is it sustained in the hyphenated term African-American. Hence the black American application is considered to be more generic because of its widespread use and its natural applicability, and because the opposing option constitutes a less-favorable designation of nationalism. Actually, applying of the term "African-American" at this late date in our American residency smacks of the classic rebuttal lines of a disenchanted stepchild who tells his disciplining stepfather, "You're not my *real* daddy anyway."

There are other reasons for preferring the use of "black American." The first of those reasons is that the descendents of other immigrant groups in America do not all hyphenate their American nationality. So, unless and until all Americans, the native Americans, the English, the Irish, the Germans, the Jews, the Poles, the Italians, and all other ethnic groups are prepared to hyphenate their American nationality, then neither should black Americans hyphenate theirs. Another reason is—and this one is much more personal—I believe fervently that America belongs as much to the black Americans as descendents of the African immigrants as it does to the white Americans as descendents of European immigrants. Therefore, I believe that to apply the modifier "African" before American is to suggest that there are "Americans" and then there are "African-Americans." This designation seems to imply that the descendents of the African immigrants are somehow one tier removed from being "true" or "real" Americans. I take strong personal exception to any such implication, or allusion. Another reason for not using the hyphenated term is because Mr. Nelson Mandela does not refer to himself as an African-South African. And if Mr. Mandela—former president of South Africa, a man of worldwide recognition, and winner of the 1993 Nobel Peace Prize—is comfortable describing his nationality and that of his associates as "black South Africans," then what greater validation can there be for the black American community's use of "black Americans" as an equally appropriate designation of their nationality?

Black Americans should abhor the use of any word, term, notion, or thought that would, in even the most remote way, suggest that they, as descendents of the Africans, are not deservedly as American as others. Furthermore, they should also refute the use of "African-American" as insufficient to characterize their American heritage, one that has been handed down to the black American community by ancestors who gave of themselves in much the same manner as those who served and died on the nation's battlefields gave of themselves, to build this great and powerful nation. The black American community should hold in disdain any assertion that suggests they are more African than American. They should do this not because they love Africa less, but because, to paraphrase Shakespeare's Brutus, they love America more.

The next, and perhaps more convincing reason for discontinuing the use of the African-American designation is because members of the eleventh generation (1806–1835) voted to discontinue using it. At a black American convention held in Philadelphia in June of 1835, convention members voted to direct black Americans to stop referring to themselves as "Africans." That decision was made one hundred fifty-eight years ago by a generation of black Americans who were considerably more in touch with their African roots than members of either of the current black

American community generations can boast. They also directed their members to stop identifying their businesses as "African." Instead, they were to allow the names of their business, organizations, and institutions to reflect their American nationalism rather than their African past.

Such arguments as these and others contained throughout this commentary are submitted as cautionary notes to the black American community and to those who, for whatever motives, are seeking to construct an African-centered national identity for the black American community. To achieve such an objective would be the equivalent to putting the black American community on an ethnic reservation. In a sense, such an approach would have the black American community patterning itself into a new kind of reservation community. Establishing such a reservation within the social ethos of the black American community would have the unfortunate effect of being *in* America, but not *of* America. I would argue—and our heritage supports this contention—that the black American community is *of* America, and not just *in* America. All socioeconomic indicators will support the premise that the social and economic integration of the black American community is far more beneficial to its advancement, both socially and economically, than if it segregates itself from the mainstream. The real beneficiaries to a resolution of this dilemma will be black American children. Today, caught up in the confusion of who they are and where they fit, instead of seeking to become increasingly more and more integrated into the mainstream of American life, wherein is the promise of their socioeconomic advancement, they are instead, increasingly caught up in a dead-end mode of social and cultural protest; hosting attitudes and engaging in activities that will ultimately prove to be counter-productive to their own career objectives.

According to U.S. Census Bureau data, there are approximately eight to nine million black American boys and girls currently in the twentieth generation (1986–2015), those born since 1986. It is time to tell them they are not children of a lesser god, nor are they children of a lesser America, but are of the same America. Therefore, my final exception to the use of "African-American" as a favored definition of our nationalism is on behalf of black America's children. One need not be a practitioner of the social or psychological sciences to appreciate the potentially harmful effect such an identity crisis can have in the lives of these children. Understanding who they are and where they fit in is a valuable asset to the maturation process.

Integration into the mainstream of American life does not mean that members of the black American community must ignore their own particular mores and traditions. Even the idea of America as a melting pot does not require ethnic homogeneity. Actually, life in America is much more like a family reunion than a true melting pot. Consider the example of a typical family reunion where the heads of the extended family unit are a Mr. and Mrs. U. R. America. They live in a small town we'll figuratively call Main Town, USA. At their family re-union in the bi-centennial year 2000, Mr. and Mrs. U. R. America's five adult children; their nine adult grandchildren; and their twelve great-grandchildren, all minors, were in attendance. Even though this family reunion was a relatively small affair, there were fifteen different nuclear family units present. The analogy is that, even though there were fifteen different nuclear families at Mr. and Mrs. U. R. America's family reunion, they were all of the same family. And that is also how the cultural structure of America operates. The melting-pot phenomenon provides the basis for a single cultural and national identity while recognizing the uniqueness of each individual ethnic community. Metaphorically, all in attendance were members of the Mr. and Mrs. U. R. America's family reunion, yet each nuclear family present had its own distinct family name, its own respective other-family affiliations, and each lived in different hometowns. So in spite of all the ethnic diversity in America, as with the Mr. and Mrs. U. R. America family reunion, America's unity is not challenged nor is the integrity of its cultural fabric offended. The individual nuclear families participating in the reunion are reflective of the many different ethnic communities existing in America.

Each has its own particular identity, origins, traditions, and operational mores but all share a common American affiliation. And all are steeped in the fundamentals of a cultural and national American identity.

The issue of national identity is not the only area where this commentary will challenge the conventional way of viewing things. Therefore, be advised that, as you read on, you will notice the use of other "politically incorrect" applications. In two such instances, the Africans who were brought over to America are referred to in this commentary as "immigrants" rather than as slaves. And, they are referred to as having been "enslaved" rather than being referred to as "slaves." The allusion to the Africans "being enslaved" as opposed to "being slaves" may be a relatively minor point so many years later, but I am inclined to think it more consistent with the focus of this commentary. For while history does record that the Africans were enslaved, it does not record that they *became* slaves. That is, history does not assert that the Africans acquiesced to slavery. On the contrary, the number and frequency of protests, sabotages, insurrections, and revolts clearly suggest that though they were enslaved, they never "became slaves."

The other instance in which a question might be raised is in my referring to the Africans as "immigrants," again avoiding use of the term "slaves." This designation is used, even though the traditional approach has always been to refer to them as "slaves." My reasoning for the different approach is, on the whole, rather simple. As history records it, the Africans left Africa—the circumstances of their leaving notwithstanding—and subsequently settled in America. That simple statement also describes all other immigrants that ultimately settled in America. There may be any number of valid arguments against the use of "immigrants" rather than "slaves," but since an immigrant is defined simply as "one who leaves a country to settle permanently in another," it is not possible to disqualify the Africans from being rightfully described as "immigrants." After all, this definition makes no distinction as to whether those who were leaving a country were doing so of their own free will or were being forcibly relocated. Often, immigrant groups consist of war refugees, refugees from famines, persons fleeing for, or being deported for other reasons. Such immigrants were also being forcibly relocated. So whether one is relocated as conscripted labor or otherwise within the latitude of the definition, they would be immigrants. Therefore, we were obliged to accord the Africans brought to America the same definitional status as other "immigrants." Even as this is being written, there are black Americans of a particular view who will protest that the Africans were not immigrants but slaves. The contention can be seen as being analogous to a hitchhiker out to catch a ride. Simply because a would-be hitchhiker catches a ride before he or she has the opportunity to stick out a thump does not preempt his or her claim of being a hitchhiker. In the same context, it does not matter that the Africans were forced to immigrate to America. It is entirely possible that with the ever-increasing frequency of European ships trading in and out of African waters, the Africans might have, of their own volition, chosen to immigrate to American in much the same fashion as the millions of other foreigners did.

Besides, despite all the apparent differences between the status of the 1619 Africans and the 1620 Pilgrims, there were a number of similarities. Accordingly, the English immigrants—the Pilgrims—sold themselves into indentured servitude prior to leaving Europe, and upon their arrival in America, they began serving their European "masters" for the terms of their indentures. Conversely, the African immigrants were sold into indenture upon their arrival at Jamestown. Also, while it is true that the Africans were abducted from Africa and brought to America against their will, some Europeans were also abducted from Europe and brought to America against their will. They, too, were sold into indenture upon their arrival at Jamestown.

Part One

THE AFRICANS

"About the last of August,
came a Dutch Man o' Warre
that sold us twenty Negroes"
      The Diary of John Rolfe

1

LEGACY OF THE 1619 AFRICANS

On April 12, 1990, at 11:58 P.M., my first grandchild, Briana Robinson, was born. Her birth, though precious to me, her grandfather, was in all other regards indistinguishable from the birth of a countless number of other American babies born that same month and date. However, because Briana is of African descent and because she was born between 1986 and 2015, she does bear a measure of genealogical distinction. As a black American born during that particular time period, she is representative of the twenty generations of Africans and the descendents of Africans who have called America home since that fateful day toward the last of August in 1619. It was in that year, 1619, that John Rolfe (friend, suitor, and husband to the famed native American princess Pocahontas) wrote in his personal diary, "About the last of August, came a Dutch Man o' Warre that sold us twenty Negroes." In what can surely be termed one of history's grandest understatements, John Rolfe's unembroidered notation, in retrospect, hardly seems an adequate or appropriate bugle call for the social and political drama that was to be played out in this country as the result of the arrival of those twenty "Negroes." From this beginning—the 1619 docking in Jamestown, Virginia, of a Dutch ship, characterized by John Rolfe as a "Man o' Warre," and the sale of twenty Africans he identified as "Negroes" (the Spanish word for people with black skins)—began a saga that would call into account the morality of the social and political thought of America and, ultimately, of the world.

The arrival of those twenty Africans, though they were not the first Africans in America, represented the vanguard of an institution and an industry that would, for 246 years, survive in the unkempt median lying between the merging lanes of the sociopolitical practices of the past and the advancing sociopolitical concepts of the future. Unlike the simple annotation in Rolfe's diary announcing the arrival of the 1619 Africans, the concept of advanced sociopolitical thinking arrived on the scene with the proverbial bang. Whereas Rolfe's announcement was a precursor to the institution of slavery, the new concept of natural individual rights was a precursor of the demise of that *peculiar* institution. Entering the sociopolitical spectrum from the lanes of evolving religious freedom, the notion of the natural rights of the individual was ultimately destined to clash with slavery's abject denial of such rights. Slavery, in all of its various forms, reprehensible as it is and was even then, had always managed to survive within the social and political systems of the nations of the world as integral components of their socioeconomic franchises. The convergence of these two events, as though engaged in a turf war over morality, would, years later, crash into each other with the sound of cannon fire at Fort Sumter. Actually, that proverbial bang manifested itself as two separate bangs. The first—more like bang, bang, bang—occurred as the resultant sounds of Martin Luther's hammer as he nailed his ninety-five theses onto the door of the Castle Church in Wittenberg on October 31, 1517, almost one hundred years before the 1620 arrival of the Puritans in America. That action would subsequently be interpreted as the beginning of the Reformation movement. More properly called the Protestant Reformation, it began as a movement against what Luther considered to be papal abuses by the Catholic Church. Instead of internal reformation within the Catholic Church, his revolt actually signaled the beginnings of an entirely new denominational doctrine. The doctrinal revisions were not simply about church structure and disciplines but also in the fundamental concepts of the individual's relationship to God and the church. Under the movement, the individual was defined not as an insubstantial link in the chain of beings, but essentially as executor of his own religious, social, and political estate.

History of Slavery as a System of Labor Management

At one time or another, almost all the world's countries have utilized slavery. Institutionalized slavery as a labor distribution system dates from the time of the ancient Babylonian empire. While details surrounding the social life of the average Babylonian four thousand years ago are scant, it is known that as early as 2100 B.C. Babylonian society was made up of both free persons and slaves. Babylonian business transactions written onto clay tablets speak of Babylonian landowners or plantation owners using slave labor to work their farms. From the time of Babylon until its gradual emancipation during the later part of the 1800s, slavery in its various forms had been utilized as the accepted and almost exclusive system of labor management and the distribution of labor. The use and institutionalization of slavery in Europe began with the Greeks in the eighth century B.C. and spread rapidly. Almost three thousand years ago, in 750 B.C. certain events occurred that caused the Greek civilization to face a large and sudden demand for additional manpower, not unlike the one Europeans encountered following their discovery of the Americas. To meet such demands, the Greeks enslaved their European war captives. Almost two thousand years later, in the face of similar demands, the Europeans enslaved African war captives. The parallels between the action taken by the ancient Greeks and those taken two thousand years later by the Europeans are striking. They are not the only similarities. Around 700 B.C. the Greeks had greatly expanded their influence in the region in and around the Black Sea and; like the western Europeans of the much later sixteenth century, were enjoying the benefits of being the most advanced civilization of their respective period. The industrial achievements of the seventh-century Greeks were tantamount to the seventeenth-century industrial revolution of Europe. It was also during that time that the oppressive rule of Greek noblemen was beginning to have a negative impact upon the living standards of the Grecian peasantry. In response, large numbers of the peasants and farmers sought new lands to harvest that were outside the control of the nobles. Conversely, although in sixteenth-century Europe the issue was not land, the oppression of religious freedoms had a very similar effect upon the European peasantry.

Greek merchants, supported by an increasing industrial capacity, were also seeking greater outlets for their goods. Their trading stations, located among the primitive Europeans who inhabited those distant regions, offered the disconnected farmers of Greece plenty of land with which to begin life all over again. Prior to the 600 B.C. expansion, the farmers and trading merchants had encircled the Black Sea with an assortment of settlements and villages. At the eastern end of the Mediterranean, the Greeks had colonized practically all of the large islands of Cyprus as far away as Egypt across the Mediterranean and had sought and received permission to establish trading sites. One such site was located at the very spot where, hundreds of years later, another Greek, Alexander the Great, would establish the city of Alexandria. But even with all the expansion the Greeks had made into the eastern region around the Black Sea and to the south into Egypt, they still had not ventured much westward. That area had not been charted by any ocean voyages and had remained virtually unknown to them.

In later years though, this unknown West would become the "America" of the early Greek colonialists. The Greeks explored Western Europe, a land they might have called the Dark Continent. Flourishing cities like Corinth, located on the isthmus of the Mediterranean, sprang up throughout the region. Their trade dealings with the western coast of Greece helped push the expansion northward along the Grecian coast. It was only a short voyage from the western coast of Greece to the coast of Italy. These coastlines were to the seventh-century B.C. Greeks what the

Americas were to the fifteenth-century A.D. European explorers—new worlds. The Greeks discovery was every bit as momentous for them as the discovery of America was for the Europeans. By 750 B.C., Greek colonies begun to be established in the new "western world." And within a hundred years their settlements and towns were all the way past present-day Naples. (As a point of note, the city of Naples had its beginning as a Greek colonial settlement. The colonizing Greeks called the city "Neopolis," or "New City.") The colonizing of America produced similar new cities such as New York, New Hampshire, and New Orleans. Greek settlements in this particular region of southern Italy became so numerous that the area became known as "Greater Greece." Again, a parallel exists between the Greeks, "Greater Greece" and the European's "New England." Just imagine: Had the Greeks elected to colonize Africa rather than Western Europe, it would have been an African archaeologist who would be pondering the ruins of past Europeans civilizations. As the Greek colonists crossed over into Sicily, they continued to live in the relatively affluent lifestyle of their homeland. As a result, they demanded extensive distribution of Greek-made products. Their colonial expansion, with the growth of industries in the Greek cities, worked almost like an overlay for the events that would follow more than two thousand years later.

Improvement in the manufacturing techniques and expansion among businessmen and manufacturers' interests led to some rather profound changes in the structure of Greek society. The new colonies of Western Europe not only had needs of their own, but they also made connections with the inland native peoples. This opened the extensive regions of Europe as a market for product made in Greek factories. As the colonizing Europeans influenced the lives of Native Americans, it was also from the much-superior Greek civilization that the primitive cultures of Europe were first introduced to things such as writing, literature, architecture, and art. Before very long, great commercial fleets of Greek trading ships carry Greek metal works, woven goods, and pottery to far distant communities.

They brought back finished products and raw foodstuffs and materials such as grain, fish, and amber. To meet the increasing demands for manufactured goods, the Greek craftsmen were forced to enlarge their small shops, which had heretofore been only large enough to supply the wants of a single estate and now had to be expanded to meet the need of a growing world market. The demand for additional manufactured goods placed large and sudden demands upon the available Greek labor supply. In response to this demand, Greek proprietors, unable to find the necessary workmen, began buying European war captives from the Greek military for use as slaves who were then trained to work in the shops and factories. Even though slavery was introduced into Greek society because of the specific need for an increase labor supply, the institution of slavery took hold and remained entrenched in Greek society for at least the next twenty-five hundred years.

As slavery was with the Greeks, so it was with the Romans. After the decline of the Greek empire, Rome—which had been among the beneficiaries of the Greek colonial expansion—emerged as the region's prominent political power. Between 200 and 150 B.C., the Roman Empire expanded rapidly. To support that rapid expansion, the Romans utilized and maintained large military forces. Drafted into its military ranks were a large number of men who normally would have been making their living by working small family farms. While these farmers were serving out their military enlistments away from their farms, more and more farming acreage was being left unattended. Worse yet, as more and more land was being left unattended, the military, through conquest, was at the same time bringing more and more lands under Roman control. So while the small family farmers were out fighting the wars, wealthy landowners back home were buying up huge estates. To meet the large and sudden demand for manpower, those wealthy landowners began buying war captives from the Roman military for use as slaves. These persons were then trained to work these large farms or plantations. Over the years, the Roman system for utilization of slaves as a labor force evolved into a system of shared harvest. Under this system, which served as the model for the use of share-croppers in the post-Civil War American South, the persons actually working the land would share the harvest with the wealthy landowner. This system, by giving those who worked the farms an actual interest in the harvest, allowed the landowners to live away from the plantation; with perhaps only an overseer remaining on the property to look after things.

Roman slavery as characterized in the Catholic Encyclopedia:

> "The Roman laws, in the heyday of the empire, treated the slave as mere chattel. The master possessed over him the power of life and death; the slave could not contract a legal marriage, or any other kind of contract; in fact he possessed no civil rights; in the eyes of the law he was not a "person." Nevertheless the settlement of natural justice asserted itself sufficiently to condemn, or at least disapprove, the conduct of masters who treated their slaves with signal inhumanity"

Feudalism as a System of Labor Management

As the Roman Empire declined, its labor management and distribution system gradually evolved into the system of medieval feudalism that dominated the whole of Europe by the fourteenth century. Feudalism, as a labor management and distribution system, relied heavily upon the relationship between a lord and his vassal. Down in hierarchy from the vassals were the serfs. The lord was like the plantation owner, and a vassal was comparable to a plantation overseer, who was himself a slave. The vassals would actually operate the farm on behalf of the lord, and the serfs would work the farm. Whereas the social positions of lord were subject to mobility, the position of the vassals and serfs were not. If you were a serf on a particular farm, you would remain so all your life, as would your children and their children. You could not move nor leave the plantation, and you, your children, and grandchildren would be forever owned by the lord of the manor, and after him, by his children, and after them, then by his children's children. Serfs could not obtain their freedom except by governmental emancipation. To the serfs of Europe, emancipation came very slowly. While the French emancipated their serfs during the latter part of the fourteenth century the English across the channel, continued the use of Feudalism for another hundred years. Feudalism was finally abolished in England during the mid part of the fifteenth century. In other European states such as Prussia, serfdom continued until 1807; and in Austria, Poland, Italy, and Spain, serfs were not emancipated until the mid part of the nineteenth century. In Russia, where living conditions and social disenfranchisement of serfs were quite possibly even worse than those of the average enslaved black American, emancipation did not come until March 3, 1861, just two years, eleven months and twenty-seven days before President Abraham Lincoln issued the Emancipation Proclamation that abolished slavery in America. (Coincidentally, as President Lincoln was assassinated following his issuance of the Emancipation Proclamation, Emperor Alexander II of Russia was also assassinated soon after issuing the Emancipation Proclamation that freed the Russian serfs.)

With the decline of feudalism and the emancipation of the serfs throughout most of Europe, workers, most of whom were peasants, gradually began to take charge of their own employment opportunities. These were undoubtedly the conditions that existed when the discovery and colonization of the Americas placed a sudden demand upon Europe for large supplies of workers. Since settlements in the New World were obviously too scarcely populated to meet the large-scale demand for workers, the colonies turned to Europe for manpower. This sudden demand prompted the creation of a new form of labor management and distribution. Actually, it was not so much a new form as it was a revisited version of feudalism, a system that was then being phased out, as free-enterprise capitalism was rapidly becoming the dominant factor in economic management. Although most of Western Europe had, with the advent of free enterprise capitalism, emancipated their serfs over a hundred years before, those serfs were, with some modifications, summoned back into servitude in an effort to meet the rising labor demands brought on by the discovery of the New World. It is appropriate to note here that it was this same neo-feudalism that would ultimately be translated as slavery when applied in the New World. Meanwhile, participants in the new modified labor management and distribution system were referred to as indentured servants.

In indenture agreements, the persons serving the indenture—usually peasants—agreed to go to the colonies and work there for a number of years, usually four to seven, in exchange for the cost of their passage. After working for the number of years, they had agreed to, they were then given a change of clothing; some land, a gun, and were set free to pursue their own fortunes. Although the indenture program was generally entered into willingly, there were numerous abuses wherein persons were simply kidnapped from the streets of England and sold into indentured servitude.

Feudalism as a System of Labor Management in the New World

During the seventeenth century, more than half of the manpower demand of the North American colonies were met not by slaves but by persons who had either signed themselves into indentured servitude or been kidnapped or consigned from prison, or had fled persecution and been involuntarily signed into indentured servitude. Initially, these were European peasants—mostly English and Germans—who met the demand for labor. In relatively large numbers they entered or were coerced into these indenture agreements with major development companies, such as the British East India Company, which were chartered by the king to develop the newly established colonies. However, as the demand for workers in the

North American colonies continued to increase, the British East India Company turned its attention away from Europe as a source of manpower and toward Africa.

The Portuguese, who had been trading in Africa for nearly a hundred years, by then had, as a proxy for Spanish interest, already turned Africa's West Coast into an a virtual manpower supply depot in their own efforts to meet the ever-increasing demands from the Spanish-held colonies of Central and South America. The demand for laborers from Africa came after the Spaniards' initial source of labor was being exhausted. Upon arriving in South and Central America, the Spaniards had enslaved millions of native populations to work in their gold and silver mines. However, succumbing to European diseases for which they had developed no immunity, millions of indigenous peoples died, depleting the local populations and thus the Spaniards' primary source of labor. This prompted the Spaniards to seek other sources for their much-needed labor supply; and because the Portuguese were already in Africa, and because Africans were generally already skilled as farmers and miners, Africans made ideal candidates for the labor markets of the New World.

Consequently, the British East India Company tapped into the African market already established by the Portuguese and Spaniards for their own labor needs. However, whereas the indenture agreements where European servants were concerned were generally accepted as legal and binding, they were less so when applied to the indentured Africans. The African immigrants, not being British subjects and thousands of miles from their own homelands and governments, lacked the course of redress or grievances available to their European counterparts. Therefore, landowners soon began violating the terms of the indentured agreements they held with their Africans tenants. Generally, this was accomplished by extending the length of their indentured service. Unscrupulous landowners, taking advantage of the Africans' lack of familiarity with the English language and law, came up with assorted trumped-up reasons for extending the length of their indentured service. This practice became so commonplace that the Africans soon found themselves locked into indenture agreements for life.

From Feudalism as a System of Labor Management in the New World to Slavery as a System of Labor Management in the New World

At first, the children of these lifetime-indentured servants were free to pursue their own lives. But many colonies soon passed legislation proclaiming that the children of these lifetime servants would themselves be in permanent bondage. This ruling defined the origin of slavery in America. Under the system of lifetime indenture, or slavery as it become known, the landowner was no longer required to release servants purchased under the indentured servitude program nor was he required to absorb the expense of sharing his profits with departing indentured servants.

From these sketches on the background of slavery, one should be able to recognize that the same forces that prompted the seventh-century Greeks to draft European war captives to work in their shops and factories—and later on the Romans use of war captives to work their fields—also prompted to European to draft millions of Africans to work their fields, mines and factories. The operative forces that powered the manpower demands of the ancient Greeks and Romans and the one that built the trade of enslaving Africans into a worldwide industry were one and the same. The issue of interest here is that the focus of these forces—market forces, as they are appropriately called—was truly as unconcerned about the race, religion, skin color, or place of origin of the potential work force as they were about their table etiquette. Workers were workers—no more, no less. There was no concern as to what the language, creed, culture, or ethnicity of the workers was; availability was the single, most significant criteria. The market force mechanism did not care whether the work force came from India, Africa, Europe, or China. It cared even less whether a worker's skin color was white, black, brown, yellow, or polka dot. Its simple and unaltered direction was, and continues even to this day to be, the availability of enough workers to meet the demands for farmers, field hands, shop workers, factories workers, fruit pickers, railroads workers, or even computer operators. And so it was with the slave-trading industry that captured Africans off the coasts of Africa and transported them thousands of miles across the ocean to the Americas. It was not simply an issue of race nearly as much as it was an economic issue. However, to the degree that slavery ever enjoyed even the remotest semblance of moral innocence, such innocence was definitely lost during the Europeans' enslavement of the Africans. Further, enslavement became not just a supplier to industry but an industry unto itself. And as such, it induced all who had the capital to invest to do so. Men, women, bankers, speculators, governors, kings, and queens alike engaged in it. Well-meaning and good folk, as well as the unscrupulous and speculators, engaged, whether directly or by proxy, in the slave trade, an activity that even in its own time was being categorized as barbarous and scandalous. From as early as the fifteenth century, the Africans were being enslaved and traded as commerce. This practice continued unabated for more than 350 years. When it finally came to an end, those who traded in the enslavement of the African people had abducted, orphaned, cajoled, shanghaied, kidnapped, murdered, maimed, raped, molested, and transported an estimated ten to fifteen million Africans to work in an assortment of places. At no other time in recorded history were such a large number of people forcibly dispersed over such a great distance over such a long duration. While to their families and friends they were loved ones and acquaintances, to the market forces of labor and of greed they were the serfs of Russia, the day-laborers of Germany, and the coal-miners of Japan's Battleship Island. They were, quite simply, expendable sources of labor.

Contrary to a point of view long held by members of the black American community, it appears that the mere availability of the supply of African workers counted far more than who they were and what their skin color was. The use of Africans as slave laborers and the trade in the enslavement of Africans itself were not fed by the racist motives of redneck bigots but by the well-refined, boardroom strategies of politicians and venture capitalists. This assessment is by no means an attempt to assuage the guilt deservedly assigned to those involved in the enslavement of the Africans, but rather to put their behavior in a perspective proper to its time and circumstance. Those politicians and venture capitalists were people who, in the modern context, may have done no more than invest their resources in an apartheid economy or to assist or hire illegal immigrants to work in their homes or businesses. It could be surmised that considerations such as the race and character of the enslaved peoples were inconsequential to such people except when used conveniently to mitigate their own personal and social guilt. If enslavement of the African was not based upon racial bigotry, one might ask what other forces could have prompted the Europeans—particularly the British, who had only about a hundred years earlier abolished feudalistic slavery—to have resorted to such enslavement.

Why Enslave the Africans?

While the answer to this question may seem obvious, some historical precedents render it less obvious. Historically, a number of other reasons exist for why peoples were enslaved. We have already discussed the fact that economics played a major role in the Greek and Roman enslavement of the people of Western Europe. But about eight hundred years before that—in and around the year 1490 B.C.—the pharaoh of Egypt issued what we today would perhaps call an executive order that enslaved more than two million Hebrews. The Hebrews, as a family clan of less than a hundred people, had migrated into Egypt over four hundred years earlier as guests of the Egyptian government. In the course of these four centuries years, the notion that they were guests of the government was forgotten.

As the Hebrew population grew, the government became increasingly suspicious of their national loyalty. The reigning Egyptian pharaoh ordered that all Hebrews were to be enslaved basing his action on the government's perception that the Hebrew population had grown so much that they had become a potential threat to Egypt's national defense. So, in an effort to ward off the risk that Egypt's large Hebrew population might one day join in battle with Egypt's enemies, the pharaoh had the rights of the Hebrews revoked and the people placed into bondage.

Another and much more recent example of this kind of government's reaction occurred in the United States. In the 1940s, Japanese citizens and Japanese nationals who lived along the west coast of the United States found themselves in a similar situation, but with considerably less stark circumstances than the Hebrews of ancient Egypt. On March 8, 1942, United States President Franklin Roosevelt issued Executive Order Number 9066, which required that the 112,000 Japanese living in the western United States be rounded up and transferred to internment centers. This order suspended the constitutional and civil rights of all west coast residents of Japanese descent. Persons covered by the order were to be apprehended and sent to one of the various camps located throughout the country. Although the action did not officially declare that the Japanese were being enslaved, for all practical purposes they were. Under the United States' judicial system, incarceration and imprisonment outside of requirements of due process are tantamount to enslavement. The federal government justified its action by saying that 112,000 Japanese living along the western coastline constituted a potential threat to the nation's security. The government's premise was that since the United States was engaged in a war with Japan, questions regarding the loyalty of the Japanese people were sufficient to warrant their detention.

However, since the Africans of the seventeenth century obviously did not pose a threat to the defense of the colonies, as was claimed of the Hebrews and of the Japanese, enslavement of the African would have to have been based upon other reasons. All indications are that this reason was the market forces of the English economy. The same forces that caused the Europeans to tap into the available pool of African labor projected an even greater profit picture if the labor supply were under permanent bondage. There existed certain economic benefits and advantages under the system of enslavement that would not have been available had the Africans simply been indentured or paid wages, as was beginning to be done in some parts of Europe. At first, the indentured-servant system was an acceptable labor management approach, but later this system was abandoned in favor of a higher yielding bottom line. For under the indenture system, an indentured servant was obliged to serve only for a limited period of time, generally four to seven years. After that time the landowner was obliged to release the indentured person and reward the departing servant with a parcel of land, a gun, and a change of clothing. Also, since European indentured servants were still citizens of their respective countries, landowners who failed to live up to the terms of the indenture agreement could be, and frequently were, taken to court. They also still had family members back home who could lobby the government on their behalf and also could, and often did, petition the colonial courts to intercede whenever a disagreement arose between them and their masters over the terms and conditions of their indenture agreements.

Although the same market forces are fully active today, they manifest themselves differently than they did then. Nowadays, when a company, a society, or a government needs more manpower, it will seeks, if a company, to hire; if a society, to import; and if a government, to draft the additional needed manpower.

In those times, however, manpower needs were met by more forceful means. And so, when the governments of Europe, Holland, Portugal, Spain, and most notably, England, went after the Africans to man the farms, factories, and shops of the New World, they went at it with force rather than with wage offers. In so doing, the English government appears to have violated the laws of its very own Magna Charta. The text of that 1215 document states that,

> "No freeman shall be taken or imprisoned, or disseized, or out-lawed, or banished, of anyway destroyed, nor will we pass upon him, nor will we send upon him, unless the lawful judgement of his peers, or by the law of the land. We will sell to man, we will not deny to any man, either justice or right."

Since the Africans were free, at least as long as they remained in their homelands, it would appear that King James and subsequent monarchs, in permitting the taking, disseizing, and imprisoning of the Africans, did indeed break the laws of their own land. Additionally, and according to Thomas Jefferson's comments in his draft copy of the Declaration of Independence, the king also violated the natural laws by denying the Africans their inalienable rights as human beings. While the details surrounding the enslavement of the Africans were likely considerably more complex, an attempt has been made, utilizing the available historical data, to reconstruct the most likely sequence of events that occurred, leading up to the implementation of slavery. It boils down to this: economic forces drove the English merchants and the English government to implement slavery in their pursuit of profits.

Two Americas:

Freedom for the Pilgrims and Free Enterprise for Jamestown

The Pilgrims, who began the formal settlement of America, belonged to a religious group called Separatists. While the Separatist movement had a relatively modest following, it was part of a much larger religious affiliation generally referred to as the Puritans. The Puritans, or Separatists had factored into their faith notions of the individual rights of man. Evidence that these same ideas accompanied the Puritans on their migration to the

Americas can be seen in the social and politically enlightened ideas expressed in the agreement jointly signed by the Pilgrims upon their arrival in America. The agreement they signed is called the Mayflower Compact and essentially establishes the first independent government structure in the New World. The 1620 settlement of the Pilgrims was not the first English settlement in the New World a region known as Virginia. The region, named in honor of England's Queen Elizabeth, the virgin Queen, and the region stretched from present-day Virginia to what is now New England.

A few years before, in May of 1607, another settlement a few miles farther south consisting of a hundred men and four boys arriving on three small ships had navigated from the coast up a river inland and established a settlement at a site along the river. They had named the settlement Jamestown in honor of their king, James I. The idea for the Jamestown settlement was not the brain-child of a persecuted people seeking a peaceful place to worship, but of entrepreneurs, mostly merchants, who had appealed to the king and been granted a charter that permitted the establishment of colonies in the New World. The colonies that they sought to establish were to be manned by their fellow Englishmen, men and boys who would labor for the first seven years in return for their ocean passage. After the seven years were up, they would be become free men and could then pursue their own riches. The enterprising aspect of the Jamestown settlement is not the only feature that makes it different from the Pilgrims' settlement. For whereas the Pilgrims had settled Plymouth as an act borne out of their own inspirations, the Jamestown settlement was a venture capitalist operation from its very beginning. And whereas the Pilgrims' settlement at Plymouth Rock operated locally under a somewhat mutual agreement contract—the Mayflower Compact—it was not so at Jamestown. Having been established and chartered to the British East India Company, it was required to operate with a profit motive by its overseers and shareholders.

The operating principles of the Jamestown settlement were in stark contrast to the founding principles of the Puritans' settlement. It was the Puritans who transported the notions of individual merit as espoused in the arguments of the reformation movement, from Europe to the shores of the Americas. Those notions and Thomas Jefferson's subsequent and esteemed application of the political ideas of John Locke, can be said to have, for all practical purposes, put slavery and the political and economic ideas of the Jamestown settlement on a virtual collision course with the ideals of the Pilgrims. The initial clash between the arguments of the politicians and venture capitalists and those of the reformation movement actually began over the issue of independence for the colonies. However, the colonies did not win their independence until about 150 years after the Mayflower landing. The English government's continued refusal to grant the colonies their independence finally resulted in the Revolutionary War of 1776. After the Revolutionary War, and even though the English government withdrew its military and mercantile interest from the colonies, certain relics of its colonial occupancy remained behind. Slavery as an institution was one such relic. Among the others was a tendency on the part of the Americans to continue utilizing the language of the monarchy. Some members of the newly independent nation contended that George Washington should become not the nation's first president, but its first king. They also continued the use of certain courtesies, honors, royal titles, and even the use of wigs as part of formal attire. All these habits and practices were leftovers from the days of the British monarchy. The tendency of the newly independent Americans to continue such practices reminiscent of their days as English colonies had to be overcome by those who envisioned a republic rather than a monarchy. Even though the choice of becoming a republic was mutually endorsed, there were still detractors who wished to retain features of the British monarchy.

Slavery, unfortunately, did not go the way of the trappings of the monarchy. Even by 1776, the roots of slavery had grown deep into the soil of

American socioeconomic society. The thirteen colonies, having inherited slavery from their former government, as it were, were split almost immediately over its presence within their new country. Most of the newly independent colonies voted to abolish slavery almost as soon as they became independent of the English government. Others—those where slavery's roots had grown deep into the soil of their economies—were not nearly as eager to abolish it. By this time also, slavery had become so interwoven into the political, cultural and economic fabric of the newly formed United States of America that even in the face of social and political opposition, it had enough staying power to survive. In his book, *The Great Rehearsal*, author Carl Van Doren made this observation regarding the sentiment of George Mason, one of the Virginia's delegates to the Constitutional Convention of 1787:

> "Like other Virginia delegates, Mason was opposed to slavery on principle, regretted the existence of it in their state, and desired to see slavery abolished if this could be done without destroying the economy of a society which had inherited its slaves as it had its land and its laws."

On another occasion, George Mason is quoted as referring to slavery as that "infernal traffic" that had begun "in the avarice of British merchants." The colonies that depended heavily on the use of enslaved laborers to work their farms were resistant to the abolition of slavery. Their reluctance, though morally reprehensible, when taken in context of the time and circumstance, is not necessarily so difficult to understand. As the regions of the country whose economies depended primarily upon the planting, harvesting, and marketing of agricultural products, one can understand why they felt the need to hold on to the use of their labor supply. Social values, customs, and economic systems as features of a country's behavior do not change as rapidly as the historical events that underlie them. For example, although the English people repudiated the monarchy in favor of a republic more than three hundred years ago, England, at great national expense, still maintains a royal family. England, during its 1668 "Glorious Revolution," opted for a government based on the supremacy of the parliament rather than on the monarchy. Britain has been a republic since that revolution. Yet, the mindset of most Britons retains the notion and reverence for a royal family.

Also, consider that for at least twenty-five years following India's 1947 independence from Great Britain, the Indian people continued to observe a ten-day Christmas holiday. This indicates that after more than three hundred years of English colonization, India's government and people had fully integrated the custom of observing Christmas into their own social ethos. When the British government withdrew from India, as when it withdrew from America, certain relics of its occupancy remained. The Indian people's apparent reluctance to give up the Christmas holidays does not necessarily signal their partiality to Christianity but rather the resiliency of certain social and cultural paradigms. And those periods of social and cultural change are considerably longer than the periods required for the historical events to change. And in the case of another historical event, a similarly much-delayed closure occurred. On May 17, 1954, a little more than fifty years ago, the U.S. Supreme Court ruled that segregated schools were inherently unequal and therefore unconstitutional. In that event, the black American community in the person of Justice Thurgood Marshall, then an attorney for the NAACP, made an eloquent and impassioned argument regarding the ills of segregated schools. His argument prevailed, and he succeeded in convincing the justices of the court that segregated public schools were discriminatory and offensive to the aspirations of black Americans. As a result, the U.S. Supreme Court ordered that all such school systems be integrated with all "deliberate speed." It is now over fifty years later and segregated public schools are still with us.

However, before we rush to the conclusion that it's all because of the racist's attitudes of white Americans, we might do well to look not at people's attitudes, but at people's interests. True, over fifty years ago the black American community, in the person of Thurgood Marshall, made the argument that segregated education was contrary to the successful development of black Americans. But today, that same black American community is petitioning the courts to spare segregated black American colleges. If segregated schools are bad for black America's children, then are not segregated colleges equally offensive to the socioeconomic interest of black America's young men and women? Of course, we acknowledge that the social impact of these examples pale in comparison with America's internalization of the enslavement of the Africans, but in terms of their social and cultural entrenchment, they appear to operate out of the same paradigmatic properties.

Slavery's Indelible Footprint on the American Mind

For more than four generations, from July 2, 1776 to April 4, 1860—eighty-four years, nine months, and ten days—the opposing arguments in the evolving social and political character of America came closer and closer to engaging each other. Finally, on that fateful day, April 4, 1860, the two converging ideologies collided. That collision, the second of the proverbial "bangs" was announced to the nation by the sounds of cannon fire as the army of the Confederate States of America fired upon Fort Sumter, a United States military garrison. And even though the firing on Fort Sumter occurred nearly 250 years after the Jamestown and Mayflower settlements, it was nevertheless the cumulative effect of a long and persistent ideological dispute. The effects of the collision plunged the nation into the Civil War. The war that followed was the nation's most painful and bloodiest conflict. It was also one of the most profound commentaries upon the character of the young American nation. And to the extent that the national character has not changed, the historicity of that war is also a present-day commentary upon the character and moral fiber of what America is meant to be. However, even though the nation's successful prosecution of the Civil War resolved the problem of slavery, this resolution did little to remedy the socio-psychological damage and the socioeconomic disparity that existed between the former natives of Africa and the former natives of Europe.

If the nation's resolution of the issue of slavery was not enough to settle the question of socioeconomic disparity and socio-psychological damage, it was even less sufficient to assuage the national guilt. To that end, America has failed to avail itself of many very conventional remedies. As recounted in the Bible, when Jacob, the father and patriarch of the Hebrew clan in Egypt, died, his sons tended their guilt of having sold their brother, Joseph, into Egyptian slavery and speculated among themselves saying, "What if Joseph holds a grudge against us and pays us back for all the wrongs we did to him?" They were convinced that Joseph held a grudge against them and intended to seek retribution. To offset such intents and to assuage themselves of their guilt, the brothers sent a message to Joseph saying, "Your father left these instructions before he died. 'This is what you are to say to Joseph: I ask you to forgive your brothers the sins and the wrongs they committed in treating you so badly.' Now please forgive the sins of the servants of the God of your father." The Bible states that upon receiving this message, Joseph wept.

Remarkably enough, it was this simple act of contrition and forgiveness between the offenders and the offended that healed what was otherwise an open wound. It is unfortunate that the white American community has not been as forthcoming or as successful in remedying its guilt of the enslavement of its brothers as Joseph's brothers were in assuaging their guilt over his enslavement. Why the appropriate remedies were not applied is a question for historians; but suffice it to say that by all appearances, it has not been applied. Perhaps, speculatively speaking, sociological remedies were not applied because healing from having been enslaved was taken for granted in much the same manner as healing from other traumatic experiences was, until more recently, taken for granted. However, it would appear that healing from severe, painful, and persistent injuries apparently does not occur without the application of significant, and in the case of black American enslavement, sociopolitical therapy. Had such a remedy been implemented, it is reasonable to assume that the sense of unrepented injury, so active in the mindscapes of many black Americans today, would not be present. That this sense of injury is present within the black American community can be verified simply by asking any one of its thirty-five million members. Or for the more skeptical, by reading the vast array of government and non-government committee reports that have been published on the subject. Even more convincing are the number and frequency of civil disturbances and riots. However, the most painful symptom of this sense of injury is more evident in the black American community's difficulty in embracing the American dream as their own. Nations, governments, and peoples have long recognized the therapeutic benefits that can result from erecting monuments or memorials to honor victims and to assuage the injury suffered by the survivors of great disasters and painful tragedies. Consistently, almost all nations on earth has established various kinds of memorials to serve as healing symbols for injuries suffered by their people. In the United States, there are literally hundreds, perhaps even thousands of memorials—national cemeteries; battlefields; statues, and other kind of war memorials—that serve the nation in this capacity. Throughout the world, nations have erected popular symbols to alleviate their pain. In America, it's the Tombs of the Unknowns at Arlington National Cemetery; in England, it's the Tomb of the Unknown Soldier maintained in Westminster Abbey; and in France, it's the Tomb of the Unknown Soldier that lies beneath France's famed Arc de Triomphe. Most recently, the United States erected the Vietnam War Memorial as a tribute to the veterans and survivors of the Vietnam War. By all accounts, the memorial wall has served as an effective instrument of healing the nation's wounds that resulted from the war in Southeast Asia. And of the Nazi concentration camps, perhaps the greatest tragedy of the modern era is the killing factories at Auschwitz, Dachau, Sachsenhausen, and Buchenwald, which are preserved as memorial museums to assuage the sense of loss among their Jewish victims and the generations of injured victims that succeed them.

To remedy the sociological injury that evidently continues to plague the black American community, even into this twenty-first century, the nation must be motivated to implement some manner of societal healing. Programs are needed that will enhance the hospitality of the current social, civic, and legal environment in such a fashion as to tend the sense of injury held by many people within the black American community. The emphasis or design of the program should be such that it is able to convert the current environment, perceived by most black Americans as being hostile to their interest, to one that is perceived as hospitable toward their interest. The need for such a remedy is simple. Hostile environments deter growth and effectiveness while hospitable environments encourage growth and effectiveness. It is not enough to simply declare the environment non-hostile. It must be altered to such an extent that black Americans, particularly young black Americans, perceived it as being definitely non-hostile. Obviously it is preferable that the environment be perceived as definitively hospitable. If white Americans, especially young white Americans, must struggle to succeed in a nurturing and hospitable environment, then most assuredly young black Americans should not be burdened to succeed within a societal environment that they perceive as being against them from the start.

To effect such a change in the current environment, Americans can esteem the American Civil War as a catharsis of national healing. The Civil War should become a significant component of any program aimed at validating the wholesomeness of America's relationship to its Declaration of Independence and its relationship with black Americans. The Civil War needs national promotion as the appropriate symbol to promote sociological healing not just between black and white Americans, but also between

Americans in the Northern states and those in the Southern states. The war in which so many died over so great an issue must be elevated to the status of a national resource. The U.S. Department of the Interior would do well to incorporate the Civil War as a national memorial, a testament to or a statement of purpose of, the nation's moral views and its resolve to defend those views. Currently, the Civil War is an event observed by only a few Americans, and even then mainly by history buffs or military strategists. In the meantime, its usefulness as a source of moral reinforcement lies untapped in a million history books and other publications. It should instead be raised to the top of the list of things celebrated by all Americans, particularly on Independence Day. What good, for instance, would a Fourth of July celebration be if the values emphasized in the Declaration of Independence had not been defended at Bull Run, Antietam, Vicksburg, and Gettysburg? If we accept the premise that slavery was indeed a relic left over from British colonialism, then the Civil War was effectively the closing chapter of Britain's colonial occupation. If that can be argued, then the Civil War should becomes a validation, a testimonial to the fact that the nation took the question regarding individual and natural rights seriously. And it indicates that not only did the country accept the premise conceptually, but that it was prepared to go to war even with itself, to defend its beliefs. The American Civil War should be esteemed as one of the commanding heights of American values and the price of freedom.

Secondly, America needs to establish a monument of tribute or memorial dedicated to the millions of African immigrants and their American descendents who, even though in bondage, willingly rendered service to their country on behalf of the hope and aspirations of a progeny yet to be summoned. Those Africans who were enslaved and transported to this country deserves to have a monument dedicated to them, to their lives, to their deaths, and to their contribution to nation building. To paraphrase Sir Winston Churchill, "Never have so many worked so hard for so little."

Besides, monuments are a part of our national heritage. The thousands of national memorials and monuments that already punctuate the national landscape are not there just for tourist attractions. They were placed in their respective locations in tribute or dedication to a number of occasions, issues, and events. Yet, in spite of the grievous circumstances of their contribution, no national recognition has been paid to the thirteen generations or to the millions of Africans and their descendents who died in the world's most exacerbating and tyrannical abuse of human rights. For a fitting redress to remedy this deficit, I suggest that the U.S. Department of the Interior, or another federal agency assume administrative control of at least one of the numerous Negro colleges located throughout the nation. And if only one is selected, then I suggest the Tuskegee University in Tuskegee, Alabama. What could be a more fitting tribute to the Africans and their descendents than a university that was founded and built by one who himself yearned to be free, and rose up to be such an able and articulate representative of their hopes and aspirations. As a memorial and scholarship institution, the university that is selected would serve as a public and living symbol of the nation's commitment to the memories of the thirteen generations of men, women, and children who lived, worked, and died under a system of enforced enslavement. Under the Department of the Interior or other agencies, the educational institution, coupled with the national observance of the Civil War, would become the core of a program of environmental healing. Funding and other administrative issues would be managed under the Department of the Interior as they currently are with other memorial institutions and facilities. In addition to acquiring administrative control of the university, federal agencies would be required to establish and maintain a perpetual and commemorative scholarship program. The scholarship program would of course be open to all American scholarship candidates.

Beyond the environmental hospitality benefits of this approach, it would serve as a great milestone toward enhancing the academic skills of

American youths. Operation and funding of such programs could be handled on the same basis and in the same manner now used to operate and fund the scholarship programs administered at the various military academies. A second or backup option drops assumption of a college or university but maintains the perpetual scholarship program. Under this option, no university would be acquired, but the establishment of a scholarship program, with a keen focus for selected black American youths, would be the order. The scope of the scholarship program would again be equal or comparable to scholarship programs currently made available to youths through the nation's various military academies. The scholarship program, like the university in the first option, would be dedicated to the memories of the first thirteen generation of African immigrants and their American descendents—those Africans who having had their U.S. citizenship immorally and unconstitutionally withheld, and were obliged to served their entire lives as disenfranchised aliens. Under both options, federal agencies would also be required to acquire all remaining relics regarding the history of this nation's enslavement of the Africans and to maintain them or assure they would be maintained as national museums of tribute. The benefits of such a program, apart from its own legitimacy, is the signal it would send to black Americans at large and in particular to the youths of the black American community. Such an undertaking would go a long way toward demonstrating the nation's disposition toward being a hospitable environment rather than a hostile one to the interest and aspirations of the black American community. That such a revision in the social environment enhances one's self-esteem is affirmed by this account from authors Gregorio F. and Sonia Zaide in their chapter "On Our American Heritage," from their book, *Philippine History & Government.*

"During the Spanish period the Filipinos acquired an inferiority complex because the arrogant Spaniards looked down on them, considering them as indios who belonged to an inferior race. Thus they [the Filipinos] became servile and meek. During the American regime, the people's manners changed. Influenced by democracy's tenets that all men have the inherent right 'to life, liberty, and the pursuit of happiness,' and that 'all men are equal before the law, irrespective of race, color creed and social position,' they broke the shackles of their colonial servility. They became more assertive of their rights."

It is therefore evident that to a large segment of the black American community, the nation has not completed its task of assuaging the injury that still lingers in their hearts. The argument is that the simple act of righting a constitutional injustice, as was accomplished by the Emancipation Proclamation and the Thirteenth, Fourteenth, and Fifteenth Amendments were remedies for the civil rights of all Americans. But they are not perceived by the black American community as a national acknowledgment of the fiduciary-like responsibility that the national government had toward the generations of Africans and black Americans that were enslaved and deprived of their rights and privileges as citizens. The defense of a United States citizen's citizenship rights would appear, by all conventions, to have been the federal government's primary obligation. And as was ultimately demonstrated by the Civil War, the federal government commanded all the means necessary to assure its citizens of the legal rights awarded them under the United States Constitution. In the case of the African immigrants however, the federal government apparently abrogated its responsibility, presumably in deference to those who argued from the platform of states rights. The states may have won the argument, but when the action within the states began to compromise or threaten United States citizens' protection under the Bill of Rights, the federal government, as it ultimately did in the 1954 *Brown v. Board of Education* case, was obliged to intervene on behalf of the citizen. As is apparent in the Constitution, and specifically the Bill of Rights, the federal government could no more have communicated the legal rights of the African immigrants to the state's disposition than a federal judge could communicate the prosecution of a case to the plaintiff in the case.

It is acknowledged that this argument is in conflict with the Supreme Court's decision as handed down in the Dred Scott case. However, since all subsequent legal and legislative decisions and actions acted upon by the nation's courts and the legislatures have, in fact, repudiated the opinion of Chief Justice Roger B. Taney, it is morally fitting and appropriate that we do so here. After all, Judge Taney's decision was in direct conflict with the founding premise of the nation that "We hold these truths to be self-evident: that all men are created equal, that they are endowed by their Creator with certain unalienable Rights." If these rights are truly "unalienable," then Judge Taney's ruling obviously represented a lapse in his sense of jurisprudence and was thus based on his own prejudices rather than upon the moral foundation of the law of the land. Not only does history in retrospect discount the Judge Taney-led decision as a miscarriage of justice, but also America's prosecution of the Civil War itself testifies that the nation disagreed with the decision of Judge Taney's court. One can easily conclude that President Abraham Lincoln's Gettysburg Address also took exception to the ruling of the Taney court when in the address President Lincoln stated that, "fourscore and seven years ago our fathers brought forth upon this continent, a new nation, conceived in liberty, and dedicated to the proposition that *all* men are created *equal*."

The scholarship programs, and the designation of Tuskegee University as a living memorial would go a long way toward remedying the erroneous moral perspective that Judge Taney held of the nation's laws, not only for his errant views but for a thousand of other violations of the human, moral, and civil rights of the African immigrants and their descendents. The environmental hospitality generated by such an approach would contribute far more to the black American community and to society in general than current quest for financial reparations. The positive remedial effect of this approach would be to reshape the social landscape with the intent of stimulating growth, self-esteem, and productivity, rather than the government handout that would be like fertilizing the roots of plants growing in a desert. The black American community would also benefit by the increases in the community's literacy rates as more and more young black Americans would become encouraged to complete their education. They would benefit also from a meaningful lessening of the number of black Americans who drop out of school; and significant increases in the number of black Americans enrolling in colleges and trade schools would play a major role in the black American community's quest for socioeconomic parity. On the other hand, there should also be an ongoing decline in the number of teen pregnancies and welfare applicants, and in the scope of inner-city riots and gang violence. Also, an assortment of other social ills currently associated with high unemployment and underemployment would show promising responses to such changes in the sociopolitical and economic environments. A program of environmental hospitality would visit upon the black American youths an atmosphere of self-esteem commensurate with that visited upon the little cinder girl of Perrault's fairy tale. Abused and mistreated by her stepmother and stepsisters, her environment suddenly and magically changed one day from one of abusive hostility to one of encouraging hospitality. When such changes in the environment are defined as being necessary to effect certain changes in social behavior, it is certain to elicit comments from some segments of the population expressing a "there you go again" refrain. However, it should be noted that proposals such as these seek to encourage a more productive environment and in this context, do not seek nor cater to, another state of altruistic benevolence.

2

Who Were the 1619 Africans?

- *Who Were Their Families?*

- *Who Were Their People?*

- *What African Countries Were They Citizens Of?*

- *What Was Their History?*

- *What Were Their Religions?*

- *What Were Their Cultural Values?*

- *What Was Their World View?*

In answering these questions, we have employed a variety of innovative techniques to provide the reader with a decided advantage in understanding the history of ancient Africa. Those countries that maintained written histories made it possible for us to travel, figuratively speaking, on the wide boulevards of their published histories. However, in those countries that maintained only oral histories, we were restricted to travel—again figuratively speaking—the narrowest of footpaths in our trek back through their histories. Details of our journey into Africa's pre-colonial and pre-slavery history are transferred like snapshots onto a collage of twenty-six historical descriptions of the life and circumstances of the African people as they lived, worked, and governed themselves before the dark ages of the

African Holocaust. The collage is arranged in a clockwise pattern that covers the entire African continent. The first of these snapshots features the lives and circumstances of North Africa. Next, the journey takes us through northeastern, eastern, and central east Africa. From there snapshots of the people and places in the southeast, the south, and the southwest nations are presented. As we close out the last phase of the journey, we submit brief histories of the people and governments in the central African, West African, and finally northwest African regions. The snapshot-like recounting of historical people and events on the following pages represents an effort to give a maximum amount of information to the reader in a minimum amount of time.

This approach, it is hoped, will provide insight into the worldview, the cultural values, the religious beliefs, the histories, the citizenship, the people, and the families of the twenty Africans who arrived in Jamestown in 1619. Having done so will enhance the understanding of the thirty-five or so million black Americans who have succeeded them. The best historical perspective of pre-colonial and pre-slave trade Africa can be gained by comparing certain key features in the area of America's own growth and success. To accomplish this we have made a limited comparison between America's commercial, industrial, and technological main operating centers, and such centers that existed in Africa's history. Additionally, brief comparative sketches have been drawn between the racial diversity and living standards of Americans versus those of historical Africans.

The bulk of America's industrial, technological, and commercial activity has traditionally been concentrated within in the northeastern part of the country. Currently, the nation's standard of living is generally the highest in the world. As to its racial or ethnic diversity, the majority of immigrants arrive through three principal ports or access areas. These regions, all along the nation's coastlines, accounts for the vast majority of the country's racial or ethnic diversity. Almost without question, the state that has achieved the greatest commercial success in the country is New York. After all, Wall Street is in New York, and plays host to both the New York and American Stock Exchanges. The Commodity and Maritime Exchanges also call New York home. New York has the largest trade and transportation centers in the country. It is home to over one thousand advertising agencies. Of its work force, fully one third are engaged in tertiary or service occupations. New York is also home to the nation's radio and television broadcasting industries. Additionally, it boasts of other high-profile names, such as Madison Avenue, Chase Manhattan Bank, the Empire State Building, Rockefeller Center, and Times Square. It has, since it's founding in 1625, become the nation's major commercial center. The history of, and the reason for New York's success is not a part of the focus of this chapter since, primarily, this is a chapter on the history and demography of Africa. However, suffice it to say we recognize that New York, for whatever providential reasons, was favored by history and circumstances to become the commercial center of the nation that it is today. Whether that accomplishment is attributable to the abundant labor supply provided by the large number of its early immigrants, the abundant capital available through its concentration of foreign investors, or its proximity to a world-class seaport and harbor is unknown.

Whatever the factors were, the fact is that even though there are fifty states and thousands of other cities in the United States, only one, within reason, has achieved the commercial success New York has. When one looks at the history of Africa, the perspective of one New York per America must be carried over to understand the one-Egypt-per-Africa perspective. In every way that New York is the leader of this nation, and indeed of the American continent, so was historical Egypt the leader nation of the African continent. Africa is a vast continent of enormous variety. Yet in all of its history, it has had only one super commercial center of operations, as we would say in today's vernacular. Also America, like Africa, appeared to be allowed only one such mega-metropolis, the emerging role of California notwithstanding. And like New York, ancient Egypt ranked far above all its competitors in the area of socioeconomic and technological developments. Even today, its historical visibility accounts for an overwhelming majority of all things popularly known of African history. Egypt was historically a leader nation, one whose achievements in the areas of science, politics, culture, religious, and architectural supremacy continues to awe, baffle, and confound a humanity enlightened by an additional six thousand years of learning.

And if New York has become almost without question the center of commercial activity in our nation, then areas around the cities of Chicago, Detroit, Milwaukee, Columbus, and Cleveland indisputably became the focus of the nation's industry and technology. All located within a contiguous northeastern region—an area that comprises less than twenty-five percent of the geographical area of the nation—this region represented more than ninety percent of the nation's industrial and technological activity. Detroit, the center of the auto industry, played host to at least six of the major producers of motorcars in the western world. Such industry giants as General Motor, The Ford Motor Company, and Chrysler are located in Detroit. And the smaller motorcar manufacturers—Hudson, Nash, Packard, Studebaker, and Willys—were also situated within that fertile crescent of industrial activity. Again, it is not within the purview of this chapter on African history to offer detailed analyses of the success of this particular pentad of cities but simply to recognize their leadership role in the nation's industrial and technological growth.

More recently, Los Angeles and other cities on the West Coast have also made substantial progress and have become key centers in the nation's technological and industrial success. As in America, so also it was in Africa. The five cities that represented the bulk of American industrial technology were all located in the Northeast. In Africa, similar centers of industrial activity were also concentrated in one general area. The great cities of Alexandria, Cairo, and Tripoli situated along the Mediterranean basin operated through trade routes with cities like Meroe, Kilva, Axum, and Khartoum to form an equally imposing assortment of industrial and technological centers that were, for their time, comparable to the Chicagos, Detroits, Milwaukees, Columbuses, and Clevelands of our time. They didn't build motorcars, but they did have a major role in the mining industry and were engaged in the smelting of gold, silver, copper and iron. The ancient city of Meroe was the iron smelting capital of the region in its heyday. In a way, and much like Pittsburgh is the steel city of our times, Meroe was the iron city of its time. Alexandria, the largest city on the Mediterranean was the major trading center along the Mediterranean Basin and boasted of a city library that contained over three-quarters of a million volumes.

The cities and regions of the United States noted above are the ones most frequently cited whenever America is the subject of a discussion. This is so even though the area covered by these particular cities lies within a single region of the country and represents less than one-third of the nation's area and a lesser percentage of the nation's people. But what should historians say of the rest of the nation? Must the history and demography of the entire nation rest upon this area alone? What of those who lived in the less-accomplished areas, the cities and regions in the wide openness of the plains states or those of the Rocky Mountain and southern states? What of necessity must future historians say of them? Should historian erroneously declare that they had no part in the matter of success of the United States? That they are discountable because they lived in the other two-thirds of the nation? Or should it be said that the merits of their existence can be ignored or relegated to the pedantic, simply because the history of their cities and regions was not sustained by skyscrapers and great historical landmarks? If the historians of tomorrow are anything like those of today—at least those who have written African history—then two-thirds of the Americans who do not live in the skyscraper capitals of industrial centers will be written off as insignificant non-achievers. As with the remaining two-thirds of America, so are the remaining areas of Africa. As the historians write, they had no part in the matter of the successes recorded in their continents' history. Why was it Egypt and not an area in the western regions of Africa that succeeded so well? Why did New York succeed rather than Charleston? If Detroit, Chicago, Milwaukee, Columbus, and Cleveland succeeded as industrial giants among the lesser cities, why did Biloxi, Corpus Christi, Birmingham, Des Moines, or Bismarck not succeed? And if no validation were required to explain the difference between the achievements of some American cities over others, then why would the question be asked of some African cities over other cities?

In pre-slavery, pre-colonial Africa, as in modern-day United States, extreme variations existed in the way people lived. Some people lived in big cities, and others in small villages or towns. There were people who lived in nice homes constructed of wood and masonry, and there were poor people who had no permanent homes. Whereas in the United States you might live in cities like New York or Detroit, a comparable lifestyle in that time of Africa's history would have found you living in places like Kilwa, Cairo, or Axum. If you are affluent and live in a place like San Diego, as an affluent African, and if you liked the beach, you would probably have lived in a city like Kisimani. If your San Diego home were comfortable and modern, you would have probably been right at home in similar comfort in the city of Kilwa or Alexandria. On the flip side of the coin, if you lived in a rural area of Iowa, Nebraska or Kansas, or in Mississippi, Georgia, or Louisiana, you would probably have worked on a cattle ranch in the country of Zanj, or you might have lived in Sotho or Swazi of in South Africa. In any of these rural places, you would undoubtedly have found yourself having to get up early in the mornings to milk and feed the cows and tend to other farm animals, before going to the fields to work.

Africa, like America, had its share of racial and ethnic diversity. Certain African cities were located on coastline areas that were subject to a large influx of foreign immigrants, invaders, or traders. And like the American cities of New York, Los Angeles, or Miami, the residents in these cities undoubtedly incurred substantial miscegenation of the races. Those areas farther inland, and away from coastal contact—as America's Midwest, for example—would have, by virtue of their location, suffered very little mixing of races. Consequently, cities like Alexandria, Carthage, Tripoli, like Los Angeles, New York, and Miami, were areas of great cosmopolitan diversity. Situated on the Mediterranean coast, their indigenous African populations were exposed to frequent incursions of Arab, European, Asian, and Semitic races. The racial characteristics of the residents of these areas reflect the thousands of years of their exposure to the multitude of different races. A number of the history books utilized in preparation for this chapter made note of the racial difference between the Africans who lived in these areas and those who lived farther inland. The notations, however, were more by way of disclaimers than analysis. They suggest that although people in Africa achieved certain accomplishments, African people did not make them. Such historical reporting causes one to wonder whether these same historians would write of accomplishments by Americans in Miami as being made by Latinos and not Americans; or of Los Angeles's achievements as points of merits for Asians and not for Americans; or of Atlanta as achievements for Africans but not of Americans; or of New York to say that the achievers were Jewish, but not Americans. And in a few thousand years of American history, as with Egyptian history, will the racial features of Miami, Los Angeles, and New York residents possess the same characteristics as they do now? It is an unfortunate commentary upon the discipline of history that some historians have, by all indications, attempted to sever the continental integrity of the African people to assuage their own biases.

SNAPSHOTS OF THEIR AFRICAN HISTORY
NORTH AFRICA—Egypt, Tunisia, Algeria, Libya, and Morocco
Approximate Area: 2,066,029 square miles

In my commentary on North Africa, I have selected Egypt as a twelfth-to-nineteenth century barometer of the social, political, and economic currents that were active in that area and during that time. Throughout recorded history, the most prominent area of the African continent has been the land of the Egyptians. Situated in the upper northeast quadrant of the continent, even during the fifteenth, sixteenth and seventeenth centuries, Egypt remained a significant point of world influence. For comparison's sake, one can think of the Egypt of past history as the America of current history, or in an earlier time, as the great British Empire. Egypt, the land of the pharaohs, has throughout the millennia been like a boulder placed in the middle of the rushing streams of history. While historical events have come and gone, like the ebb and flow of the annual rainfalls, the land of the pharaohs has remained almost constant in its mystique and status as the fountainhead of cultures.

Because of its unique location along the Nile River delta, Egypt is recognized as being one of the first places on earth where erstwhile nomadic man settled for a period long enough to develop the art of plant cultivation. It is accorded that the act of settling down in one place, as opposed to wandering back and forth as the traditional nomads did, served as a catalyst to the invention of the cultivation plow and the process of crop irrigation, and it was due to their efforts to predict the annual flow of the Nile and the flooding of the Nile delta that the first Egyptian calendar was invented. The plow and the process of irrigating that which he plowed allowed early man to not only feed himself, but perhaps even more importantly, to accumulate a surplus of food. Because of the need to monitor the flow and distribution of the irrigation water, it is said that the process of writing and the use of numbers significantly advanced the use of writing and a need for civil authorities, and therefore civil government. Like a stone thrown into the middle of the pond, the waves emitted by those simple inventions evolved into the sophisticated structures that we now regard as civil government, bookkeeping, and taxes.

Of such prominence was Egypt, upon the history of Europe, particularly in the late Stone Age, that historians, who were not otherwise inclined toward crediting Africa's role in the technological development of European history were obliged to recognize it. J. H. Robinson and J. H. Breasted, authors of *Outlines of European History*, published in 1914, wrote in a chapter titled "Late Stone Age Europe and The Orient:

> "There are certain traders whose wares these Stone Age villagers inspect with eagerness. They come from the coast and they are already threading the alpine passes leading northward from southern Europe—roads which are yet to become the great highways of the early world. These traders entertain the villagers of the European interior with the tales which circulate among the coast settlements, telling how huge ships—which make their own rude dugouts look like tiny chips—ply back and forth in the eastern waters of the Mediterranean. Such ships have many oarsmen on each side and mighty fir trunks mounted upright in the craft, carrying huge sheets of linen to catch the favoring wind, which drives them swiftly without oars from land to land. They come out of the many mouths of the vast river of Egypt, greater than any river in the world says the tale and they bear crowded cargoes of beautiful stone vases, strings of shining blue-glazed beads, bolts of fine linen, and above all, axes and daggers of a strange, heavy, shining substance, for which these European villagers have no name. They listen with awe-struck faces and rapt attention; and in their traffic they desire above all else the new axes and daggers of metal which take a keener edge than any they can fashion of stone.

> "Strings of Egyptian blue-glazed beads, brought in by traders, wandered from hand to hand and people to people in western Europe; and we find them now lying in graves among the ornaments once worn by

the men of the late Stone or early Copper age in England. In the East the people of a late Stone Age village on the low hill in north western Asia Minor where later rose the walls of Troy; likewise the people of another settlement of the same age near the north shore of the Island of Crete, yet to become the flourishing city of Cnossus; and other communities scattered through the Aegean islands—these eastern people have even seen those marvelous ships of the Nile with their huge spars and wide sails and have trafficked with them on the seashore."

The foregoing was written in the early 1900s, a period when racially sensitive European historians routinely identified Egypt as a place separate and distinct from "Africa." Indicative of that practice is the following passage from the same Robinson-Breasted book, which references Egypt as part of the Orient (Asia). To illustrate the point, references to Egypt as being of the Orient have been struck through and "Africa" or "African" has been inserted; thus, the sanitizing reassignments employed by the authors become very obvious. Such efforts, while they might have been more palatable to European sensitivities, failed to properly credit the African continent's role in the development of civilization on the European continent, and through it, the world.

"[Thus at the very dawn of European history, barbarian Europe looked across the Mediterranean to the great civilization of the Nile, as the native Americans of North America must have fixed their wondering eyes on the first Europeans who landed in America and listened to strange tales of great and distant peoples. But these late Stone Age men had now (about 2500 B.C.) reached the limit of their resources. Without writing (for the records of business, government, and tradition), without metals (save the trader's copper ax and dagger) without stanch ships in which to develop commerce—they could go no further. Perhaps the late Stone Age villagers recalled a dim tradition of their father that grain and flax, cattle and sheep, first came to them from the same wonderland of the far East [Africa], whence now came the copper ax and the blue-glazed beads. It was after receiving such contributions as these from the Orient [Africa], that Europe went forward to the development of a higher civilization, and in order to understand the further course of European history, we must turn to the Orient [Africa] whence came these things by which the life of our European ancestors entered upon a new epoch.

"Let us remember as we go to the Orient [Africa] that the age of man's prehistoric career lasted some fifty thousand years, and that on the Orient [continent of Africa] he began to enter upon a high civilization in the historic epoch during the thousand years from 4,000 to 3,000 B.C. (in eastern Europe a thousand years later). Civilization is thus between five and six thousand years old. It arose in the Orient [in and around the continent of Africa] in the eastern Mediterranean region, and civilized supremacy both in peace and war shifted slowly from the Orient [the regions of Africa] westward. It was not till about 500 B.C. that the Greeks became the leaders in matters of civilization. The Romans gradually subdued them, with the rest of the Mediterranean world, until Roman power was supreme and practically universal not long after 200 B.C. We have, therefore, first to trace the career of the Orient [Africans], and then to follow civilization as it developed among the Greeks and Romans."

From the above passage, it is easy to see that commerce from the areas in and around Egypt was active, perhaps through an assortment of different peoples, beyond Africa and the Mediterranean basin to Europe some three thousand miles away.

Egypt

Geo-Political Description

Historical Background of Region: With minor exceptions, the countries that have historically occupied this area of North Africa have remained fairly stable as far as territories and name changes are concerned.

Current: Area currently occupied by the countries Morocco, Algeria, Tunisia, Libya, and Egypt.

People: These people were ethnically Arabs, Berbers, Semitic, Yorubas, and Edo.

Political System: The political system consisted of sub-kings to the Ottoman sultan.

Government Structure: The government utilized civil servants.

Religion: The religion consisted of Christianity, Islam, and other regional religions.

Educational System: The education system was conventional as required under the Islamic religion.

Legal System: Laws were codified consisted with the Islamic religion.

Languages: They spoke Egyptian and Arabic languages.

Arts: The arts consisted of poetry, music, literature, dance, sculpture, and drawings.

Major Industries: Major trading ports made up the primary industries.

Imports: Goods were imported from as far away as China, Europe, and the African interior.

Exports: Cotton and gold were exported to China, Arabia, and Europe.

Foreign Contact: During the fourteenth through the nineteenth centuries, North Africa was invaded for the second time by marauding Islamic Arab tribes.

Currency: Various forms of currency were utilized throughout North Africa.

Economic System: Interior-to-overseas-trade was a prominent facet of the Egyptian economy.

Military: The Egyptians maintained a standing army.

Medicine: An assortment of western medicines and some local medicines were used. Most local medicines consisted of herbal portions based upon strong religion reliance.

Dress (Clothing): Cotton and other fabrics, both imported and domestic were used.

Housing: Houses were routinely built of wood or of stone.

Food (Staples): Rice, maize, game, fish, and butchered domestic animals made up the diet.

Agricultural Crops: Mostly cotton and later on, some maize was grown.

Domesticated Animals: Their domesticated animals included, sheep, goats, cattle, fowls, elephants and various pets.

Roads: There were main crossroads to all major trade routes coming from the African interior.

Cities and Towns: Major cities were Cairo and Alexandria.

Rural Areas: Typical homestead families and some were farming with animal husbandry.

Prominent Statesmen: The pharaohs were the prominent statesmen.

Descriptive Quote: "Strings of Egyptian blue-glazed beads brought in by traders wandered from hand to hand and people to people in western Europe; and we find them now lying in graves among the ornaments once worn by the men of the late Stone or early Copper age in England." (*Outlines of European History*)

NORTHEAST AFRICA—Ethiopia, Sudan, Djibouti, Somalia

Approximate Area: 1,693,970 square miles

As we depart Egypt on our journey along the historical thoroughfares of Africa, we come upon the less prominent, yet well documented, civilization of the Ethiopians. Ethiopia, like Egypt, has an established history dating back to at least second century B.C. However, unlike Egypt, Ethiopia (the Greek word for sunburnt faces) did not play upon the world scene, as did the Egyptian civilization. The worldview of the Ethiopians appears to have been shaped more by their relations with the Arabs of Yemen and the Jews of Israel than with any direct contact with the Greeks, Romans, or much later, the Portuguese.

The people of Ethiopia have possessed the art of writing since early in their history and boast of having the oldest written histories in Africa. They can ostensibly trace their royal lineage all the way back to Solomon, the tenth-century king of Judah and Israel. They base their claim upon the historic visit to Israel by the Ethiopian queen, Sheba. Accordingly, during her visit, the Ethiopian queen became pregnant by Solomon and after returning home, gave birth to a male child whom she named Menelik I. Ethiopian tradition holds that Menelik I returned to Israel as a youth with a contingent of soldiers and took possession of the Ark of the Covenant, whether for safekeeping or otherwise, and carried it back to Ethiopia where it is claimed to remain to this day.

Ethiopia

Geo-political Description

Historical Background of Region: Ethiopia's history dates back to the time of the Queen of Sheba. Ethiopia, which essentially became a Christian state in 300 A.D., is the oldest, continuously Christian state on earth.

Current: The northwest area is now occupied by Sudan, Djibouti, Ethiopia, and Somalia.

People (Ethnicity): Ethiopian and some Semitic.

Political System: Monarchy (claims of royalty from Biblical Solomon).

Government Structure: Monarchy: ruled through a cabinet of noblemen.

Religion: Christianity and Islam.

Educational System: Conventional educational system.

Legal System: Civil laws.

Language: Ethiopian, Hebrew.

Arts: Written poetry, music, literature, dance, sculpture, and paintings.

Major Industries: Farming, cattle ranching, gold mining, and trade.

Imports: Firearms, Clothing fabrics, tobacco, jewelry, and other consumer goods

Exports: Cotton, gold.

Foreign Contact: Visited during the fourteenth through nineteenth centuries, for the second time, by Islamic Arabs missionaries.

Currency: Currency was utilized.

Economic System: Interior-to-overseas trade was a prominent facet of the Ethiopian economy.

Military: Standing army.

Medicine: Variations from western Medicine to the use of herbal-based religion served as treatment in more rural areas

Dress (Clothing): Cotton and other fabrics, imported and domestic.

Housing: Houses were routinely built of wood or of stone.

Food (Staples): Rice, maize, game, fish, and butchered domestic animals.

Agricultural Crops: Crops consisted mainly of cotton, maize, dry rice, and millet.

Domesticated Animals: Domesticated animals consisted mainly of sheep, goats, cattle, fowls, and elephants.

Roads: Main roads crossroad to all major trade routes coming from the African interior mining industries.

Cities and Towns: The main city, Addis Abba, is the capital of Ethiopia

Rural Areas: Farming, cattle ranching, and fishing.

Prominent Statesmen: King Lalibela (twelfth century), builder of Roha.

Descriptive Quote: "Ethiopia is the oldest surviving continuous Christian state in the world." (*A History of East and Central Africa*)

EAST AFRICA—Uganda, Kenya, Rwanda, Tanzania, and Burundi

Approximate Area: 701,910 square miles

From here, we depart the historical thoroughfares and turn off onto one of the many simple paved roads of history as we continue to visit other prominent points of fifteenth, sixteenth, and seventeenth century African civilizations. This area, lying just to the south of Ethiopia and along the Indian Ocean, was home to the Swahili states, one of the most active commercial centers on the East African coast. The states of Swahili, like most of the countries of Africa, felt the impact of the arrival of the European. In 1497, the Portuguese explorer Vasco da Gama visited the major trading city of Kilwa, and eight years later the Portuguese returned to attack and loot the city.

Geographically, the Swahili states were located in approximately the same area along the Indian Ocean now occupied by southern Somalia, Kenya, portions of Uganda, and Tanzania. During the second century, a trading and mercantile community developed along the East African coast. Their Greek trading partners called it Zanj, the Arabs called it Zingis, or Zingion. This community served as the export/import center for the countries within the interior and for other less-developed towns and cities along the Indian Ocean coastline. The various Greek and Arab historical sources indicate that the city-state of Zanj flourished as the major trading point for goods imported by the various African states and for those being exported from those states to places as far away as India, China, and even Europe. It was African gold, perhaps gold being exported from this very shipping port that the thirteenth-century English King, Henry III, used to supply the London Mint for coinage.

Kingdom of Zanj

Geo-Political Description

Historical Background of Region: Historically, the kingdom of Zanj occupied the area reaching from present-day Kenya along the coast to the border of Zimbabwe.

Current: Area currently occupied by the countries of Uganda, Kenya, Rwanda, Burundi, and Tanzania.

People (Ethnicity): Shirazi.

Political System: Monarchy.

Government Structure: The monarchy ruled through provincial governors or sub-kings of each city-state within the empire.

Religion: Regional religions, but from the early fifteenth century, strongly Moslem.

Educational System: Education occurred primarily through private tutoring in the subjects of religion, custom history and the arts and through apprenticeships for skill in trades.

Legal System: Laws evolved from religion, customs, and business and were enforced.

Languages: Swahili (a Bantu language).

Arts: Oral poetry, music, dance, sculpture, paintings, and storytelling.

Major Industries: Iron mining and iron smelting, ivory, and gold mining, shipbuilding and overseas commerce to India, Java, and Sumatra. They also engaged in copper and silver mining.

Import: Clothing fabrics, jewelry, citrus fruits, and other consumer goods.

Export: Gold ingots, ivory, iron products shipped to as far away as India, Sumatra, and Java.

Foreign Contact:

1. Arab shipping companies
2. Portuguese sacking and looting of Kilwa in 1503
3. Chinese trading partners
4. Zimbabwe
5. Visited in 1497 by Portuguese explorer Vasco de Gama.
6. Visited in the fourteenth century by the historian Ibn Battuta

Currency (Second Century): Coins of copper and silver.

Economic System: Iron mining; trade.

Military: Standing armies.

Medicine: Medicine men were skilled in an assortment of medical practices and treatments of the time.

Dress (Clothing): Wealthier people wore clothing of woven dyed cotton, and silks. Poorer people wore coarse cotton fabric.

Housing: Houses were usually made from wood, stone; some were probably of mud-brick and thatched roofs, much like the building materials used by some of the American Indians and early American settlers.

Food (Staples): Rice, millet, fish, oranges, and lemons.

Agricultural Crops: Rice and millet

Domesticated Animals: The domesticated animals included, sheep, goats, cattle, fowls, elephants and various pets.

Roads: There were roads between major trading centers.

Cities and Towns: Of Kilwa and Pate, it is said; "Their kings and leading merchants lived in palaces of stone, often finely decorated with windows and niches of carved coral that were filled with splendid plates and vases from Persia and China." (*A History of East and Central Africa*)

Rural Areas: Very much like Texas in the mid-1800s, some farming but mostly cattle ranching.

Prominent Statesmen: King Ali bin al Hassan (thirteenth century) minted the empire's first coins.

Descriptive Quote: Of the town of Kilwa, an Arab historian wrote, "It was a town of many fine houses of stone and mortar, with many windows…and very well arranged in streets. The doors on the houses are of well-carved wood and with excellent joinery. Around the town are streams, orchards and fruit gardens."

Additional Quote: Vasco da Gama, the Portuguese explorer who also explored parts of the Americas, upon arriving at the Mozambique port of Quilimane in 1497–1499, wrote in the logbook of his flagship, the San Gabriel, "When we had been two days at this place two gentlemen of the country came to see us. They were very proud and valued nothing that we gave them.... A young man who was visiting with them...had come from a distant country and had already seen big ships like ours (ibid.).

CENTRAL EAST AFRICA—Malawi, Zaire, and Zambia

Approximate area: 1,241,189 square miles

The political history of the region situated in between the kingdom of the Congo on the West and the kingdom of Zanj of the East, began around the time of Christ—around two thousand years ago—when Bantu immigrants arrived into the area. By the early Iron Age, these Bantu people had established a village chief, who headed a community of small villages. The communities consisted mainly of farmers, metalworkers, and traders.

By the early fifteenth century, another immigrant group, the Luba of Katanga, had joined them. During this time period (around 1450–1500) and by virtue of their military conquests, they had built the region into a rather large city-state. Then, instead of being governed by village chiefs, the state was ruled instead by a king. Fifty years later in 1550, the Luba king had succeeded in defeating a number of lesser chiefs and extending his kingdom all the way to Lake Kisale. Having established control throughout the region, the king then proceeded to increase his state's trade. Their export items consisted of gold and iron. So plentiful were gold, copper, and tin that the region is littered with the remains of such ancient mines. The Lubas exported these minerals and imported other goods from around the world. Among the items imported from the Americas were planters' seeds for maize, tomatoes, and cassava (manioc). These products augmented the regular millet crops and were accepted by the farming community. Their addition greatly improved the food supply, and this increase in food availability led to the region's population growth. In 1600, the kingdom of Luba united with Lunda, another rapidly expanding kingdom in the region, and became the Lunda-Luba Empire.

The Luba-Lunda Empire

<u>Geo-Political Description</u>

Historical Background of Region: The Lunda-Luba Empire consisted of the combined Lunda and Luba kingdoms; the Rotse Kingdom; the kingdom of Kazembe; the city-states of Ovimbundu, and other city-states of the Kwango area.

Current: the countries of Zaire, Zambia, and Malawi currently occupy the area

People (Ethnicity): Luanda.

Political System: Monarchy (inherited by royal primogeniture).

Government Structure: King ruled through a cabinet of appointed department heads and city mayors. Each new king had to reappoint his cabinet members.

Religion: Regional religions.

Educational System: Compulsory for boys; all males had to attend one year military school.

Legal System: Laws evolved out of religious values, customs, and business needs, and were enforced. The legal system espoused this maxim, Quote: "Molau sefofo, obile otle oje mong waone." ("Not even judges can be above the reaches of the law.")

Language: Bantu.

Arts: Music, dances, storytelling, wood sculpture, and paintings.

Major Industries: Copper mining, salt mining, farming, fishing, iron ore mining, smelting, and logging.

Imports: Maize, tomatoes, and tobacco (from the Americas), firearms, gunpowder from Europe.

Exports: Salt, copper, timber, and iron ingots.

Foreign Contact: The Portuguese visited the Kingdom of Congo during the fifteenth century.

Currency: Katanga cross (a small copper cross).

Economic system: Exports of iron ingots, salt, and timber.

Military: Maintained large military reserves, mandatory draft for all males.

Medicine: Medical men practiced medicine, often in conjunction with spiritual application. Herbs were the principal source of medication.

Dress (Clothing): Cotton fabric and a cloth woven from raffia.

Housing: Houses were constructed of stone and of wood. Some were also made of woven reeds and featured thatched roofs.

Food staple: Manioc, maize, tomatoes, game, fish dairy products, and butchered livestock.

Agricultural crops: Maize, manioc, tomatoes, and harvested groundnuts.

Domesticated Animals: The domesticated animals included, sheep, goats, cattle, fowls, elephants and some pet animals.

Roads: Major trade routes extended outward from the center of the Luba Empire at Katanga 800 miles to Luanda on the western coast and about 600 miles to lake Moero on the eastern coast.

Cities and Towns: Mwibele, near Lake Boya, was the capital. The kingdom was made up of modest-size cities and an assortment of small villages and towns located throughout the kingdom.

Rural Areas: Thinly populated areas consisted of homesteads and subsistence farming, fishing, and domesticated animal husbandry.

Prominent Statesmen: Kalala Ilunga (1550) established strong central government throughout the kingdom.

Descriptive Quote: "During the seventeenth century the Lunda people founded a large empire. It stretched from the Kwango River in the West to Lake Moero in the East and it covered vast tracts of territory in Angola, Zambia, Katanga and Kwango. Moreover, the Lunda people founded the Rotse Kingdom in Zambia, the chiefdoms of the Ovimbundu in Angola and many smaller states in the Kwango area of the Congo. By the end of this period the whole savanna was permeated with Luba-Lunda states." (*The Dawn of African History*) Note of Interest: The Lunda people had a cemetery over a mile long along the scenic banks of the Congo River.

SOUTHEAST AFRICA—Zimbabwe, Mozambique

Approximate area: 460,297 square miles

As we continue on the major thoroughfares and roads of African history, we come to the great walls of Zimbabwe.

Although the sixteenth king of Zimbabwe (Monomapata) sent letters to the king of Portugal and engaged in treaties, the citizens in the streets of Zimbabwe had not yet learned the art of writing. The bulk of the history from this area is taken from an assortment of documents and reports accumulated by the Portuguese subsequent to their contact with ancient Zimbabwe. Other accounts of Zimbabwe's history come from Africa's own account of its history as maintained by its oral historians. Zimbabwe, before it was sacked and looted by the Portuguese in the early 1500s and conquered and colonized by the British in the 1890s, was an empire of impressive stature by any reckoning. Its beginning can be traced to the early 1400s. The founders, a Shona people call Karenga who, for the previous two hundred to three hundred years, had been migrating to the area from the North.

Mutota, the leader of the Shona people and a military man of some note, united the different Shona groups into a number of smaller city-state-like units that were subjected to one central government. Under the British, the empire of Monomapata was renamed Rhodesia after its European founder and financial backer, Samuel Rhodes.

Zimbabwe

<u>Geo-Political Description</u>

Historical Background of Region: Historically, Zimbabwe began in the 1400s as the capital city of the great empire, Mwanamutapa.

Current: the countries of Mozambique and Zimbabwe currently occupy Area.

People (Ethnicity): MaKaranga and MaShona.

Political System: Monarchy (kingship was divine).

Government Structure: King governed through a cabinet of eight ministers appointed annually:

1. Chancellor of the kingdom
   a. Vassal kings
   b. Provincial governors
2. Court Chamberlain
3. Head Drummer
4. Military Commander
5. Keeper of fetishes
6. Head doorman

7. Chief cook

8. Queen Mother

Religion: Monotheistic; worshiping Mwari (God).

Educational System: The nobility sent their children to the Monomatapa court to be educated as pages and soldiers.

Legal System: Laws were based upon religious values, social customs, and business needs in much the same manner as the judicial systems of Europe and America.

Language: Bantu languages.

Arts: Poetry, music, literature, dance, sculpture, and drawings.

Major Industries: Gold mining, ivory, farming, and cattle ranching.

Imports: Cotton from India, brassware and jewelry from China, pottery, and porcelain.

Exports: Gold ingots, ivory, and silver.

Foreign Contact: A Portuguese traveler, Antonio Fernandes, first visited Zimbabwe (Mwanamutapa) in the year 1516.

Currency: Copper and silver coinage.

Economic System: Gold mining, local and overseas trade, cattle ranching, and metal working.

Military: The kingdom maintained a standing army.

Medicine: Medical men practiced medicine, often in conjunction with spiritual application. Herbs were the principal source of medication.

Dress (Clothing): Clothing generally made of cotton fabric imported from Europe.

Housing: Homes were generally constructed of wood or daga (a kind of cement) or of mud-brick. All were routinely constructed using thatch for roofing.

Food (Staples): Manioc, maize, fish, game, and butchered animals.

Agricultural Crops: Manioc, bananas, rice, maize, tomatoes.

Domesticated Animals: The domesticated animals included, sheep, goats, cattle, fowls, elephants and various pets. Heavy emphasis was placed on cattle ranching.

Roads (Trade Routes): Most significant trade occurred via ocean-going vessels.

Cities and Towns: Buildings in the capital were made from stone. The capital was surrounded by stonewalls.

Rural Areas: The rural areas consisted mostly of cattle ranches and farms. Royal family, nobility. Upper class consisted mostly of large cattle ranchers, lower class mostly of farmers

Prominent Statesmen: Emperor Mutota (who reigned from 1437–1450 united the kingdom under a single authority.

Descriptive Quote: The following is quoted from a letter written in the 1630s by Dom Philipe, King of Portugal, to Mavura, the King of Monomotapa (Zimbabwe). "Most noble and powerful King Monomotapa, I, Dom Philipe, by the grace of God King of Portugal, of the Algarves, and of the sea on both sides of Africa, Lord of Guinea and of the conquest, navigation, and commerce of Ethiopia, Arabia, Persia and India, etc., greet you well, as one who I love and esteem as a brother." (*A History of East and Central Africa*)

SOUTHERN AFRICA—Republic of South Africa, Swaziland, Lesotho, Botswana, and Namibia

Approximate area: 1,021,509 square miles

Settlements in the area known to the world today as South Africa actually began with a group of Bantu-speaking immigrants from an area north of the Lipopo River. Archeological records suggest that by the tenth century another immigrant group that called themselves the Kopje people joined these early South Africans. These new immigrants were mostly farmers and metalworkers. They manufactured such products as iron spear points for hunting and defense, and metal hoes for farm use. It was the introduction of the metalworking skill and of maize and cassava crops from America during the sixteenth century that allowed the area's food production to increase for the first time. By the eleventh century the two groups had established small, self-governing villages. Whereas they had begun living in mud-thatch houses, they now began using stone as a building material. Two other groups, the Shona-speaking Sothos and the Ngoni-speaking Mapungubwe Bantu people who were also migrating down from the grasslands of the Congo had also joined them. Along with these new immigrants came new ideas of government. They extended their political control of the area by bringing a considerable number of local towns and communities into large city-states under a central government.

Fundamentally, this area of South Africa remained a land of farmers, metal workers, and cattle-ranching communities until the arrival of the Dutch settlers in the 1760s. After their arrival, and subsequently, that of the English, all other events in the history of South Africa are eclipsed by the influence and history of the kingdom of the Zulus.

South Africa

Geo-Political Description

Historical Background of Region: States of Sotho, Swazi, Kingdom of the Zulus, (1818).

Current: Botswana, Namibia, Lesotho, Republic of South Africa, Swaziland.

People (Ethnicity): Ngoni, Xhosa, Sotho, Khoisans, Swazi, and Tswana.

Political System: Consisted of a monarchy and mainly small city-states in which the king or ruler reigned.

Government Structure: King ruled through vassals.

Religion: Regional and cultural religions.

Educational System: Tutorial and apprentice formats were utilized to develop training in religion, metalworking, history, and social customs.

Legal System: Laws evolved from religions, customs, and business requirement.

Languages: Bantu, Ngoni.

Arts: Poetry (oral), music, storytelling (literature), dance, sculpture, and painting.

Major Industries: Farming, cattle ranching, metalworking.

Imports: No direct import; received maize and cassava plants from America.

Exports: No substantial exports, perhaps ivory and some gold.

Foreign Contact: No foreign interface until they engaged the Dutch settlers in 1757.

Currency: All transactions were conducted via the barter system.

Economic System: Mainly subsistence farming.

Military: No standing army.

Medicine: Medical people (doctors) utilized herbal medicines and often invoked spiritual connection with illnesses.

Dress (Clothing): Clothing fabric woven from raffia or palm tree tissues.

Housing: Regional buildings materials vary from stone and wood to thatched baked mud brick and reeds.

Food (staples): Millet, maize, manioc and cassava.

Agricultural Crops: Millet, sorghum, imported maize, cassava, manioc, and potatoes.

Domesticated Animals: The domesticated animals included, pigs, chickens, sheep, goats, cattle, fowls, elephants and various pets.

Roads (trade routes): No substantial trade engaged in outside the immediate region.

Cities and Towns: Towns and villages in these areas probably served as the principal site of government offices and as markets where goods and services were exchanged or bartered, much like the small towns and villages of the early American frontiers.

Rural Areas: Communities consisted mainly of independent families engaged in subsistence farming consisting of agricultural crops and domesticated animals such as pigs, sheep, chickens, and cattle.

Prominent Statesmen: The most significant statesman of this area came during the nineteenth century in the person of Shaka, King of the Zulus.

Descriptive Quote: "Mefecane"

SOUTHWESTERN AFRICA—Congo, Angola, and Gabon

Approximate area: 716,744 square miles

Over the past 1400 years, from around the sixth century, the area imme-diately south of the river Congo and just north of the Kwanza River on the southwestern coast of Africa has been home to an assortment of rural communities, city-states, nations, and kingdoms. One of those kingdoms, the Kingdom of Congo, has a rather unique place in African history.

In 1492, while the Portuguese expedition led by Christopher Columbus was venturing into the Americas, Portuguese missionaries, embassy per-sonnel, blacksmiths, carpenters, masons, bricklayers, and farm workers were visiting the Kingdom of Congo.

Also, two members of the Congolese royal household traveled to Rome to visit the Pope. One of the visitors, baptized in the name, Dom Henrique, became the Bishop of Utica.

Kingdom of Congo

Geo-Political Description

Historical Background of Region: The Kingdom of Congo was subdi-vided into six separate provinces.

Current: the countries of Congo, Gabon, and Angola now occupy this area

People (Ethnicity): Bantu.

Political System: Elected monarchy.

Government Structure: The monarchy ruled through the nobles and the six provincial governors. Taxes were collected by the provincial governors and forwarded to the capital or national treasury.

Religion: Roman Catholicism (Introduced in 1492) plus other local belief systems.

Educational System: The Portuguese introduced reading and writing in 1641. Subsequently, a number of youths were sent off to attend the college of Santo Eloi at Lisbon, Portugal. Local schools located throughout the country.

Legal System: Justice was administered in accordance with civil laws and as established by custom (Congolese common law). Note: After arrival of Portuguese embassy officials, missionaries and traders, the judicial system consisted of a Portuguese magistrate if the plaintiff was Congolese, and a Congolese magistrate if the plaintiff was Portuguese.

Language: A Bantu language.

Arts: Poetry, music, literature, dance, sculpture, and drawings.

Major Industries: Iron and copper mining pottery works, woven straw mats, cloth weaving, farming, hunting, and iron—and copper-smelting.

Imports: Portuguese technology, blacksmiths, masons, bricklayers, tools, books, field laborers, and consumer goods.

Exports: No substantial export activity.

Foreign Contact:

1. "The Congolese showed an enthusiastic willingness to adopt the ways of western civilization which anticipated that of the Japanese 350 years later."
2. Portuguese explorers/traders arrived in 1483.
3. Follow-up visits by Portuguese diplomatic envoys, missionaries, artisans and teachers1588 visited by Portuguese Duarte Lopes.
4. 1649 visited by Italian Capuchin friars.

Currency: The Nzimbu.

Economic System: Mostly cottage industries. Royal treasuries operated from taxes, fines, and tolls.

Military: Mostly armed with bows and arrows.

Medicine: Medical professionals were highly esteemed by the Portuguese.

Dress (Clothing): Clothing fabric woven from raffia or palm tree tissues.

Housing: Official buildings were frequently of stone, but homes were regularly made of thatched baked mud brick and reeds. Churches and schools were generally built of stone when located within the city walls and of other local materials when built in the rural areas.

Food (staples): Millet, maize, and manioc.

Agricultural Crops: Millet, sorghum, imported maize, manioc, citric fruits, and potatoes.

Domesticated Animals: The domesticated animals included, sheep, goats, cattle, fowls, elephants and various pets.

Roads (trade routes): Trade routes to the sea 150 miles long.

Cities and Towns: The capital, Mbanza, Congo, later renamed Sao Salvador, had an estimated population of around one hundred thousand people.

Rural Areas: Farming communities maintained such animals such as pigs, sheep, chickens and cattle. They used metal hoes and axes.

Prominent Statesmen:

1. King Nzinga Mbemba (1506–1543) who assumed the Christian name of Dom Afonso I, and adopted Roman Catholicism as the kingdom's official religion. Regarding the trade in African slavery, he wrote an angry letter to the king of Portugal in which he com-

plained that "the slave trade was doing great harm to his country. Together with certain Bakongo thieves and men of evil conscience, Portuguese traders were grabbing and selling his people, even including members of his own family." He also demanded that Portugal recall its traders, "because it is his [Affonso] will that in the Kingdoms of Congo there shouldn't be any trade in slaves, nor any market for such slaves." He further stated that he wanted nothing from Portugal except priests to teach in his schools, and wine and bread for the Lord's Supper.

2. Bishop Dom Henrique, Bishop of Utica.

Descriptive Quote: This comment is made of the Congolese King, Dom Affonso, (Nzinga Mbemba); "[he] learned to read and write Portuguese, and he studied so hard that he often fell asleep over his books from sheer exhaustion."

CENTRAL AFRICA—Niger, Chad, Nigeria, Cameroon, C.A.R.

Approximate area: 1,764,709 square miles

The Bornu-Kanem Empire first came into historical focus sometime during the early part of the ninth century. Before being organized into an empire, it consisted of six smaller, loosely confederated city-states located in the region of Lake Chad. The six city-states—Daura, Gobir, Kano, Rano, Katsina, and Zegzeg—in addition to being located in the Lake Chad region, were also, more importantly, located on one of the major West African trade routes. The trade route was a principal corridor for the ivory, salt, kola nuts, and other goods coming from the West African states, and for the horses, salt, fine metalware, and copper coming from Egypt, Nubia, and other African states to the north. Trade became one of the principal industries of the Bornu-Kanem Empire.

The Bornu-Kanem Empire saw its greatest territorial and political expansion under one of its best-known emperors, Idis Alooma whose reign lasted from 1580 to 1617. He became one of the most powerful and politically adept leaders in the history of the empire. Unfortunately, or perhaps unavoidably, the empire of Bornu-Kanem funded its governments operations largely by colonial expansion. As a result, there were extended periods of times during which the empire took on the characteristics of militaristic expansionism.

Bornu-Kanem Empire

Geo-Political Description

Historical Background of Region—Bornu-Kanem consisted of six small city-states, Daura; Gobir; Kano; Rano; Katsina, and Zegzeg.

Current: The countries of Niger, Chad, Nigeria currently occupy the area of Central African Republic and Cameroon.

People (Ethnicity): Kanuri and Hausa.

Political System: Monarchy (king semi-divine).

Government Structure: The king governed through a cabinet of twelve provincial governors, and a general of military operation.

Religion: Islamic (fourteenth century), local belief systems.

Educational System: Reading and writing were introduced in the twelfth century.

Legal System: A single system of law and order was established throughout the country.

Language: Hausa.

Arts: Poetry, music, literature, dance, sculpture, and drawing.

Major Industries: Iron ore mining, farming, leather working, bronze castings works, fabric weaving and dyeing, iron ore smelting, domestic and foreign trade, blacksmith forging, hunting and fishing. Note: The city of Meroe's main industry was iron smelting. Meroe's fame in iron ore smelting ranks it as Africa's equivalent of Birmingham, England, or Pittsburgh, Pennsylvania.

Imports: Horses, fine metalware, firearms, salt, copper, ivory, kola nuts, and ammunition.

Exports: Iron, mutton, cotton, iron products.

Foreign Contact: the sultan of the Ottoman empire visited Idris Alooma. Trade with the Portuguese and North Africa.

Currency: Cowry shells, brass pieces, and barter.

Economic System: Major trading center.

Military: Wore armor of mail and imported firearms as early as the seventeenth century.

Medicine: Extensive use of herbal medicine.

Dress (Clothing): Homegrown, homespun, and dyed cotton was the primary fabric.

Housing: Houses were built of wood; roofs had skylights, rooms were square and houses were built close together along wide, straight streets.

Food (Staples): Maize, pineapples (imported from the Americas), fish, and game.

Agricultural crops: Cotton, maize.

Domesticated Animals: The domesticated animals included, sheep, goats, cattle, fowls, elephants and various pets.

Roads (Trade Routes): Situated adjacent to the busy trans-Saharan trade route.

Cities and Towns: Walls of stone were built around cities and around some smaller towns.

Rural Areas: Rural areas consisted mostly of small homesteads. They maintained subsistence farming, animal husbandry, and small ranches.

Prominent Statesmen:

1. Idris Alooma expanded the empire and its influence throughout the eastern region.

2. The Sefuwa kings and emperors whose dynasty lasted for eight hundred years.

Descriptive Quote: Of the Bornu-Kanem Empire, "What the Kanuri and their allies and subjects were able to do, over a very long period, and in a region of great importance, was to bring the advantage of a single system of law and order to a great many different people, and it was through this large empire that West Africa kept in regular touch with vital centers of civilizations beyond the Sahara, and especially Egypt." It was through Kanem that the goods of Egypt and other northern lands, horses, and fine metalware, salt and copper, came into West Africa by way of the eastern Sahara; and it was often through Kanem that the goods of West Africa, notably kola and ivory, were taken in exchange to those northern lands." (*A History of West Africa*)

WEST AFRICA—Senegal, Gambia, Guinea Bissau, Guinea, Sierra Leone, Liberia, Ivory Coast, Burkina Faso, Togo, Benin

Approximate area: 883,804 square miles

In a manner similar to the area of northwest Africa, this area, the home of the sixth to the fifteenth century kingdoms of Benin and Oyo, was one of the principal areas from which enslaved Africans destined for America were captured. Most of these Africans came from an area of West Africa stretching from the site of present-day Ghana, northward toward the coast of Morocco, and southward to present-day Angola. The countries that presently occupy this area of our ancestry are Morocco, Spanish Sahara, Mauritania, Senegal, Mali, Upper Volta, Gambia, Guinea, Sierra Leone, Ivory Coast, Liberia, Ghana, Togo, Dahomey, Nigeria, Cameroon, Gabon, Congo, and Angola. Alex Haley's *Roots* led him back to the country of Gambia to find his African ancestors.

Before the trade in African enslavement began, however, the states of Benin and Oyo were the dominant political forces in the area. Oyo, a small city-state, the citizens of which were mostly ethnic Yorubans, was located inland and maintained its capital near the river Niger. Benin, on the other hand, was located closer to the Atlantic coast and was inhabited by ethnic Edo people. At the time Christopher Columbus was discovering America, or more specifically toward the end of the fifteenth century Benin was described by Paychec Pererica, a Portuguese explorer. Pererica, while scouting for available sources to establish trade in slaves, visited the city and described it as approximately three miles long, surrounded by a protective wall. The area of the Benin state or kingdom was described as extending some 250 miles from east to west. By the middle of the eighteenth century, the kingdom of Benin and the state of Oyo had united with other city-states in the area to form the Ashanti nation, which was ultimately overwhelmed by European forces during the slave trade and the advent of colonial expansionism.

The Ashanti Nation (United States of Ashanti)

Geo-Political Description

Historical Background of Region: The United States of Ashanti consisted of the states of Oyo, Benin, Dahomey, and Ashanti and was united into a single kingdom. The image of the golden stool, a symbol of royalty, was the national icon or flag.

Current: the countries of Senegal, the Gambia, Guinea Bissau, Guinea, Sierra Leone, Liberia, Ivory Coast, Burkina Faso, Ghana, Togo, and Benin currently occupy this area.

People (Ethnicity): Yoruba and Edo.

Political System: King, inherited by royal primogeniture.

Government Structure: The king governed though a cabinet of provincial kings and governors. Civil servants staffed governmental bureaucracy.

Religion: Christianity introduced in the fifteenth century.

Educational System: Schools varied from full-fledged academies to home class rooms and taught subjects as varied as medicine, trade, law, religion, history, and politics.

Legal System: Civil laws were based upon religion and social customs.

Language: Housa.

Arts: Poetry, music, literature, dance, sculpture, and drawing.

Major Industries: Salt mines, iron ore mining, hand-manufacture of farming, tool, knives, fish hooks, kitchen utensils, and household furniture.

Imports: Military equipment, consumer goods such as cloth, tools, mainly from Portugal.

Exports: Salt, ivory.

Foreign Contact: Fifteenth-century visit by Portuguese Paychec Pereira.

Currency: Cowry shells, copper pieces, and barter.

Economic System: Depended heavily upon the mining and exporting of gold.

Military: A standing army of mounted cavalry.

Medicine: Consisted of herbal medicines combined with a prominent religious application.

Dress (Clothing): Clothing fashioned from locally grown cotton and from imported cotton fabrics.

Housing: Houses were built of wood and stone, and some were built of baked mud and thatch.

Food (Staples): Maize, games, pigs, and homegrown vegetables.

Agricultural Crops: Pepper, maize, and cotton.

Domesticated Animals: Pigs, cattle, and horses.

Roads: Trade routes to the Atlantic coast.

Cities and Towns: The capital of the empire was a city three miles long with a wall around its entire perimeter. It was described as having great streets with neat rows of houses on each side. The king's residence was described as an enormous royal palace with courtyards and galleries and magnificent brass figures and plaques.

Rural Areas: Rural areas consisted mostly of small homestead, subsistence farming, animal husbandry, and small ranches.

Prominent Statesmen: (a) King Obalokun, during the sixteenth century he improved the salt-mining process, and opened up foreign trade with white people. (b) King Osei Tutu of Kumasi and Okomfo Onokye, his chief priest or prime minister, inaugurated the Union of Ashanti in the latter part of the seventeenth century.

Descriptive Quote, or Observation: During his reign between 17241732, the king of Dahomey issued a royal decree banning the enslavement of Dahomey citizens. Additionally, he launched a military campaign to assure compliance with his prohibition against the taking and selling of Dahomey citizens as slaves.

NORTHWEST AFRICA—Mali, Mauritania, West Sahara

Approximate area: 899,900 square miles

Ghana, which was located northeast of its current site, was a major African empire. Its borders ran roughly along two of the more prominent trade routes on the northeast and extended as far as the southern borders of present-day Mali and Guinea. Also, the information that survived reveals that the ancient empire of Ghana traded in kola nuts, iron, ivory, gold, and a number of other goods. Some of its trading partners were as far away as Europe and Asia. It endured until around 1240 when it collapsed under the influence of internal factions and the Islamic invasion of North Africa that had begun during the eighth century.

Following the decline of the kingdom of Ghana, a smaller but equally notable state emerged. Mali, the new empire, is perhaps best known because of Mansa Musa, its emperor. Mansa Kan Kan Musa came to power in 1312. Under his rule, Mali became one of the largest and wealthiest empires in the world. In 1324, while on a pilgrimage to Mecca, emperor Mansa Musa carried and dispensed so much gold that when he passed through Cairo, Egypt, his purchases and gifts in gold upset the value of trade on the Cairo market. Under Mansa Musa, Mali had ambassadors and royal agents established in Portugal, Morocco, Egypt, and in other major trading centers. The capital of Mali was often visited by North African and Egyptian scholars and upon his return from his pilgrimage to Mecca; Mansa Musa brought Egyptian scholars back to Mali and to Timbuktu. Mali remained a strong empire and exerted influential control over the West African regions that would become the main source of African slaves two hundred years later.

Shortly after the 1400s, Mali began to decline. Beset by warring states within the empire, it came under siege by the Moslems whose sweep across the region had begun with their overthrow and the destruction of the empire. When the Portuguese arrived on the west coast of Africa in the latter half of the fifteenth century, the empire was already in decline. The ruler of Mali at the time appealed to the Portuguese for help, but to no avail. Across the far plains and slow ascending hills of Western Sudan, the authority of the old empires was now at an end. By 1619, the imperial power of Mali had practically disappeared. In its wake, however, rose the kingdom of Gao, which would remain a political force in the region until overcome by the force of European military might in the mid-nineteenth century.

Ghana/Mali/Gao Kingdoms

Geo-Political Description

Historical Background of Region: The kingdoms of ancient Kingdom of Ghana in the fourteenth century gradually evolved into the Empire of Mali in the eleventh century. Upon its decline, it gave rise to the Gao empire.

Current: the countries of west Sahara, Mauritania, and Mali currently occupy the area.

People (Ethnicity): Mandinka and Songhay.

Political system: Monarchy.

Government structure:

1. An emperor or king
2. Provincial governors

3. A cabinet of six departments:
   a. Department of Finances
   b. Department of Justice
   c. Department of Home Affairs
   d. Department of Agriculture
   e. Department of Forestry
   f. Department of White People

Religion: Regional religions, Islam, perhaps some Christianity. Their temples were decorated with religious icons.

Educational System: University at Timbuktu taught a variety of subjects, among which were theology, Islamic law, rhetoric (philosophy), grammar, and literature.

Legal System: Laws were established in response to custom, religion and business interests. Enforcement of the laws was the responsibility of the emperor through the Department of Justice.

Language: An assortment of Bantu languages.

Arts: Poetry, music, literature, dance sculpture, and paintings, woodcarving.

Major Industries:
1. Trade in salt from Saharan salt mines.
2. Mined iron ore.
3. Iron smelting
4. Blacksmithing
5. Farming
6. Worked copper mines
7. Copper smelting

8. Worked Bronze

9. Cattle ranching

10. Trade in gold, horses, cloth, swords, books, and haberdashery from Europe

Imports:

1. Finished products from Europe

2. Salt and gold and lumber from countries of the south

3. Finished products from countries of the south

Exports: Salt, lumber, gold, and diamonds.

Foreign Contact: (a) Visited in 1513 by a young Arab named al-Hassan ibn Muhammad, who later wrote on African history under the name of Leo Africanus. (b) Moslems from the Western Sahara captured Ghana in 1077 (c) Ghana was visited by ibn-Battuta in June 1353.

Currency: Copper coins and barter system.

Economic System: The state maintained ownership of the gold and diamond mines as royal monopolies.

Military: Maintained a standing army of 200,000 soldiers, 40,000 of whom were still armed with bows and arrows.

Medicine: Consisted of herbal medicines combined with a prominent religious application.

Dress (Clothing): Fabrics woven from either imported or domestic cotton.

Housing: In the towns and more prosperous areas, homes were constructed of stone, but in rural areas homes were often constructed of woven straw mats.

Foods (Staples): Maize, kola nuts, games, fish, and meat from the slaughter of domesticated animals.

Agricultural Crops: Primarily corn and cotton.

Domesticated Animals: The domesticated animals included, sheep, goats, cattle, fowls, elephants and various pets.

Roads (Trade Routes): The trans-Saharan trade routes and trade routes to the Atlantic coast.

Cities and Towns: Timbuktu and al-Ghaba (the Ghanain capital).

Rural Areas: Localized homesteads with houses of wood, mud-straw bricks, and thatched roofs. Farms generally included farming, animal husbandry, cattle ranching.

Prominent Statesmen:

1. Twelfth-century Emperor Mansa Munsa put the empire of Mali on the fourteenth-century European map. During his pilgrimage to Mecca he carried so much gold with him that when he passed through Cairo, Egypt his expenditure of gold created an inflationary effect upon the Egyptian currency.

2. As king, Askia the Great (1493) united the greater part of western Sudan into the Gao Empire.

Descriptive Quote: The historian Leo Africanus, an Arab converted from Islam to Christianity, said the following of the city of Timbuktu. "There are numerous judges, doctors, and clerics in Timbuktu, all receiving good salaries from the king. He pays great respect to men of learning. There is a big demand for books in manuscript, imported from Barbary. More profit is made from the book trade than from an other line of business."

SUMMARY

In summary, it is said that a picture is worth a thousand words. Since we have neither pictures nor actual word descriptions of the activities of ancient Africa, we have attempted the fore-going alternative. By utilizing a type of narrative, or snapshot questionnaire answers to each of the six questions posed at the beginning of the chapter, we believe we have achieved what otherwise required many more words in straight narrative. The responses to the questions are attempted via use of a pseudo-questionnaire format. The purpose was to formulate historical data in such a manner as to make it more visually accessible. It is from these semi-narrative/snapshots of the economic, cultural, and political characteristics of pre-slave trade Africa that a clearer picture of modern Africa can be reassembled. It is hoped this innovation has allowed the reader to see at a glance, so to speak, the kinds of people that the African ancestors of today's black Americans were. The particular historical periods and cultures portrayed in these snapshots do not, of course, represent all of the ethnic or cultural groups present during the centuries covered, but the ten geographical areas and the cultural groups located within them will provide some answers to the six questions originally posed.

Moreover, I hope that by implication at least, we would also have put into perspective some of the more personal questions, not just who those 1619 Africans were, historically and geographically, but what kind of people they were. Who were their mothers and fathers? What subjects were taught in their schools? What was their national interest? Who were their chiefs, kings, queens, or emperors? What religions did they follow? Were they Christians, Moslems, or did they belong to religions of which we are unaware? How did they live? What kind of houses did they live in? What kind of foods sustained them? What kind of clothes adorned them? What kind of jobs skills did they possess? Were they farmers? If so, what crops did they grow? Did they mine gold, iron, or copper? Did their governments draft for the military? Since it is often reported historically that a number of the ancient Africans people left no written language, how did they learn history and science? How did they write to relatives and friends?

How did they study in school? What kind of lessons were they taught? And lastly, what view did they have of cultures other than their own?

It is hoped that these snapshots have allowed the reader to better understand that Africa—though often described as if the historians had their non-European perspectives tied behind their backs—was essentially no different, no better or worse, than any other nation or groups of peoples. In some instances African life support circumstances were decidedly better than other nations or peoples. For instance, Roland Oliver wrote in *The Dawn of History of Africa*, "We may be sure that an easier life was lived in the round houses of Africa than in the cottages of Europe's medieval serfs and free peasants. Certainly the African peasant enjoyed more leisure." Therefore, it would appear that when these "snapshots" are assembled and viewed together as a sort of collage, it should become apparent that the pre-slave trade cultures of Africa were fundamentally no different than that of other countries during their respective culture's evolutional period. Some national governments were well organized and functioned effectively and their people lived in degrees of comfort and social sophistication. There were, however, other cultural groups whose people were considerably less developed and lived in considerably less comfort and social sophistication.

Egypt is an example of a well-developed African country whose people lived comfortable and sophisticated lifestyles. By their own historical documents, their history can be traced back to not hundreds, but thousands of years. Many other countries whose civilizations also date back thousands of years could also be mentioned, but here I quite deliberately limited my focus to Egypt. Some will certainly say, as has been said regarding the great stonewalls of ancient Zimbabwe, that the great civilizations of Egypt that dominated the political, cultural, and economic forces of the Iron Age circle were not truly African. They would say that the inhabitants of ancient Egypt were not of the same racial stock as are the traditional or sub-Saharan Africans. The main point of their argument was that the people who established cultures as developed, sophisticated, and enduring as those of Egypt, Nubia, Carthage, Zimbabwe, and Ethiopia were not characteristically Africans.

When America begins to count its history in thousands of years, the miscegenation process will undoubtedly have turned the ethnic face of its West Coast citizens away from western Europe and become decidedly Hispanic and Asian. If and when such a time occurs, should the contributions of those non-European Americans be discounted from the whole? Of course they cannot. It is the blend of cultural mixes that occurred in the coastline cities of North Africa and of both coasts of America that has enhanced the growth of cultural and technical innovations. The founding premise of America's melting pot phenomenon is that the growth of the United States itself has been enhanced because of its ethnic diversity. If you separated the major coastline states of New York and California from the United States of America, you would have seriously diminished the cultural and technical status of the country. With due respect to the southern states, if the level of their technology fifty years ago was all that constituted the cultural and technological development of America, we would have been little more than another third-world country. It fact, the variation that exists between the degree of development in some geographic areas of America versus that of other areas is also reflected by what the snapshots show us about pre-slave trade Africa. It is reasonable to assume that whatever forces were at work in the distribution of technical development in pre-slave trade Africa also might have been at work in the distribution of technological development in America.

The east coast of America (and specifically, metropolitan New York) has for years been the cultural, economic, and political centerpiece of the country. Of course, California (and more specifically, Los Angeles) has been prominent in these regards during recent years. But to understand historical Africa apart from a platform of perpetual bias, it is necessary to retain a view of Africa as an assortment of cultural developments that are similarly diversified. On the east coast there was Egypt, historical and constant, the cultural and economic centerpiece of Africa. The ancient Hittites, Phoenicians, and Greeks trafficked here. The first iron tools of the barbarians of western Europe came from here. Alexander the Great built his famous port city here. Anthony met Cleopatra here. Even though Africa was not united into a single nation, interaction between the various governments occurred through their engagement in transcontinental economic and cultural trade. As pointed out in the introduction of this chapter, no attempts or efforts have been made to buoy the cultural credentials of the African people. In all regards, the only consideration is to "render unto Caesar that which is Caesar's." Or render unto the Africans that which belongs to Africans. This was the period of iron-age technology. It would appear that movement of the Iron Age technology occurred through Africa, Asia, and Europe at practically the same pace. Radiating outward from the Mediterranean Iron Age circle at a rate of approximately three miles per year, its movement covered the entire three-continent land mass. It went no farther until the technology spun by it was capable of taking it across the ocean to America in 1492.

And so we can see that time and circumstance played a key role in the flow of the currents of technological growth. To attempt to understand why these currents did not flow through the heartland of the African continent would be the same as pondering why the present Pacific ocean currents do not irrigate the Mojave Desert. For example, from the initial origin of the Iron Age in 1650 it took an additional three thousand years, until the fifteenth century, for the currents of that technology to flow five thousand miles across the Pacific Ocean or the three thousand miles across the Atlantic to the inhabitants of the Americas and of Australia. And yet today, it is America that is the predominant player in the technological age.

3

AN AFRICAN HOLOCAUST

"He [King George IV] has waged cruel war against human nature itself, violating its most sacred rights of life and liberty in the persons of distinct people, who never offended him; captivating and carrying them into slavery in another hemisphere to incur miserable death in their transportation thither. This piratical warfare, the opprobrium of infidel powers, is the warfare of the Christian King of Great Britain. Determined to keep open market where MEN should be bought and sold, he has prostituted his negative for suppressing every legislative attempt to prohibit or to restrain this execrable commerce"

Thomas Jefferson, Draft copy of the Declaration of Independence

Rape, Pillage, Loot, and Burn

The quotation above is taken from language contained in the closing article of the original draft copy of Declaration of Independence proposed by Thomas Jefferson. Because the language of the article contained such a strong social, political, and moral indictment of Europe's practice of the enslaving and establishing mercantile trade in the citizens of Africa, it was omitted from the final ratified version of the Declaration of Independence as a compromise gesture to win the support of southern delegates to the constitutional convention. Although excised from the final version, the text and the sentiments are nonetheless a reflection of the beliefs of its author. And although the indictment against the king and the trade in the enslavement of the Africans was not formally ratified, it still functions as an effective barometer of the feelings and points of view that existed in the minds of some Americans during the mid-eighteenth century.

In his assessment, Thomas Jefferson levied a strong and passionate indictment against Great Britain's reigning monarch, King George III, whose policies regarding the trade in the enslavement of the Africans and the institution of slavery itself played a significant role in the determination as to whether the colonies retained or abolished slavery. It is appropriate to keep in mind that when Jefferson wrote these words into the Declaration of Independence, the Revolutionary War that resulted in America's independence, had of course not yet been fought. And so the colonies were still very much under the laws and government control of the British's king. In his accusations against the king, Thomas Jefferson charged that the monarch's trafficking in the African slave trade was tantamount to having waged a war against human nature itself (In current human rights terms, his actions would undoubtedly be viewed in the context of crimes against humanity). The sentiment expressed in this statement would tend to rebut the arguments posed by some black and white Americans that the Declaration of Independence's declarative statement regarding the natural rights of human beings did not apply to the African immigrants. Jefferson's charge that the king was waging war against nature itself is a clear vindication of what he meant when he wrote that particular statement in the Declaration of Independence. The charge was that the British monarch was violating the African peoples' most sacred rights of life and liberty. Taken to its logical extension, the statement would suggest that the colonists would have rid themselves of slavery—or if not slavery itself, then certainly of the trade in enslaved Africans—by the eighteenth century, had the British king not opposed their actions and instead forced his "execrable commerce" upon the settlements and peoples of the New World.

John Rolfe's account as recorded in his diary, of the arrival of twenty Africans into Jamestown in 1619 has served and continues to serve as the flagship statement signaling the arrival of the first enslaved Africans into the New World. And more than simply recounting their arrival to the United States, it also signaled how rapidly agriculture was becoming a prominent source of revenue in the New World. The settlement at Jamestown had been in operation only since 1607, and yet in just twelve years, it had already become productive enough to require a labor supply beyond its own indigenous labor source. With its Native American labor source severely taxed and the European indentured system apparently unable to satisfy the demands, the colony now turned to those who traded in the enslaved Africans. The African people therefore became a commodity and the slave traffic a business enterprise. As the years progressed, the Africans would suffer enormous, social, political, and economic losses that are directly attributable to the increasing demand for additional supplies of workers driven by the New World's growing agricultural and industrial activities.

Of those twenty Africans, we know very little except that they arrived onboard a Dutch warship. Additionally, we know that, unlike the one hundred and twenty English immigrants who arrived a year later at Plymouth Rock, the Africans were not destined to become enshrined in American folklore as heroes of nation building as were the 1620 Pilgrims. Rather, the arrival and role of the twenty Africans have been relegated to historical footnotes. Or when rising above a mere footnote, they were subjected to the scornful critique of twentieth-century hindsight. In a way, though, both groups of immigrants—the one hundred and twenty Pilgrims and the twenty Africans—were destined by the uniqueness of their circumstances to be the vanguard elements of movements in political morality that would ultimately spread throughout the rest of the world. The Pilgrims, fresh from a reformation Europe, came with the innovative notions of politics of the future, and the arrival of the Africans, caught up in Europe's political economics of the past, caused the two to become merged into a single philosophy—human rights.

It is not possible to know the moral or philosophical questions that John Rolfe and the other Jamestown residents may have asked of themselves as they undertook such a fateful purchase, but we know that the erstwhile "business as usual" transaction was to ultimately have a most profound affect upon the moral values of the nation they were attempting to build. Its effects were not only upon the people whose backs bore the brunt of the lash and the task, but upon the taskmasters also. Or, as the writer of the Ecclesiastes put it, "there is a time when one man ruleth over another to his own hurt." For indeed the presence of slavery in America was a hurt. It was like the proverbial "thorn in the side" thrust directly into the ideals of the country's pretenses of moral enlightenment. And like a thorn, it continued to fester until 1860 when it erupted into a bloody and costly civil war. What we can readily acknowledge, though, is that John Rolfe's account of the arrival of those twenty African signaled a connection between America and the continent of the Africa that would play an increasingly prominent role in the fate of each. The purpose and focus of this chapter is not so much upon John Rolfe's twenty Africans but to see them merely as the triggering event that set in motion an industry that would ultimately result in the African holocaust.

Black Americans have strong feelings about having been abducted from their homeland, enslaved, and brought to America, and justifiably so. But there is another side to the story that black Americans rarely reflect upon. It concerns the impoverishing agony that was heaped upon the thousands and thousands of African families who were themselves victimized by the sudden and painful disappearance of family members and other loved ones. For over thirteen generations, nearly three hundred years, men, women, and children were routinely abducted from their home and shipped to labor camps around the world thousands of miles away. Millions of people were seized and forcibly transported on a one-way journey that permanently severed ties with family members, languages, and landscapes. They were transplanted more than four thousand miles away to the Americas. In the following pages, I shall attempt to speak, not of those that were enslaved, but for the suffering of those millions of families left behind. My comments are not meant to be from a historian's point of view but rather from that of a humanitarian whose own moral conscience is founded upon and articulated by the behavioral edits of a Judeo-Christian society. In contemplating the full measure of those dark years on the shores of West Africa, we realize that it is impossible to fully fathom the depth of human trauma that most assuredly occurred. And one would undoubtedly have to have been present at that time in order to grasp the magnitude and degree of sheer human misery that those African families most likely endured.

The national experiences of Americans do not lend themselves to easily understand such degrees of sheer horror. Therefore, even though the vocabulary of the average American might contain words like catastrophe, calamity, tragedy, cataclysmic, disaster, havoc, misfortune, inferno, annihilation, extermination, massacre, or slaughter, none of these words has been sufficiently expanded by national experience to convey the plight of those African families. None of these words would have the alarming effect that yelling "fire" in a crowded theater would have. It is not our intent that the word used should inspire terror but rather, that it elicits empathy for pain and losses that occurred nearly five hundred years ago. Although the world has been generous in its aid when famines have visited Africa, it is wished that it would be equally generous in remembering. To the best of my knowledge, there has been no published recognition of Africa's pain.

For the survivors of the six million Jews that were kidnapped and exterminated in the gas chambers of the Nazi holocaust, we have constructed monuments and museums in an assortment of sites around the world. These bear witness to, and assist survivors in memorializing the victims.

But for the survivors of more than ten million Africans who were kidnapped and taken from their families, no such monument stand, nor such healing devices. The nations and peoples that engaged in the "execrable commerce" of slavery have erected no reminders, no witness marks as memorial commemoration to their victims' only remnants of the festering sores where the wounds occurred. Even black Americans, busy feeling sorry for themselves, have failed to recognize or pay heed to the grievous agony suffered by the families, friends, and loved ones who remained in the African homeland. Their pain was certainly no less than that of those who arrived in America. Even the misery of having lived under slavery in the various labor camps and plantations of the New World would still have to take its place among the miseries suffered by the Africans left at home.

In the final analysis, after surveying and contemplating many other words and expressions, I feel that only the word "holocaust" has been sufficiently energized, both in America and in the rest of the world, to effectively communicate the degree of horror surely suffered by the African peoples during the three hundred years that this "execrable commerce" was carried out. Therefore the chapter's title, "The African Holocaust." This word works primarily because most people and particularly Americans can relate to a holocaust. Europeans and Americans already possess the depth of feeling prompted by the Jewish Holocaust to appreciate the pains the Africans underwent. It is for this cause that Americans and Europeans should have sufficient a depth-of-trauma experience to translate what could only be described as unparalleled human suffering and devastation. Although it is this human suffering the Africans were compelled to undergo that prompts the application of this term, pain-and-death suffering alone were not the only dimension of the African holocaust. To reflect on the full dimension of the impact the enslavement of the Africans and the trade associated with it had upon the peoples of the African continent, we must look beyond the obvious. We must look, not only to its more obvious social effects, but also, even if only speculatively, to the effects such actions had upon the economics, the governments, the religious institutions, the educational system, the family structures, and the pain-and-death suffering of the people.

Of the social effects, we shall, figuratively speaking, visit the families of those who were abducted. Beyond that, we shall attempt to look at the political consequences resulting from the devastation caused by those who had turned African families, mothers, fathers, and children into a marketable commodity. Our plan is to see what effect the shortage of up to ten or more million Africans had upon the local, regional, city-state, and national governments, as well as governments at the empire or kingdom level. After that, we shall speculate as to the effect the trade in the enslavement of the Africans had upon the economies of the African countries most affected. Obviously, to look back in history and speculate on what might have been could earn the dubious characterization of dealing in the make-believe. Be assured, though, that even in our speculation, we shall deal only with those arguments, which are grounded in the facts recorded in historical records. When opinions are offered, they shall be base on logical probabilities sustained by comparative analysis. Along that line of thought, it is reasonable, particularly since the impact the Europeans have had upon Africa has had been so profoundly significant, to speculate upon the alternative courses of development the African peoples might have taken, had the foreign policy of the Portuguese government been different. If, for instance, the Portuguese government's policy had been one of cultural and technical cooperation with the peoples of Africa rather than one of exploitation, then it is quite possible that the nations of Africa would have had quite a different role in the growth of the industrial revolution. For instance, had the African nations, particularly the Kingdom of Congo, been given access to the advanced technologies then existing in Europe, who can presume what might have occurred. In his *A History of East and Central Africa*, the author, Basil Davidson, commenting on the tendency of the citizens of the Kingdom of Congo and its King Nzinga Nbemba to emulate the ways and things of the West, says that they "preceded the Japanese in this regards by some three hundred and fifty years." If the Congolese were as inclined toward things Western as the account suggests, then it is reasonable to think it probable, or at least possible, that the Congolese might very well have adopted Western technology and become a developed nation by the twentieth century as did the Japanese.

Since Mr Davidson used Japan in his reference, we shall take the liberty to continue the analogy. To use Japan as a comparative example, we need to go back to the history of the Japanese people. Until the mid-nineteenth century, the Japanese lived mostly under a feudal system. The average person was a serf or lived under circumstances similar to that of a serf. Whereas the serfs of Europe had been emancipated, at least three hundred to four hundred years before, Japanese peasants were still living in a deplorable state of servitude and poverty. Regional and despotic noblemen, known as Samurai, ruled the country. Peasants lived their lives in abject obedience to the wishes of the Samurai. In 1549, a Jesuit priest missionary, Francis Xavier, described Japan as a country devastated by feudal wars. Three hundred years later, when Commodore Perry landed in Japan, he saw a country still ruled by the same terrorizing Samurai. The Japanese were awestruck by the advance technology and sophistication of the steam power engines used to power Commodore Perry's fleet of ten American ships. However, realizing their national vulnerability and seeing how medieval and technologically unsophisticated their nation was, the Japanese Samurai coalesced around the emperor to form a central government. Which then made a national commitment to improve its industry. It also committed large portions of its resources, both financial and human, to move itself out of feudalism to become an industrialized power. For the next fifty years, the Japanese government worked man and beast to achieve its objective, and by 1899, as the twentieth century dawned, the industrial strength and military might of Japan had become almost comparable to that of its mentor, Great Britain.

Therefore, since the Japanese were able to move from a state of medieval feudalism to that of an industrial super-power in roughly forty years, it would therefore be reasonable to suppose that, had the Portuguese government used its technological resources to aid rather than to enslave, the Congolese people might indeed have become awash in the waters of the industrial revolution as far back as the seventeenth century. However, as the saying goes, you can't lose that which you never had. So is it not possible to contend that the absence of industrial growth on the part of Africa can be tabulated as a loss attributable to the impact of the Europeans. However, there were other areas in the economic, political and social lives of the African people that suffered specifically because of the invasions of the Europeans.

Since the political and economic structure of most African countries were, apart from their foreign trade, heavily dependent upon the stability of their cottage industries, the influx of vast amounts of cheap European products, tools, consumer goods, etc., went a long way toward undermining those industries and thus the political and economic structures of various African governments. Evidence of this detrimental effect is apparent when we take a comparative look at the countries and governments that were intact and effective during the pre-slavery era versus those that remained intact and effective after the trade in the enslavement of the Africans had begun. Some economic and political tragedies confronted Africa during those dark days. Unfortunately, these acts alone were not the worst tragedies. The impact upon the institutions of the time, though unfortunate, could be reasonably expected. The world was not an enlightened place then as it is now, and the maxim "to the victor goes the spoils" was more than a vague and extant quotation; it was the order of the day. To recover from economic or military defeat one needed only to defeat the offending nation and take back his country.

On the other hand the real tragedy, the African holocaust, dealt not only with the breakdown of government institutions, but also with the awesome human trauma as previously stated. During the course of the European trade with Africa many of the indigenous African cottage industries failed to compete with the technologically superior products, both in quality and supply available through European trade. The breakdowns that would have occurred in the economic and political stability of many of the African countries would have resulted in an African Dark Ages, much like the Dark Ages that occurred in Europe during the eighth century. Whereas the European Dark Ages were primarily the lost of enlightenment resulting from the collapse of the Roman Empire, the African Dark Ages would have resulted from the lost of political and economic stability. It was mainly during this period of time that the enslavement of the African people began. Before enslavement of Africans ended, almost three hundred years later, millions of Africans would have been abducted from their homeland and packaged as cargo into specially designed ships bound for American plantations. Millions more were sold into various European countries. It was this act, the depopulation of thirteen consecutive generations that qualifies for application of the term "holocaust."

Have You Seen Me?

In America, the Justice Department reports that as many as four hundred thousand people, mostly youngsters, are kidnapped from their homes each year. The agony from these losses has produced a tidal wave of responses. Over a hundred different agencies, some public and many others private have come into being. They publish, print, and issue millions of newsletters, flyers, mailers, milk-carton photos, and use a myriad of other methods to spread the word across the entire country. All this effort is aimed at recovering and preventing the disappearance of four hundred thousand loved ones each year.

In addition, local and federal government law enforcement departments and agencies have established special services that also help to locate these four hundred thousand missing persons. All these agencies and activity are brought into play because those who are disappearing are leaving behind families, friends, and loved ones who love and miss them sorely. The same agony felt by these American families was certainly felt by the families of the more than ten million people abducted from Africa. What might the parents of the abducted Africans have done when their sons, daughters, fathers, mothers, failed to return home? How long might a mother have stood staring out of her doorway, longing, hoping, and perhaps praying? How did the Africans that remained in Africa handle such agonizing losses? In her book, Protect Your Child, Laura Huchton, tells of her experiences with the parents of American children who were abducted, kidnapped, or for some other unknown reason, just disappeared.

"I could tell you stories that would break your heart. I could tell you stories that would horrify you because they horrify me. I could show you pictures of missing and murdered children that would haunt you forever. They will haunt me forever.

"There is no way to take you through the empty rooms of missing children. You can see their toys gathering dust on the shelf, or reach out and give a missing child's grieving parent a hug. I can take you into an emergency room to hear the terrified cries of a molested child."

The passage, though describing the agony experienced over the disappearance of children in America, might just as well have been written of the mother of an eight year-old African girl that we in America have come to know as little Phyllis Wheatley. Or, for that matter, it could be written regarding any number of the millions of men, women and children who were taken from their families by villains whose occupation was to capture and trade in the enslavement of Africans. As such, the missing children would become missing sons or daughters. The toys on the shelf might just as well be the clothes of their sons and daughters still hanging in the closets, or their teenage friends who still comes over to visit, even though they know that their friend has disappeared, never to be seen again. And they are aware of their parent's ample warnings, "Don't go any place by yourself and always come home before it gets dark. Do not talk with strangers, white or black, and if they approach you, run as fast as you can." Even in the face of the odds, it seem obvious that there were mothers who banded together, just as they now do in America, to try to find their children and to prevent the disappearance of still others. Africans, like Americans today, must have bonded as a unit of support around a thirteen-generation subculture of disappearing people. The seemingly recent incidences of missing persons in America are causing American families considerable anxiety. It is inconceivable that African families suffered less anxiety.

There have been several well-publicized disappearances that can serve as windows into the circumstances of the African disappearances. In one instance, an office manager in a California firm left home one day en route to work and just disappeared. Although later found, his disappearance was never the less the mainstay of office conversations. Co-workers relaxed their own anxieties by speculating upon known aspects of his disappearance. They constantly probed the unknowable to try to understand what might have happened to him. Television crews went to the office and filmed a show in an effort to assist the family in locating the missing husband and father.

In another instance, a young California woman disappeared while on her way home from visiting friends in a nearby city. Soon, posters and billboards were posted along local freeways in the hope that someone would come forward with information. Often, such devices remain in an area for months and perhaps even years, in an attempt to locate a missing loved one. In a third instance, a man from Utah disappeared while on his way to visit his sister. Subsequently, she; along with television crews and a national TV audience, combed the area of his disappearance in the hopes of locating him. If the reaction and disposition of American families is in any way the barometer of people's sentiment, then it is not difficult to imagine the absolute bedlam that most assuredly visited African families during the wretched trade in their enslavement. In America, that reaction has inspired an entire industry geared around the security of America's children. It has spawned security services; motivated special television programs, and inspired the writing of books on child protection.

With all that, is there any reason we should not expect that African families were equally torn apart by the disappearance of their loved ones? And perhaps even more so, because those disappearances continued uninterrupted for thirteen generations, parents, grandparents, all the way through great-great-great-great-great-great-great-great-great-great   grandparents lived through this epoch of African history. It is a period in humanity—or inhumanity—unparalleled in the history of mankind. For nearly three hundred years, from the mid-sixteenth century until the mid-nineteenth century, African parents and loved ones were continuously victimized by the tragically misguided morals of a people whose socially enlightened minds were pre-empted by greed and the arrogance of ethnic passions. During this period grandparents of children orphaned by slavery's merchants of severed and broken families were obliged to tell their grandchildren why they had no parents. Why there was no mother to nurse them, to cuddle them, or to tuck them into bed at night. No mother to school them thoroughly in acts of self-defense. To tell them not to stop and speak with strangers, not to open doors to strangers, and when they must be outside, not to travel alone. And to always, always watch when approaching wooded areas. Even though some parents and loved ones may have known, or at least hoped that their loved ones had reached the Americas, their absence was nevertheless so permanent and final as to be reflective of their deaths. To have been kidnapped by such merchants meant there was no opportunity to say good-bye or to get a going—away kiss or a hug from a husband or wife. It was like dying. It meant being there one day and not being there anymore forever. To disappear in such way was to deny the family the opportunity of ever hearing from or seeing that person ever again. It was that final. It was, to adopt a term from the language of American penal institutions, "cruel and unusual" punishment.

In spite of all the agony inflicted upon the Africans as a result of their enslavement by the Europeans, there are those who would say, "Sure, we see your point regarding the human tragedy, but don't forget that there were also a number of Africans involved in the trade and enslavement of the Africans. Were their immoralities not equally taunting and repulsive." My response is, yes, there were, and yes their acts were equally reprehensible. But even so, it does not indict the Africans as co-conspirators any more than the Nazis' drafting of Jews into service to assist in their attempted extermination of the Jews indicts the Jewish people as co-conspirators of that holocaust. While there were Africans who participated in the enslavement of other Africans, there is no reason to see their behavior as more repugnant than that of the Europeans who initiated and profited from the trade of enslaving the Africans. And the Americans plantation owners, by any moral critique, went one step further. They not only sold their fellow countrymen, but because they often sired them, they sold their own children.

Historical records are replete with incidents of white American men who, having sired children by their enslaved women, either enslaved them on their own farms or sold them off to others who enslaved them. How they could have morally justified such transactions is difficult to explain. The moral argument could not have simply been that the children were black, because a fair number of these children's skin complexions were as white, or nearly as white, as that of their fathers. Even the stigma of an African selling an African cannot, in any scheme of cosmic morality, match the inhumanity of a father who would sell his own children as slaves.

Pseudo Biographical Sketches

In King Nzinga Nbemba's Kingdom of Congo alone, it is estimated that between 3.5 and 5.0 million Africans were abducted and carried off to Brazil. The social, political and economic chaos resulting from so many disappearances would have been sufficient to decimate the foundation of any government and the economy of any country as it ultimately did in the Congo. So devastating was the result of the trade that in 1526, the Congo king wrote a letter to the king of Portugal complaining that the slave traders were literally depopulating his country. Among such abducted people were the following (pseudo biographical because the descriptions and data are fictional additions made by the author):

Antony

- Name: Antony
- Date of birth: August 4, 1592
- Age: 27
- Height: 5'10"
- Eyes: Brown
- Hair: Black
- Weight: 182 pounds
- Sex: Male
- Date missing: September 11, 1619

Isabella

- Name: Isabella
- Date of birth: Jan 3, 1595
- Age: 24
- Height: 5'5"
- Eyes: Brown

- Hair: Black
- Weight: 112 pounds
- Sex: Female
- Date missing: September 15, 1619

Antony and Isabella were among the first twenty Africans to brought to America. They came onboard that infamous warship dubbed a Dutch Man o' Warre by John Smith. They were the parents of the first child born of that party, and perhaps of the first child born in America to African-born parents. They named the boy William Tucker.

Charlie Smith:

- Name: Saude Montu
- Date of birth: December 15, 1848
- Age: 12
- Height: 4'10"
- Eyes: Brown
- Hair: Black
- Weight: 102 pounds
- Sex: Male
- Date missing: October 25, 1860

Charlie Smith who was captured when he was twelve and sold into slavery in Virginia. During interviews with him before his death in 1978 Charlie Smith, reportedly 130 years of age at his death, told of how he remember his abduction from his African homeland.

Phyllis Wheatley

- Name: Kibi Swanan ("Little Sister")
- Date of birth: February 20, 1753

- Age: 8
- Height: 4'1"
- Eyes: Brown
- Hair: Black
- Weight: 56 pounds
- Sex: Female
- Date missing: October 25, 1761

She was a frail young eight-year-old African girl who, arrived in Boston as a slave and was sold to a Mr. John Wheatley. I am obliged to ponder under what circumstances would even a 1761 America not have considered the abduction and removal of an eight-year-old child from home and family criminal kidnapping.

While slavery is recognizably horrible unto itself, we must acknowledge that different cultures and nations have, on many occasions, utilized slaves as a labor supply source. And, as unforgivable as the institution was, precedents were set long ago in faraway places. As far back in history as the ancient Babylonians and ancient Greece, slave labor was used for an assortment of tasks varying from the construction of the hanging gardens of Babylon to the manufacture of consumer goods in Grecian workshops. So slavery existed in spite of its low rating on the morality scale. Even putting all that aside, should the abduction and sale of an eight-year-old child be considered fair game for such an industry? After all, before little Miss Africa, Phyllis Wheatley, became a slave, she was a kidnap victim. The act of being enslaved occurred only after she was sold to the party of the second part. Prior to that she was simply kidnapped. Can we envision her mother wandering about from village to town, asking if anyone had seen her eight-year-old child? Hoping against hope that she was simply lost and not abducted. And yet knowing in her heart that it had become her child's most probable fate.   It is hard to find grounds to consider such an act anything but a crime. It is unfathomable that just because the government of the child's country was economically, politically, and militarily unable to prosecute her abductors, the penalty for their guilt should be less, even 232 years later. Throughout the history of man, criminal acts have always been subject to punishment. Such a deed as this would have earned the abductors capital punishment, even as far back as the Code of Hammurabi. Even in Greek mythology, kidnapping was considered such an offense that when Pirithous and Theseus kidnapped Helen of Troy, it plunged the two nations into war. On the more recent front, the 1668 English Bill of Rights morally condemned such an abduction.

Oloudah Equina (Gustavus Vassa)

- Name: Oloudah Equina
- Date of birth: February 15, 1749
- Age: 26
- Height: 5'10"
- Eyes: Brown
- Hair: Black
- Weight: 152 pounds
- Sex: Male
- Date missing: September 11, 1775

Oloudah Equiana, later renamed Gustavus Vassa, in 1789 (the year George Washington became president) wrote and published his biography detailing his life when he lived in Benin, West Africa, under his real name of Oloudah Equiana.

Cinque of Manis, Mendis

- Name: Cinque
- Date of birth: November 20, 1810

- Age: 29
- Height: 6'1"
- Eyes: Brown
- Hair: Black
- Weight: 164 pounds
- Sex: Male
- Date missing: July 26, 1839

Cinque of Manis, Mendis, (who was not renamed), with the assistance of other Africans on board his ship, overpowered the crew and sailed into the Boston Harbor. They filed a petition against the ship's captain and sued the Commonwealth of Massachusetts for their freedom.

Kunta Kinte

- Name: Kunta Kinte
- Date of birth: □□, 1734
- Age: 16
- Height: 5'6"
- Eyes: Brown
- Hair: Black
- Weight: 142 pounds
- Sex: Male
- Date missing: September 11, 1750

He was later renamed Toby Waller and millions of Americans watched him as portrayed in Alex Haley's *Roots, The Saga of an American Family*. In that epic portrayal, we were able to see first hand just how the enslavement and trade of Africans functioned. In that drama, young Kunta Kinte was barely outside the watchful eyes of his mother and father when he was kidnapped and taken aboard *the Lord Legionnaire*, a British ship designed and rigged for transporting Africans to work the farms and mines of the New World.

Pseudo-Biographical Sketched

While all the accounts rendered above are extracted from known historical records, the following are drawn not from historical records but from the millions of other stories that were never told. And if I may be permitted the liberty, I will attempt to paraphrase for perspective's sake the very passionate and empathetic sentiments quoted earlier of Laura Huchton, the author of *Protect Your Child*. In her characterizations, Ms. Huchton was addressing the trauma and awesome plight faced by the real flesh-and-blood parents of the hundreds of thousands of real flesh-and-blood children that are kidnapped, abducted, or just disappear right here in the United States. Although the names and circumstances are fictitious, the parents and children mentioned below were no less real and the trauma and awesome plight faced by them no less painful.

Thus come with me and,

I will share with you vignettes,

Of stories that were never told,

Of millions betrayed souls,

Of lives that were ever grieved,

Of pain that was never relieved.

The Story of Tselana Denianke

- Name: Tselana Denianke
- Date of birth: February 20, 1519

- Age: 19
- Height: 5'1"
- Eyes: Brown
- Hair: Black
- Weight: 102 pounds
- Sex: Female
- Date missing: July 11, 1538

Tselana's grandmother peered out the door at the children playing in the yard, she remembered the night, almost nine years ago, that her daughter had given birth to Tselana (later to be named Phyllis Wheatley). The baby was so very tiny at birth that Jallon Futu, the midwife, as she later acknowledged, didn't expect the child to survive. Jallon said that it was only after Tselana began to cry that she believe she had enough strength to live. Even as she grew older, Tselana had remained small for her age. While the other girls in the village looked their age, she always looked like a little kewpie doll. Tears welled up in the grandmother's eyes as she remembered the expression on Tselana's father's face the first time he saw his daughter. All wrapped up in her blankets, he held her as though feared he would break so fragile a thing. Everyone in the village knows how he'd often boasted that his first child would surely be a boy. However, when he first held little Tselana, his face lit up with pride and gratitude.

"It's too sad." She spoke the words aloud although she was standing in the doorway alone. "How can you be a mother and grandmother when you can't protect your children and their children?" she went on. "And how can you care for them when those heathen out there would steal a little girl from her own mother?" She tightened her grip on the doorframe and tried to hold back the tears as her mind took her back to the last time that she had seen Namilia, Tselana's mother. She loved all her children, but Namilia was her youngest, and she felt a special bond toward her. Tselana was gone, and now Namilia was gone. Namilia had suffered what could only be described as a nervous breakdown upon discovering that Tselana had disappeared. She had gone all over the village to see if someone had her Tselana. Finally, after being told by someone that the white people had a ship anchored off the coast many miles to the west, she accepted what had most likely actually happened to here child. She never came home again. Instead, she turned her face west and began looking for the ship of the white people. Although she had never been away from her village before and had never even seen white people, she set out to look for their ship. "Surely," she mused to herself, "not even the god of the white people would make such people who would deny a child her mother, or a mother her own child."

The Story of Jenne "Bani" Futa

- Name: Jenne "Bani" Futa
- Date of birth: May 17, 1769
- Age: 23
- Height: 4'11"
- Eyes: Brown
- Hair: Black
- Weight: 109 pounds
- Sex: Female
- Date missing: August 11, 1792

Jenne (later killed by sharks when she jumped overboard and into the shark infested waters of the Atlantic), Sunni (later renamed Sally Williams), Sardina (later renamed Mary Tilden), Jallon (later renamed Ella Mae Browning) and I (later renamed Rose McWilly) grew up together in the village of Okuunriizwe. We were all blessed to have married men from the same village. There were times when I was sure the women of our new village resented how close we were. Although they made us welcome and treated well, we never quite opened up to them, because we were practically raised in the same household. Sardina, and Jallon's mother, and my mother were from the same village, and when they married brothers from the Okuunriizwe village. Our mothers became they became best friends with the mothers of Jenne's (we always called her Bani) and Sunni, their sisters-in-law.

When the women gathered together to ground the day's meal or to wash the week's clothing, all five of us would, sooner or later, come together and form our own little group. When we went visiting, it was usually just among ourselves. We would often meet at Sunni's house if she were preparing some special food because she was the best cook among us. And if we were going to sew, then everyone would come to my house. They always claimed that I could sew anything I wanted too. In this village, the younger women did their washing on the second day of the week and the older women on the third day. The usual routine consisted of all the young women meeting in the village square, and from there, we would go down to the river and do the washing. When everyone had arrived, we left for the river. As usual, it wasn't long before the five of us came together in our own little group. We would talk about everything. Among the five of us, we knew all the village talk and Bani would have something especially funny to say about her brother Kipofu (later to be renamed Leander Broomfield). Kipofu had just recently taken a wife (later to die during the mid-Atlantic passage). She was from a village to the north, and, poor thing, she was so young. Bani said that whenever her brother Kipofu left for work, his wife would immediately leave the house and return to her own village to her mother's house. Bani used to tell us such funny stories about her brother and his new wife. There would be times when she would make us laugh so hard we'd have to hold on to the person ahead of us for guidance along the footpath since our own eyes would be near-blinded by tears. Months later, our laughter turned to sadness when Bani told how her brother, Kipofu, had gone as he always did to his wife's village to fetch her. On their way back, they disappeared; and neither was ever seen again.

After that, Bani almost never laughed. From the day Kipofu disappeared, she became almost paranoid at the thought that white people were going to get her or her children. She rarely let her children out of her sight. Whenever she went anywhere she would always take them. She had two girls, Nupe and Miana, and a son, Kankanza, who was five years old. It was because of Bani's fears that her three children were with us on this washday. As is usual during the village washday, after the women got to the river, the five of us would gather at a place down river from the others. Bani had placed her children in a play area where she could see them all the time. Just as we began to get setup there was a sudden noise from the brush behind us. As we turn to look, men, some of whom had white skin, sprang from the brush and seized us. I saw Bani run for her children and I saw her fall to the ground with blood gushing from her head as her attacker struck her on the head repeatedly. As I was dragged away, I could still hear Bani's three children crying for their mother.

The Story of Mpunga Bisaland
- Name: Mpunga Bisaland
- Date of birth: April 6, 1786
- Age: 31
- Height: 5'7"
- Eyes: Brown
- Hair: Black
- Weight: 152 pounds
- Sex: Male
- Date missing: July 11, 1815

Mpunga Bisaland (later renamed Charlie Jones) was only twelve years old. He remembers how excited he had been on the day his mother told him that on the fifth day of the week, his father would take him on the village's annual one-week hunt. Every year the men in Mpunga's village gathered and launched their first hunt of the season. To twelve-year-old Mpunga, to be taken along on such a hunt was just about the greatest thing that could ever happen to him. Mpunga had just turned twelve and he had been watching his father very closely in the past few weeks to see if there was any sign that he had planned to take him on the hunt. Sometimes, if a boy did not measure up to their fathers expectation, he would not be permitted to go on the hunt. If he didn't go on the hunt nearest his twelfth birthday, he would be teased and jostled by all the boys in the village who went. And even the village girls would giggle behind the back of such a boy.

The next day, Mpunga's father and the other men set off for the hunt There were six other boys (later settled on a tobacco plantation in Georgia and renamed John Mackie, Pete McNeil, Thurmond Marshall, Harry Townsend, Scotty Hanover, and Harold Brooks) from the village who came with their fathers. The first day of the hunt passed without much activity. Some of the men were busy locating the game and others were setting traps. By nightfall, Mpunga was so proud of himself that he didn't even think about how tired he was. As they began to make camp a stranger came. He was talking to some of the men and they were pointing to the east, so Mpunga guessed that the stranger wanted directions. In a few minutes the stranger left and the men cooked the game they had hunted, and with the food they had brought from the village, they served dinner. Afterwards, everyone went to their sleeping tents. The huge fire in the center of the campsite was left burning to ward off the wild beasts.

Mpunga was awaked from his sleep by someone kicking him in his side. When he opened his eyes, he almost died of fright. There, right in front of his eyes was a man whose face was as white as the web of the bush spiders.

The Story of Jash-Sha Nxinolo, The Son

Jash-sha Nxinolo (later renamed Josh Harper) was nine years old. It had been raining in their village. For three days, his mother had kept him inside. He missed playing outside with his friend and was bored. And then he had to take care of his three-year-old sister. So when the rains stopped and the sun came out, he was immediately excited. Soon the ground dried and he was able to leave. Although the sun was hot on his face, he ran all the way to Malani's house. Malani (later renamed Byron White) had been his lifelong best friend. When he got there, Malani was just coming out of the house, he was carrying the bow and the bag of arrows his older brother, Makanjila, have given him. He and Malani would often spend hours playing big hunters. As soon as Malani saw him, they ran toward their favorite playground. As they did, Malani handed him one of the manioc cookies his mother had made. They had chosen this place as their favorite hunting ground because there the trees grew so tall they often shut out some of the sunlight and made it kind of dark. In the shaded places, the small bushes often looked like wild animals. It was the make-believe animals that made this a good hunting ground. Just as they ran up to the big tree where they always sat, they saw the strangest sight ever. There they saw two men, wearing peculiar clothes. Their faces and hands were all white. As he and Malani stopped and stared, other men grabbed them from behind.

The Story of Mweenge Magwangwara, The Father

- Name: Mweenge Magwangwara
- Date of birth: March 4, 1681
- Age: 34
- Weight: 5'10"
- Eyes: Brown
- Hair: Black

- Weight: 182 pounds
- Sex: Male
- Date missing: September 11, 1715

For nearly four decades, Mweenga Magwangwara (George Jefferson Brownley) had been one of the most important figures in his nation's government. He had served at the emperor's pleasure as mayor of the city for seven years. Before that, he had served in the service of the emperor's army for thirty years. And now that he was out of the army and no longer mayor, he had become a trader. His trading business had recently become very profitable. The family lived in a well-kept house built of stone and masonry and was located within the walls of the city. Mweenga and his wife, Hillal had four children, two boys and two girls. All were still living at home and the boys often helped their father in his trading business. A big delight in the home was the new food their father had brought home recently. The new food maize, tomatoes and manioc was not grown in their state and had been imported all the way from a place across the ocean. The ship captain called the place America. In Mweenga's trading business he bought iron ingots from the emperor's mine located in the province and timber from the emperor's forest in Ovimbundu, and he would took them overland to the Arab trading station on the East coast at Kilwa. There he traded the iron ingots and timber for cotton fabric, house wares, and farm implements, which he sold on his way, back home.

Two days ago, while returning home, Mweenga and fifteen of his servants were ambushed by a band of white people firing guns. One of his servants was killed, and two others were injured. Mweenga and the remainder of his servants were captured and carried out of the country to the white people's ships anchored offshore in the Atlantic Ocean.

The Story of a Grandmother: "The White People Have Taken All My Grandchildren"

- Name: Nupe Lumumba "Grandma"
- Date of birth: December 15, 1446
- Age: 52
- Height: 5'4"
- Eyes: Brown
- Hair: Black
- Weight: 112 pounds
- Sex: Female
- Date missing: July 11, 1499

Walking slowly and slightly bowed as though the weight of her royalty bore heavily upon her shoulders, she moved gently up the aisle between rows of pews in the newly built structure. As she walked, she thought about life in her province before the trouble began. Of the times when men could travel and trade throughout the province without fear; of how mothers could let their children play in the playgrounds and not worry about anything more harmful than a scraped knee. Then the weight of her grief, as though competing for its own attention, pierced her reflections of times past and made her to think of her agony. Of how the land had become plagued with a curse; how mothers were terrified that their children would be taken from them; how fear had spread throughout the entire province. And how even the king, himself had been unable to put a stop to the raids of the white people.

As she neared the small altar, she paused at the candle stands. There, rows and rows of candles were burning for the victims of the white people's raids. Among the flickering flames, she lit and placed six new candles. As she put each candle in its holder, she called out the names. Blessed Mother, I ask your blessing upon Antony (later renamed Andrew Wayde), my son; I ask your blessing upon Sarabella (later renamed Martha Beard), my beloved daughter-in-law; and I ask your blessings upon my three grandchildren; Wala (later renamed Sampson Riddlehouse), Isabella (later renamed Lizzie B. Booker), and especially upon little Nzinga Affonso (later renamed BoBo Hogan). And blessed mother, I pray your blessing upon the king that he will soon be able to stop the raids of the white people. When all the candles were lit, she moved across to the figure of the Virgin Mother. There she placed the scarf from her head onto the floor and knelt down upon it, her face now drenched with her tears, turned up to the figure in supplication

The Story of Aquina Akasunga, The Son and Brother

- Name: Aquina Akasunga
- Date of birth: February 20, 1790
- Age: 40
- Height: 6'2"
- Eyes: Brown
- Hair: Black
- Weight: 170 pounds
- Sex: Male
- Date missing: October 25, 1830

Kanen Alooma (later renamed Caesar) recalls the days, long ago when he worked for the emperor at the Tshombe mines.

"I hired a young man to haul the iron ores out of the mine to the place where the ores were being smelted. Although, he was not from our village, I had gotten to know him quite well. One day, just as we were leaving the mine for the day, he told me that his father had been killed during an attack on his village. He said that this had left him very sad. Now he was the man of the house and had to take care of his mother and three sisters.

I also learned that his name was Aquina Askasunga (later renamed Jim Simpson). Aquina spoke of his concern about being able to accumulate enough goods to provide good dowries for his sisters, which would enable them to marry well.

"'Look son,' I said, 'as smart and industrious as you are, when the time comes for your sisters to marry, you will have all the goods you need for more than three dowries.'

"He asked me why I thought so. I told him that if he continued to work as hard as he had been working, he'd surely be successful. For a moment, he lapsed into a kind of meditative state, then said goodnight and headed off in the direction of his village. None of us ever saw Aquina again.

"Every day, for weeks thereafter, his mother and at least one of the girls would come by the mine asking for Aquina. Depending upon who asked the question, it would always be the same. 'You miners there! Have you seen Aquina?' or at other times, 'Have any of you men seen my son?'

"Although, we were fairly certain of what had happened, none of us could bring ourselves to say, 'Aquina has been taken during one of the raids of the white people.'"

The Royal Decree and the Cries of a Nation

The man, Khama Bikuri, was known throughout the province as the man who speaks for the king.

Khama Bikuri was first minister to the king, and in the company of his advisors, rode up in front of the village mayor's house. A servant boy came around the house and took the reins of the camels while the party dismounted. They then followed the mayor, who had come out of the house to greet them. Hardly had Minister Khama Bikuri arrived before people began assembling in the village square. Though called a square, it was not a square at all but more like an extension of the front yard of the mayor's home that expanded to about a two hundred fifty feet in its midst and grew progressively narrower as it reached to the northern entrance of the village. Throughout the area were trees with wooden benches built around them. At the end of the square nearest the mayor's house was the elevated section where the mayor and his council sat. It was usually from this pulpit that criminals were judged, legal decisions rendered and public announcements issued.

After a short while in the house, the mayor came to the door and dispatched the village criers to go about the village and inform the villagers that an assembly has been called. Those already in the square just sat around, talking to one another in somber tones. Their voices were hardly audible above the din. As soon as the village criers began their rounds the square began filling up as though the people were already waiting. As the mayor and the representative from the king proceeded through the crowd toward the elevated platform, some of the villagers began speaking. While they spoke toward the mayor, they otherwise did not seem to be speaking to anyone in particular.

"This thing is barbarous, it must be stopped. The king must speak to these white people."

Across the square, someone else shouted, "The king must march on these white people and take back our people."

As the mayor walked to the pulpit to speak, the assembly grew quiet.

The mayor asked, "How many here have lost someone during the raids of the white people?" Everyone in the square raised his or her hand.

Again the mayor asked, "How many of you here have lost as many as ten people from your family?" Three women, perhaps in their sixties, raised their hands.

The mayor went on, "How many of you here have lost nine people from your family?" A man and four women raised their hands.

"How many families have lost eight people?" the mayor went on. "How many have lost seven people?" "How many have lost six people?" as the number of lost people came down, more and more people were raising their hands, and then when the mayor asked how many had lost three people, about half the people in the assembly raised their hands

The mayor then asked, "How many of you have lost two people from your family?" Everyone in the assembly raised their hand.

The mayor then turned to the village census taker, who also sat on the platform, and asked for the village current population. The census taker took what looked like an ornate walking cane sitting near him and, after gazing at it for several seconds, told the mayor that there were 863 subjects in the village. The mayor then turned to the representative from the king, and motioned him to the pulpit while he returned to his own seat.

The representative from the king began, "The king has heard the complaints from this village and all the villages throughout his kingdom. He wishes you to know that this plague has not come upon only you, for just three days ago, the royal treasurer and the king's own grandson were also taken during a raid by the white people. So you see, the kings heart burns with the same agony that burns in your hearts."

Pausing for a moment, the representative looked all around the square as though contemplating what he would say next. Finally he said, "It is because of the disastrous effect the raids of the white people are having upon your families, upon the king's own staff, and upon kingdom itself that the king has issued this royal decree. He has decreed that the taking and selling of slaves within the boundary of his kingdom is hereby prohibited. To assure compliance, the king has also decreed that the commander-in-chief of the royal army launch a campaign to stop the white people from raiding within these provinces and to enforce the ban against the capturing and selling of slaves."

Having thus spoken, the king's representative sat back down in his seat.

The mayor returned to the pulpit, held up his hands to make the people quiet down, and said, "I have directed the holy man to offer a sacrifice for god to bless and keep all those who have been taken from this village, and I have asked Mama Anicet to come and talk to all of you about how to protect yourselves and your family members from the ravages of the white people. Oh, one other thing," the mayor added, "how many of you have gun powder rifles?"

From the crowd only two men held up their hands. The mayor directed them to get additional men and let them use the gunpowder rifles to stand guard over the village.

Obviously we do not have actual specific accounts of what transpired during the capture and enslavement of Africans, but the author is offering the following fictional sketches to represent the reality of the plight and fate of those abused souls. Who were these Africans? Were they not farmers, laborers, cattlemen, mechanics, librarians, carpenters, doctors, lawyers, nurses, entrepreneurs, mothers, and daughters? Were they not sisters, brothers, fathers, parents, children, boys, girls, adolescents, cousins, granddaughters, grandsons, sisters-in-law, girlfriends, boyfriends, husbands, fiancés? Might they not also have been ministers, bankers, fishermen, hunters, politicians, miners, historian, scientists, policemen, astrologers, social workers, psychologist, traders, weavers, gardeners, teachers, bosses, students, employees, accountants, or medical men? Or might there have been others who knew them as friends, buddies, lovers, grandmothers, grandfathers, mistresses? The answers are, of course, yes. These and all other descriptions of relationship, career, and kinship that existed among people of the world during the sixteenth, seventeenth, eighteenth, and nineteenth centuries, also existed among the Africans. If, as most modern archaeologists now contend, Africa is the place where all mankind began, then the Europeans returned to the place of their incubation to foul the nest of their nurture. For the better part—or more correctly the worst part—of four hundred years, European nations, thanks to their superior weaponry and industry, had their way with Africa.

If Colonial and Pre-Colonial Africa was a woman, one could say that they had their way with her and then abandoned her. After the rape, pillage, looting, and burning of Africa, the European offered no balm for her healing, no Marshall Plan for her Reconstruction. Africa was largely left unto her own devices in attempting to cope and to restore her devastated infrastructures. Neither were there memorials or monuments erected for her pain. Great was her suffering, and yet there was no recompense to show for the millions of African sons and daughters lost. Nothing remained but their absence and the destruction of nations. Even on the personal level there was nothing but emptiness.

AFRICA: THE SOCIOECONOMIC AND POLITICAL IMPACT OF THE ENSLAVEMENT PERIOD

With such a massive and unplanned loss of citizenry, is it any wonder that almost without fail, all the African governments that had been in power prior to the beginning of the trade in the enslavement of Africans collapsed? And to add insult to injury, the collapse was not followed by reconstruction programs but by the ear-splitting sound of gunfire in the hands of the European colonizing forces that followed in the wake of the decline in the African slave trade. After the thirteen-generation exploitation of manpower the colonists came in and for an additional five generations, exploited Africa's natural resources. The political callousness exhibited by the Europeans toward Africa is tantamount to the cruelty of the rapist who rips away his victim's jewelry as a final offensive act of his molestation.

4

THE IMMIGRANTS:
AFRICANS AND EUROPEANS

All ethnic groups that migrated to America—the English, the Irish, the Scandinavians, the Italians, the Poles, the Germans, etc.—underwent a period of cultural miscegenation sometime during the first three generations of their American residency. The transition from English, Irish, Scandinavian, Italian, Polish, or German to American has traditionally been attributed to a phenomenon dubbed by Americans as the "melting pot."

AFRICANS VERSUS EUROPEAN IMMIGRANTS, AND THE MELTING POT

Fashioned on the premise that all immigrant groups would ultimately be molded into a single nationality, the melting-pot theory has been defended as an effective socialization and cultural vehicle or mechanism. It has frequently been used to explain how English, Italians, Greeks, and Germans immigrants can, for example, bring their own cultural values to America, but after a certain period of time—generally around the third generation—develop a distinctively Americanized culture and character. Whether this premise described what actually occurs is not really significant at this time. What *is* deemed significant is that the melting-pot process did result in an assortment of immigrant groups taking on a cultural identity unique to America as their new nation and that the new cultural identify was beneficial to their social, economic, and political successes in America. As noted before, the process of cultural metamorphism did not occur overnight. In fact, a summary review of the history of the English immigrants suggests that it was not until around the early 1700s before they developed a cultural identity that could be considered distinctively American.

AMERICANIZATION OF THE PILGRIMS

We can see that it would not have been the Pilgrims of the Mayflower who effected an American identity, but their grandchildren and the children of their grandchildren, who became Americans. As stated in chapter one, we've generally defined a generation as a thirty-year period that occurs on the average every twenty years. With this figure in mind, and using the English immigrants as an example, it would appear that each immigrant group required around sixty to ninety years to acquire sufficient value reorientation as to be considered *American*. With that time approximation in mind, the suggestion is that the African immigrants should have achieved their status of "Americanization" by the early 1700s as the English did. And, having done so the Africans should have gone on to establish themselves in the professions, in politics, in business, and in other enterprises with equal applications to that of the English immigrants. But of course, that did not happen.

The reason that it did not happen and the forces that interfered with the Americanization process are the primary theses of this chapter. What forces were at work in the migration of the European immigrants that were or were not at work during the immigration, or importation of the Africans? Understanding the effect and the operation of such forces will permit a better understanding of the economic and sociological elements that were at play in the Americanization of both immigrant groups. We know from the John Rolfe diary that the twenty 1619 African immigrants delivered by the Dutch Man o' Warre were purchased by the people of Jamestown. However, the fact that they were sold does not necessarily mean that they were sold into slavery. In fact, they were not. When the John Rolfe account state they were sold, it meant that they were sold into indentured servitude. So whereas the Africans immigrants were sold into indentured servitude to a group of Jamestown businessmen upon their arrival in Jamestown, in that sense they weren't much different than the Pilgrims that would land at Plymouth the following year.

COMPARISON BETWEEN AFRICAN AND ENGLISH IMMIGRANTS

The Pilgrims, unlike the Africans, sought out their own sponsors and then sold themselves into indentured servitude. Before leaving Europe, they sold their service to a group of English businessmen in order to raise enough money to pay their for passage on board the Mayflower. Additionally, there would also the added expenses of food, clothing, weapons, farming implements, other tools, and miscellaneous stuff that they would need to establish a settlement upon their arrival in America. Therefore, excepting the fact that the Africans were abducted, and brought to America, both immigrant groups arrived in America as indentured servants. However, in spite of the fact that a semblance of equality existed upon their arrivals, the economic forces that had already been set in motion would of a certainty render them quite unequal.

THE ENGLISH IMMIGRANTS—The English Immigrants, the Pilgrims, and Feudalism

Simply stated, the Pilgrims fled Europe to avoid religious persecution. However, it was not merely the free exercise of one's faith that was involved. Europe, during the time of the Pilgrims had changed considerably since the time of medieval top-to-bottom feudalism. Whereas feudalism had been abolished in large portions of Europe, it was still alive and well in countries like Germany until the seventeenth century and Prussia until the early eighteenth century. Both England and France had abolished feudalism around the fourteenth century. Feudalism, when operating, was a system of labor management that had been inherited by Europe from its political predecessor, the Roman Empire. Under feudalism, the lord had almost absolute rights over a serf. For an offense as minor as disobedience, the lord could, and frequently did, cut off the serf's ear, in whole, or in part. Or he might slit the serf's tongue; or even cut off his hand or foot. As for all major offenses such as leading an insurrection or leading an escape, a serf would most certainly have been hanged.

However, by the seventeenth century, the period of the Pilgrims, feudalism had been absent from England for at least three centuries. In those three centuries, the single candlepower of social insight that had powered the Magna Charta in the twelfth century had become candelabra of social insight by the time of the Pilgrims. For the better part of three hundred years, the Europe that nurtured the inspiration of the Pilgrims had been reflecting upon the thoughts and writings of Sir Francis Bacon, John Locke, and other such thinkers.

Advances in Sociopolitical Thought

During the seventeenth century, revolutionary thoughts in political philosophy and the rights of man were beginning to take shape in western Europe. The innovative religious insight of Martin Luther that ultimately resulted in his break with the traditions of the Catholic Church became a part of this approach. John Calvin of France also expressed Luther's premise regarding the autonomy of local congregation and his ideas about the rights of the individual. Coupled with the political philosophies of men like Bacon and Locke, they were gradually finding their way into the minds of the people on the streets of Europe. Of particular social implications were Bacon's arguments regarding the political rights of the individual. The innovative political and religious ideas that existed at the time fused themselves into a single functional social philosophy regarding individual rights. It was with this new idea that the Pilgrims set out to establish, not only new homes in a new land, but a new concept involving the religious, social, and political affairs of man. In spite of all the philosophical innovations, however, it was yet another innovation that made it all possible, and that innovation is what we've come to call the industrial revolution.

Industrial Revolution In Europe

Seventeenth-century Europe was, in addition to a place of innovative social thought, the European core of the industrial revolution. It was largely the growth in the industrial capacity of Europe that made the frequent migrations across the Atlantic Ocean a realizable aspiration. It was as if the philosophical innovations regarding the rights of man and the innovations of the industrial revolution combined and, like a mixture of ammonium nitrate and calcium carbonate, blew the Pilgrims across the Atlantic Ocean in an occurrence as natural as shrapnel projectiles from an exploding bomb. However, the impact of the explosion was not limited to the fleeing of the Pilgrims. The first governing document of the New World, the Mayflower Pact, contains all the elements of an enlightened Europe that were to find their way into the more refined documents, the Declaration of Independence and the Constitution of the United States of America, that followed it.

The African Immigrants

If the 1620 Pilgrims were blown across the Atlantic like projectiles from exploding concepts and ideas, then the enslaved Africans that followed them were most assuredly drawn across that same Atlantic by the draft currents of the explosion. Of the explosive mixture, innovations in the application of advance concepts in the areas of social, political, and economic disciplines resulted. These philosophical innovations were then harnessed together by history and the fortuitous circumstances of the times with the significant improvements also being made in the application of industrial technology. The coupling of these forces brought about expansions in Europe that the natural boundaries of the continent could no longer withstand.

As these ideas trickled down to people living in hovels, they gradually became aware that the expansions in social and political issues were, for the first time, endowing them, for the first time, with the same natural rights as those who lived in castles. This awareness resulted in civil discontent and massive out-migration. And the out-migration was supported by the continent's new ability to extend its operations over greater and greater distances. These changes, when applied to the more commercial aspects of the continent, made it possible for European merchants, entrepreneurs, and governments to engage in profitable ventures far beyond Europe's traditional borders.

The technological improvements in the designs of ocean-going vessels enabled them for the first time to circumnavigate the globe. As they traveled and opened up new frontiers to continental interest, settlements of European citizens began to follow them. As the number of settlements increased, so did the demands placed upon the manufacturing facilities of Europe. And as manufacturing increased, so did the demand for additional raw materials and new products. Moreover, each new colonial settlement sought products that it could market in Europe in exchange for money. The cash was used to buy consumer goods and more equipment. It was within this arena of events that the demand for additional manpower would ultimately set the stage for the arrival of the African immigrants.

New World Demand for Labor

Initially, the demand was met by the influx of European peasantry who hired them out to work for contracted periods. The periods, usually lasting from seven to fifteen years, were served as indentured servants to the contracting person. Under the terms of their indenture, the worker's ocean passage and other incidental expenses were paid for in exchange for that worker's labor for the agreed-upon period. Upon completion of the indenture period, the worker would then be free to leave the employ of the indenturing person or agency. After a while, however, the supply of European peasants failed to keep pace with the increasing demand for more and more manpower.

As an alternate manpower source, the indigenous people of the New World, the native Americans, were also being brought into the pool of available manpower. Their overall benefit as a source of manpower was dampened by the fact that they were not easily reconciled to the European system of indentured service. Secondly, it became increasingly difficult for the landowner, or the indenturing agency to retain the Native Americans in servitude since they could so easily and frequently did, leave the work place and return to their own homeland or reservations. Also, the Native Americans had no immunity to European diseases and thousands dies as these diseases swept though their camps and villages.

Labor Demands Shifts to Africa

Halfway around the world, Portugal, which has become a preeminent sea power, was beginning to establish trade relationships with various African nations on both the east and west coast of the continent. Among the items being imported by the Africans were maize and other foodstuffs from America, gunpowder, weaponry, tools, other equipment, and consumer goods from Europe. In exchange for these European goods, the governments of the African nations or city-states traded gold, ivory, iron ore, copper, cotton, timber, and other raw materials. As one African nation would arm itself with weapons purchased from the Europeans, then other African nations, almost as a precursor to the arms race of the twentieth century, would follow suit and arm themselves. While the demand for new weapons increased among the various African governments, the African consumers, at the same time, were demanding increases in the importation of European consumer goods. These two demands placed great burdens upon the various nations and city-states for additional capital. In some cases, in effort to increase their trade revenue, some African governments began trading their prisoners of war for European currency or merchandise. It was from transactions like these that the demand for manpower in the New World began to be met. As this demand outstripped the available supply of African prisoners of war, the Portuguese and other European governments began engaging in the practice of illegal abduction and kidnapping. This became the method of securing Africans to meet the demands of the mines and sugar plantations of Central and South America, the factories and farms of North America; and for the farms and factories of Europe and would continue for more than two hundred years.

African Immigrants Versus English Immigrants

From this account, it is obvious why the statuses of the African immigrants and that of the European immigrants were irreconcilably different. Whereas the 1620 Pilgrims had full and free access to the inculcating forces of the cultural melting pot, the African immigrants had none. Fundamentally, this is the key difference between the two immigrant groups. Amazingly, though, in spite of all the reasons why the Africans should not have become involved in the socializing phenomena, a cursory review of the lives of several African immigrants indicates that, they still developed the same strong sense of American nationalism as that of the European immigrants.

The first such example can be seen in the name that Antony and Isabella, two of the original 1619 Africans, chose for their first American-born child, a son. Although they both had Portuguese names, Antony and Isabella named their first child William Tucker. Since this event occurred prior to the formal legalization of slavery, it cannot be determined why Antony and Isabella elected to give their first-born an English name. Another act that portrays elements of American nationalism was exhibited by an African immigrant under fire in the service of U.S. military. James Forten, a fourteen year-old powder attendant on board the American vessel *Royal Louis* when captured by the British in 1778 and offered relocation and freedom in England. To which offer the fourteen year-old offer this Nathan Hale like response, "I am here a prisoner for the liberties of my country. I shall never, never prove to be a traitor to be her interest."

Why Did the Europeans Immigrants Support Slavery?

At this juncture, one might ask the question, that a reasonable person would be expected to ask. If, as we are told, the Pilgrims and the European immigrants that followed them had been so exposed to the socially and politically innovative thoughts of Luther, Bacon, and Locke that they were motivated to leave home and family in Europe and migrate to America, how then could they have become slave owners? How could the same people who embraced such explosive concepts of individual liberty initiate and play host to an institution as repugnant and vile as American slavery? Again one might ask, how they could rationalize their enlightened views regarding the natural rights of man, the rights of religious freedom, and the institution of slavery.

For an answer to that question, we need look no farther than Thomas Jefferson, author of the words; "We hold these truths to be self-evident" who at the same time maintained a workforce of enslaved black Americans. Did this conflict between ideals and practice make Thomas Jefferson a hypocrite? No, not really. Thomas Jefferson's use of enslaved labor was no more a default of his own ideals than the position of a 1990s senator who lobbies for and supports gun control legislation while owning guns makes him or her a hypocrite. Or the congressman whose vote for the North American Free Trade Agreement is in conflict with his own ideals and preferences. The conflict that existed between Jefferson's personal involvement with slavery and his own ideals of political morality cast him well within the dilemma characterized by the Apostle Paul in his Epistle to the Romans: "The good which I want to do, I fail to do; but what I do is the wrong which is against my will." While Thomas Jefferson did maintain enslaved Africans to work his plantation, it was probably a battle between pragmatism and idealism. The means for working such a plantation in those days would have been through the use of enslaved labor. Conventionally, people used enslaved labor, while some others with special beliefs and passions, like the Quakers, did not.

While the European immigrants were in the throes of new and innovative thoughts, both sociopolitical and socio-religious, their traditional labor management heritage was one wherein feudalism had been the labor management system. Under this system, the life of a serf was not measurably different than that of an enslaved Africans. Even the indentured servant system of manpower management was but a link between serfdom of the past and the free-enterprise labor management system that emerged in Europe with the coming of the industrial revolution. Under the indentured servant system, a person could sell or barter off his or her individual rights to another in exchange for money or goods. When the Pilgrims arrived in America, they were basically a different cast of European immigrants than the settlers at Jamestown. Back in chapter 1, I portrayed the Pilgrim's Mayflower settlement and the Jamestown settlements as two distinct Americas. As the first permanent European settlement in America, those who settled in Jamestown did so as an official colony of the English government. Jamestown was operated principally as a business enterprise through the management of the London Company via grants, or charters extended by King James I, after whom the settlement was named. James I was England's reigning monarch from 1603 until 1625. And it was during his administration that the 1619 Africans arrived in America. The Pilgrims' settlement at Plymouth was not a government-sponsored colony. They came to America nursing their own ideas and values. Which were not necessarily those of the English government. It was, in fact, on the basis of those ideas that they stand enshrined in American history and in the cultural ethos of the nation as the first settlers rather than the 1607 settlers of Jamestown.

Even though Jamestown was under the auspices of the English government, one must remember that the first African immigrants who arrived there were not enslaved but rather were sold into the same indentured-servant system the European immigrants were subjected to. During that period, the indentured servant system encompassed Europeans, Native Americans and Africans. Some of the problems that plagued that system had resulted from landowners or employers failing to observe the maturity dates of the indenture and trying to retain servants in servitude longer than the agreement specified. These illegal extensions meant extra dollars in the pockets of the landowner to whom the servants were indentured. For example, if a servant indentured himself or herself to a landowner for, say, seven years, the landowner would be obliged by law to free the servant at the end of that period. Under the term of the indenture agreement, the landowner was also required to provide his former indentured servant with food, tools, and resources sufficient to enable the former servant to make it on his own. Obviously then, if the landowner could forestall the indenture period for several years, he could effectively gain the extra years' worth of work for a premium price at the expense of the indentured servant.

However, such practices were much more common among African indentured servants than among the European servants.

The European indentured servants had a number of advantages over the Africans in this respect. On the one hand, the European indentured servants, who were more often than not, English, spoke the language and could speak up for themselves. And if that proved inadequate, being subjects of the Crown, they could also file a formal complaint. And if all else failed they oftentimes had family or friends who could appeal their case. In the case of the African indentured servants though, there were no such protective constituencies. Having been abducted from the country of their birth, they had no government to represent their grievances. Not being English citizens, they would have received only lukewarm support from the English judicial system. And having been abducted from their homes they had no family or friends to appeal their cases. Therefore, whereas the landowners could not tamper with the terms of the indentured Europeans, they could shape public opinion sufficiently to be able to legally alter the terms and status of the African indentured servants as they wished by utilizing dehumanizing stereotypes, and other slanderous commentary.

Eroding Status of the African Indentured Servants

That is precisely what must have occurred in 1661 Virginia when the colony legislature legalized slavery for the first time in the country. The statute declared that those Africans or African Americans already serving under the terms of an indenture agreements were not subject to it, but that all Africans brought into the colony after the statute went into effect would be enslaved. Since we said earlier that to understand how Americans could rationalize the gaping flaw between the rhetoric of their ennobling precepts of individual rights and their abysmal neglect of those idealistic precepts in their enslavement of the Africans, we have to go back and reflect again upon the character of Thomas Jefferson. And we do this because, throughout his life, Jefferson maintained at least one item as a constant fixture on his political agenda, which was, his desire to the enforce the newly ratified constitution's repugnance against the institution of slavery and the importation of slaves. He aspired to do this even though—perhaps consistent with the perspectives of his own times—he rather favored separation rather than integration of the races. Throughout Jefferson's public and political life, he continued to defend his thesis that, "We hold these truths to be self-evident: That all men are created equal, that they are endowed by their Creator with certain unalienable Rights."

A Nation's Ambivalence: The Assault on the Africans' Character

As was noted of Thomas Jefferson, it may also be said of the country as well as what Apostle Paul said of himself, that when he would do right, evil was always present, and that the things that he should do, he did not do but the things that he should not do, those he did. Certainly the political debates that were going on over the issue of slavery attest to nation's awareness that enslavement of the Africans was politically and morally wrong. However, under the influence of the authority of the English government and certain moneyed interests, it became a wrong that an enterprising young country was apparently willing to endure. By all indications, the fallout from America's willingness to tolerate slavery proved doubly harmful to the African immigrants. In the first instance, it meant, of course, that slavery would not be abolished.

In the second instance, it triggered a need in the country to morally justify its position. In its attempt to do so, a barrage of assaults was levied against the character of the African immigrants. The nature of the assaults suggests that, the maxim usually used in debates was applied. That is, if you cannot win the debate by defeating the arguments of your adversary, then win by undermining the character of your adversary. Such an approach appears to have been the basis by which the colonies adopted the tactics of diminishing the social character and intellectual merits of the African immigrants. As noted earlier, the African immigrants as indentured servants were initially treated in virtually the same manner as the European indentured servants. That is, they lived, worked, and socialized together, and even inter—marriages were common. The effect of these attacks upon the character of the African immigrants resulted in a series of legal laws being passed limiting the legal rights of the African immigrants. Ultimately, of course, like the Hebrews of ancient Egypt, all their civil rights were withdrawn, the result of which meant their enslavement.

Socioeconomic Disparity

Had the African and English immigrants been permitted equal access to all the avenues of socioeconomic growth, my contention is that the socioeconomic progress of the African's descendents would have rivaled that of the English descendents. But this did not occur since the Africans did not have the same opportunity to exercise their options as the English immigrants did. They were not permitted to write letters back home to moms and dads. And the practice of separating the Africans who spoke the same language deprived them even of inquiring among themselves about their families and loved ones back home. No other such circumstances exist in which so large a number of people have suffered such a total and finite excommunication from everything they had known. The social and cultural trauma of such a total and complete shutdown should have reckoned irreparable damage to the social fabric of the African immigrants. As if the act of segregating then was not enough, the practice of selling the enslaved Africans from one plantation to another and from one city to another raised the additional trauma of dislocation and excommunication. Under present-day insight, such action alone would constitute cruel and unusual punishment and would, at the very least, mandate hours of corrective therapy.

The African Immigrants Sacrifice United States Citizenship

More than any other immigrant group in America, the African immigrants were tasked to make an ultimate sacrifice. In much the same manner that the Egyptian pharaoh stripped the ancient Hebrews of their rights by enslaving, the Virginia legislation of 1661 did the same thing to the African immigrants. They were ostensibly stripped of all their civil and legal rights as citizens. No other immigrants have been obliged to pay so high a price for their American citizenship as they were. Perhaps this is why the American descendents of those African immigrants today are so patently passionate over issues involving civil rights.

THE DYNAMICS OF EMIGRATION

Immigrant groups almost always arrived in America essentially with the same socioeconomic status they had previously enjoyed while in their native land. To lay the groundwork for understanding the situation and plight of the Africans immigrants, it is necessary to first get a grasp of the dynamic forces at play in the movement of any immigrant group. When groups of people migrate to America, they come expecting to exercise certain elective options rather than being forcibly dispersed or relocated. Consequently, whenever such migration occurred on a large scale, the immigrant groups have almost always been able to maintain certain demographic features of their former homelands. Of particular interest here is the feature of social stratification. The occasions when this would not be observed, would of course be when the decision to migrate was not spurred by the exercise of options but when it is mandated by forced dispersion or relocation. Even when a large migration occurs as the results of life-threatening famines or hostile governments, the migrating people still arrive packaged, as it was, within the social stratification of their native homeland. The logic for this ordering is dictated on this premise. When threatening circumstances are such that people elect to leave their country, those who can afford to do so tend to leave first. The lesser privileged, having fewer resources to facilitate migration, tend to tolerate hostile conditions longer and will therefore be the last to emigrate. Following are examples from the history of various immigrant groups who settled in America.

English Immigrants

The English immigrants to America came with their social and economic structures still intact. Their family structures were retained. They were able to write letters, or have letters written home to family and friends. They were able to converse with, and discuss, mutual family and friends with recent arrivals. They were free, although it was often too expensive, to return to or visit their homes or to have those back home come and visit them. They were even able to re-establish families and social circles after their arrival. Additionally, they were always under the umbrella of their government's protection. Their settlement at Jamestown, although manned by people who had left England for the New World, was more in the context of a modern-day offshore operation than a classic case of migration. The settlement consisted of a party of one hundred men and four boys. While the settlers themselves were mostly uneducated, working-class people, they were in effect, on an expense-paid enterprise. It had been paid for, and provisioned by the Virginia Bay Company of London, a collection of well-to-do English venture capitalists, who were making this investment in the hopes of starting a successful and profitable enterprise in the New World. The one hundred four settlers were, in a way, their own venture capitalists. For not only were they being looked after during the term of their contract with the Virginia Bay Company, but also when those seven years expired, they were free to pursue of their own fortunes.

The truer of the two English settlements—that of the Pilgrims at Plymouth Rock—represents an example of poor people migrating, not so much in exercise of elective options for economic improvement, but more in response to what they perceived as threats from a hostile government.

The Mayflower settlers were made up of religious Separatists, who were followers of the teachings of one Robert Browne, a sixteenth-century reformist. They were essentially of the Congregationalist denomination but maintained a Separatist character in that they had broken rank with the English Church. They held secret religious services in order to avoid detection by the English government, which was not tolerant of the Separatist movement. To avoid persecution by the English government, they initially immigrated to Holland where greater religious tolerance was practiced. However, being in Holland offered another threat to their membership. Members of their party began marrying into Dutch families and leaving the Separatist movement. In an effort to keep the movement free from religious persecution and a compromising social environment, leaders of the movement elected to take advantage of the many opportunities to immigrate to America. Failing to get backing from wealthy sponsors, one hundred two members sold themselves into indentured servitude agreements before boarding the Mayflower at Plymouth, England. They arrived in New England and named the port Plymouth Rock.

German Immigrants

Another example of an immigrant group, and one in which the classic immigrant model is more apparent, is that of a group of immigrants from Germany. That the native demographics of a given group of immigrants remain intact can be seen in their mid-1800s migration. The initial wave of German immigrants had come from the middle-class social strata and brought large sums of money with them. Because of this, they did not have to stop in the slums of New York to seek employment but were able to travel all the way to areas of the Midwest to buy farms, farmland, and businesses. In only a few short years, these Germans were perceived as successful immigrants who had made it good in the New World. I have referred to this immigrant group as a classic example because their migration was elective and because they apparently retained patterns of their original socioeconomic stratification.

Other Immigrants Compared with African Immigrants

Those immigrant groups who chose to emigrate as a simple elective rather than those who were obliged by circumstances to emigrate were obviously more fortunate. They came unmolested by circumstances and brought the fundamentals of their socioeconomic status still intact. They came as the wealthy, the upper class, and the middle class. Upon their arrival in America, they went into the professions, opened up a business, or went into politics, just as they might have done in their native country. They corresponded frequently with the folks back home, and because they could afford it, they either made return visits or had family members come and visit them. The significant point is that when immigrants arrived in America, their social or class status, whether they were professionals, merchants, "blue collar" skilled or unskilled, or illiterate remained virtually intact. This was decidedly not true of the African immigrants. Even when Africans of wealth or of substantial social status were enslaved, they were reduced to the lowest common status. On board the ships that carried the enslaved Africans, the fact that they were members of prominent African families that may have possessed great resources meant little or nothing. They were absolved of privileges and immersed into the anonymity of African enslavement.

This is precisely what occurred when an African known as Joseph Cinque of Manis, Mendis, reached America. Reportedly of royal birth, he was abducted in Africa, sold into slavery, and placed on board a ship that contained a large number of other Africans. His status as the son of prominent and perhaps wealthy parents was of no consequence. As fate would have it, however, Cinque, perhaps because of his former social status, led a revolt among the other enslaved Africans and seized control of the ship *Amistad*. They sailed the seized vessel into the Boston Harbor where they were promptly arrested and defined as slaves. It was only after a number of years of defending themselves in the American courts—their defense team was headed by none other than John Quincy Adam, the former American president—that they were permitted to return to Africa.

Irish Immigrants

Of all the immigrant groups cited herein, perhaps the immigration of the Irish bears the closest resemblance to that of the Africans. Their plight, as it applies to the circumstance of their emigration and the conditions encountered upon their arrival in America reflects elements of the African immigrants' experience. True, the Irish were by no means enslaved, and it is equally true that they immigrated to America as an expression of their options rather than under force of arms. But beyond these differences and the fact that the Irish were European and not African, parallels can be discerned. Clearly the Irish were not enslaved and were not treated as such, but the degree to which they were exploited, both in their labor and in society's negativist assessment of their rights as citizens, compares well with the plight of the African immigrants. And as to their having chosen to emigrate from Ireland, under the circumstances, the option was probably made more *for* them than *by* them.

In 1845, prior to the great Irish migration, Ireland suffered a devastating famine that occurred as the results of an infestation of the potato plant. The potato was one of Ireland's principle food products and was a daily staple in the Irish diet. As a result of this infestation, for fifteen consecutive years, the nation's potato harvest was cut to a mere pittance of it former yield. The resultant lost in food supply caused the starvation deaths of over 1.5 million people. So while the Irish may have decided to migrate, there were virtually no other options. The choice was, leave Ireland or starve to death. Faced with this choice, they fled to America, and upon their arrival, other comparative features were experienced. The Irish were impoverished economically, they possessed limited technical skills, and they were Catholics. Either because of these elements of their immigrant status or because of something more traditional they were bitterly discriminated against.

Vietnamese Immigrants

The next example of an emigrating group occurred much more recently than the mass migration of the Irish. Following the collapse of Saigon at end of the Vietnam War, thousands of Vietnamese immigrated to the United States. Over two hundred thousand of these immigrants settled in southern California. In the seventies when the first Vietnamese immigrants began arriving in southern California, local rumor mills characterized them those gold-bearing immigrants arriving in southern California with gold, or hoards of cash money. During the arrival of the initial or first wave of immigrants, conversational fare painted pictures of wealthy Vietnamese families arriving in America with large caches of gold and cash. Stories such as these abounded about the Vietnamese alleging that they had fled Saigon with only a suitcase of gold to their name, or about the high-ranking Vietnamese military men, doctors and businessmen who came with special U. S. Government or State Department backing.

Even as obtuse and elaborate as these anecdotal accounts may have been, they were essentially founded upon the apparent logic of the event. The first wave, or group of Vietnamese immigrants did not include the poor, the illiterate, and the unskilled. These immigrants were not the subjects of Emma Lazarus's poetic plea. They didn't come to America in sampans packed with starving and indigent refugees. Rather they came over in air-conditioned airplanes with flight attendants and cocktails. When they reached their destinations, consistent with the rumors, a number of them probably were met by U. S. government representatives and were indeed put up in pricey hotels at the expense of the government. The intention here is to illustrate that during large-scale migrations, the socioeconomic stratification of a society may be stressed, but not likely upset. This first wave of Vietnamese immigrants more than likely maintained their social and economic status. If they were fortunate enough to have been a wealthy family in Vietnam, they came to America as a wealthy family. If they were perhaps not wealthy but were of upper class status, then they were able to sustain their social class status. If the family was only middle class, then they likewise would have retained middle-class status unless, of course, in the frantic pace to flee Saigon, good fortune fell into their lap and elevated their status. Of course, we can be sure that there were Vietnamese who lost everything. The probabilities are though, that if your family was poor, you came as poor people. Subsequent to the initial group immigrants, successive waves of immigrants had not fared as well. In fact they didn't fare well at all. They were the faceless mass that we all know of as "the boat people." They were those souls immortalized by Emma Lazarus' impassioned rendering of human pathos so poignantly displayed on the Statue of Liberty.

And came they did, setting sail for a distant land, girded in the knowledge they had nothing to lose and all was gain. They were not the French-speaking, credential-bearing Americanized professionals, nor were they laden with the proverbial suitcases filled with gold pieces. They were just desperate immigrants. In America, they have become the working class, the blue-collar consumer. They were not wealthy, nor have they necessarily become so. Whereas the first group of immigrants represented the wealthy the professional and the highly skilled, these successive immigrant groups—the boat people—have represented the poor, the indigent, the semi-skilled, the unskilled, and the illiterate.

IMMIGRANTS: IN SUMMATION

These examples represent the principal differences between the circumstances surrounding the emigration of other immigrant groups and those that surround the emigration of the African immigrants. Unlike any of the other immigrant groups, the socioeconomic status and social order of the African immigrants were disrupted and perhaps destroyed by the priorities of those who traded in the enslavement of Africans and the owners of large plantations. Had the African immigrants been permitted to arrive as the result of their own elective choice with their socioeconomic status and social order intact, their success in America would have been comparable to that of any other immigrant group. Had they been permitted to maintain their own native social stratification, they would have brought their own share of wealthy, professionals, upper class, middle-class, skilled blue-collar workers, and yes, poor and unskilled immigrants along, with them. Not only were certain socioeconomic and social status options denied the African immigrants, but even features as basic to humanity as common language and determined residency were pre-empted by the priorities of the institution of slavery.

Part Two

THE AMERICAN DESCENDENTS OF THE AFRICANS

5

THE GENERATIONS OF DESCENDENTS

During the more than 380 years since the twenty Africans landed at Jamestown, America has moved forward in almost quantum leaps. One hundred fifty-seven years after their landing, in 1776, America declared its independence from Europe and fought a war in its defense that allowed establishment of an independent democratic government. It then fought a civil war in defense of the ideal of that government. Now, in the early years of the twenty-first century, democracy has emerged among all the governments of the earth as the most humane application of the science of human politics yet instituted among men.

In the following table the first generation of African immigrants are shown as the "1619 Africans," and correspondingly, the first generation of English immigrants are shown as the "1620 Pilgrims." The backgrounds of all the events noted on the listings are addressed in much greater details in the various chapters and sections of the commentary. The generational list chronicles the arrival of the 1619 Africans and then proceeds to incorporate the millions of other Africans who subsequently arrived into a generational hierarchy that, beginning with the 1619 Africans, continues through twenty successive generations. A generation, as utilized here and as referred to throughout this commentary, is a period of thirty years. The thirty-year expanse is further divided into three distinct ten-year intervals. Children of these intervals or birthing periods are referred to respectively as children of the first, second, or third tripartites. All together, these three groups of children cover the entire thirty-year generational period. Within this framework, one can see that children born into the first tripartite of a given generation will overlap with the children born into the third tripartite of the preceding generation. And children born into the third tripartite will likewise overlap with those children born into the first tripartite of the succeeding generation. No such overlap occurs with children born into the second tripartite. A new generation of children begins on the average of once every twenty years. The use and application of specific generations and of the generational tripartites as keynote features of this commentary permit unique visibility into ever-changing environments into which black American children are born.

Years / Generations	Events That Defines Each Generation
1606 through 1635 First Generation	1. King James authorizes the colony that is named Jamestown in his honor. 2. The 1619 Africans arrive in Jamestown. 3. The 1620 Pilgrims arrive at Plymouth
1626 through 1655 Second Generation	1. The 1619 Africans become indentured servants 2. Slavery does not yet exist in the colonies. 3. The second generation of African immigrants arrived.
1646 through 1675 Third Generation	1. The first statutes limiting African rights are passed. 2. Africans' indenture agreements are extended. 3. English immigrants' mindset of "English"
1666 through 1695 Fourth Generation	1. Africans are now held in lifetime indenture. 2. Slavery succeeds indenture program. 3. English immigrants are still "Englishmen."
1686 through 1715 Fifth Generation	1. Slavery is under British mandate. 2. Insurrections by African immigrants occur. 3. Quakers issue formal protest against slavery.
1706 through 1735 Sixth Generation	1. Slavery still a mandate of British government. 2. African immigrants commit sabotage. 3. Many Africans revolt against slavery.

1726 through 1755 Kunta Kinte Generation	1. Slavery still held under British mandate. 2. Africans continually rebel. 3. Kunta Kinte (*Roots*) arrives in America.
1746 through 1775 Eighth Generation	1. Slavery continues to be a British mandate. 2. Black Americans fought in the Revolutionary War 3. America declared independence from Great Britain
1766 through 1795 Ninth Generation	1. Black Americans fight in Revolutionary War. 2. Americans debate the issue of slavery. 3. Seven Northern states abolish slavery.
1786 through 1815 Tenth Generation	1. New York and New Jersey abolish slavery. 2. U.S. excludes slavery from Northwest Territory. 3. Congress votes to ban African slave trade.
1806 through 1835 Eleventh Generation	1. American Anti-Slavery Society is founded. 2. Abolitionists publish "The Liberator." Newspaper. 3. Congress approves Missouri Compromise.
1826 through 1855 Twelfth Generation	1. Official abolition of the African slave trade. 2. Harriet Beecher Stowe's *Uncle Tom's Cabin* is published. 3. U. S. Supreme Court issued the Dred Scott ruling.
1846 through 1875 Thirteenth Generation	1. Abraham Lincoln elected as the 16th U.S. president. 2. The Civil War began 3. Black Americans fight in Civil War. 4. Slavery is abolished in remaining states.
1866 through 1895 Fourteenth Generation	1. Reconstruction program begins and ends. 2. Century-long Ku Klux Klan terrorist campaign begins. 3. "Jim Crow" laws are implemented.
1886 through 1915 Fifteenth Generation	1. Jim Crow laws and sharecropping are introduced. 2. Black Americans fight in Spanish-American War. 3. 50 years of continuous Ku Klux Klan terrorism.
1906 through 1935 Sixteenth Generation	1. Plow-handle-to-keyboard migration begins. 2. Black Americans fight in World War I. 3. 80 years of continuous Ku Klux Klan terrorism.

1926 through 1955 M. L. King Generation	1. Modern Civil Rights Movement is launched. 2. Black Americans fight in World War II. 3. Plow-handle-to-keyboard migration continues.
1946 through 1975 Eighteenth Generation	1. Black Americans fight in Korean War. 2. *Brown v. Board of Education* victory is achieved. 1. Civil Rights legislation passes.
1966 through 1995 Nineteenth Generation	1. One hundred years of Ku Klux Klan terrorism cools. 2. Black American middle class mushrooms. 1. Black Americans fight in Persian Gulf War.
1986 through 2015 Twentieth Generation	1.First tripartite (1986-1995) of the Twentieth Generation born. 2.Nation prepares for the twenty-first Century 3.Proposed generation for launching an internal affirmative action program within, and for, the black American community.

Table I

This table of Generations reflects some of the key events in the history of the black American community's 1619 through 2002 presence in America

The first generation of black Americans (1606–1635) referred to in Table I above as the generation of the 1619 Africans were not enslaved per se but were sold into the indentured servitude system. They did not experience slavery during the thirty-year period of their generation. However, the third generation (1646–1675) was not so fortunate. It was during the third generation (1646–1675) that the first legally binding statutes leading subsequently to enslavement of the African immigrants occurred. From the initial statutes issued in 1661 until America declared its independence from English authority in 1775, slavery had encompassed the fourth (1666–1695), fifth (1686–1715), sixth (1706–1735), seventh (1726–1755), and eighth (1746–1775) generations of Africans immigrants and had become a significant fixture in the American economy. The farming colonies' inability to free themselves from slavery was probably more in response to the dependency than political persuasion. To assault this premise, I have listed three examples of dependency over choice.

In the first examples, the United States, in response to the Surgeon General's report that cigarette smoking causes lung cancer, launched an ad campaign during the 1960s aimed at discouraging cigarette smoking. Forty years later, and although the campaign has successfully reduced the percentage of cigarette smokers, the sale of cigarettes is still a multi-billion dollar enterprise. There are, of course, more complex reasons why people smoke than the following, but sparing those, another powerful reason for the continued presence of cigarette smoking is because of its entrenchment in the country's economy and in the social habits of the American people.

Another example can be found in the nation's efforts, ostensibly to limit the air pollution caused by the use of gasoline-burning automobile engines. Again the moral content of these example pales besides the immorality of slavery, but their application is a paradigmatic model by which social behavior and responses to certain social stimuli might best be assessed. Also, perhaps through the illustration of some of the phenomena of the twentieth-century black and white Americans might better understand the behaviors or misbehaviors of nineteenth-century America. In this example, the use of gasoline-burning automobiles have become such a integral fixture within the nation's economy and so intensely integrated into its social habits that Americans continue to tolerate the millions and millions of tons of pollutants released into the atmosphere every day.

A third example illustrates the difficulty the nation might have experienced in its attempts to disengage itself from socioeconomic benefits of the cheap source of manpower made possible through the institution of slavery. In this illustration, not unlike the previous one, the nation's ambivalence towards the use of low-cost coal used to power a large number of the nation's electrical power generators can be witnessed. We have long acknowledged that the use of coal-burning power-generation systems form a significant part of the nation's air pollution problem. In spite of that acknowledgment, however, the people and the government have apparently come to some sort of understanding—seemingly being that either the nature of the problem is not as severe as announced or that to rid ourselves of the use of coal-burning power stations poses an even greater threat. In the meantime, the smoke stacks of coal-burning furnaces continue to spew out atmospherically harmful pollutants.

Finally, another sociopolitical issue that perhaps compares more favorably with the recalcitrance of American slavery is the current discussions regarding abortion. I am sure that some day in the future the issue will be resolved into appropriate legislation, or legislated into an appropriate morality. In the meantime though, millions and millions of unborn children, like the enslaved Africans before them, suffer neglect, abuse, and death at the hands of persons who claim the right of human ownership over other human beings. Certainly the nation holds strong and opposing ideas as to how to resolve the question of abortion. In a manner not too unlike these opposing notions, so did the nation hold strong and opposing ideas as to how best to deal with the issue of slavery. We can only hope that resolution of the abortion issue does not require the ninety years (1776–1865) needed to resolve the questions regarding the morality of slavery. In each of these four examples, we have seen how difficult it has been for the nation to rally around a single, solution. Do these problems exist simply because Americans like the idea of abortion as a form of birth control or that they are insensitive to the dangers of the air pollutants? We all know that's not the case. The dangers posed by the persistent and ongoing habit of smoking cigarettes has been repeatedly demonstrated. Also, the nation's love affair with the automobile, an affair that results in millions of tons of hydrocarbons being pumped into the atmosphere daily, would seem on the surface an easy one to resolve. Americans could simply switch over from gasoline to a lesser polluting fuel, or switch over from using individual automobiles to mass transit systems.

All these solutions are possible and accessible, yet the auto pollutants persist. And the acid rain from coal-burning power plants, like the automobile pollutants, also persists. Analytical solutions to these problems are not the problems that resist their resolution. Resistance is brought about by the presence of opposing and different ideas about the resolutions to be employed. From these examples, one can see that it doesn't really matter whether the issue was slavery or some other institutionalized activity. Simple knowledge of the ill effects of the activity is obviously not enough, in itself to evoke a strong enough social reaction to prompt a speedy resolution of the issue. Such were very likely the circumstances surrounding the institution of slavery following the nation's success in winning its national independence. From a given perspective, it could be said that from the years 1661 to 1860 or roughly ten generations, the market forces of the nation's economy succeeded in institutionalizing African slavery as an integral feature of its operation. And from the years 1865 to 1976, or roughly six generations, the moral forces of the nation succeeding in dismantling, or de-institutionalizing Jim Crow terrorism against the black American community.

The thirteenth generation (1846–1875) is to be celebrated as the *Generation of Liberation.* Even though the euphoria of their liberation lasted only as long as it took the terrorist to organize. From the latter half of the thirteenth generation (1846–1875) until the civil rights era during the eighteenth generation (1946–1975), thousands of black Americans were tortured, murdered, and intimidated by an assortment of terrorists' activities. Concentrated primarily in the Southern states but effective throughout the nation, the fourteenth (1866–1895), fifteenth (1886–1915), sixteenth (1906–1935), seventeenth (1926–1955), and eighteenth (1946–1975) generations were virtually shut-up within the dehumanizing confines of Jim Crowism. The last entry in the chronology introduces those persons born and to be born between the years 1986 and 2015. They are of the twentieth generation (1986–2015), and have been referred to as the academic generation. They will be the freest, the most educated, and the most socio economically accomplished of the entire string of generations. They carry in their genes the same passion to survive and the same aversion to capitulation that has characterized the legacy of their elders, their forebears, since their first arrival in America. It closes with the end of the twentieth generation (1986–2015). The year 2006 is the generational eve of the twenty-first generation (2006–2035).

The characterizations of the generations depicted are designed to emphasize the paths the respective descendents of the African immigrants have taken in the building of this nation and to call attention to the fact that the particular role played by them have been fashioned by the circumstances of the times into a consummate feature of the nation's legacy. Also, the characterizations are designed to illuminate the historical account of the indispensable part the black American community has played, not just in the physical building of America but also most assuredly in her moral foundation.

THE CULTURAL ESTATE OF BLACK AMERICA

The entire cultural and moral estate of the black American community is vested within the legacies and traditions of its six-layered generational sexpartite. More definitively this sexpartite consists of great-great-great grandparents (1886–1915), great-great-grandparents (1906–1935), great-grandparents (1926–1955), grandparents (1946–1975), parents (1966–1995), and finally, the sixth layer, the children and youths of 1986–2015. This last layer varies from those born in 1986 to those that will be born through 2015.

The Eighteenth and Nineteenth Generations of the Parents

As the process of each generation functions, the principal, or parental generations currently pertaining to the eighteenth (1946–1975) and nineteenth (1966–1995) generations have received their moral and cultural values as an inheritance from their parents, who consist mainly of those persons within the sixteenth (1906–1935) and seventeenths (1926–1955). And so the eighteenth (1946–1975), and nineteenth generation (1966–1995) parents are obliged to communicate the same moral and cultural values they received to the young adults, adolescents, children, and infants of the nineteenth (1966–1995) and twentieth (1986–2015) generations. In simple application, one can see that the process is quite similar to the way property or family estates are transferred from one generation to the next. In that scenario, children inherit shares of stocks, money, land, homes, jewelry, or other valuables from their parents. And depending upon their management of these assets during their lifetimes, they will probably bequeath the same, or increased assets to the generation that follows them.

In the same manner, then, children of black American parents must become heirs to the cultural and moral estates of their parents. Each generation of black Americans must inherit—like the inheritance of physical assets between parents and children—the cultural, moral, and meritorious values of their generation and pass them on to succeeding generations. Along those lines, if this commentary is accepted as having historical and cultural significance, then it, too, must be among the things of merit handed off by the seventeenth (1926–1955) and eighteenth (1946–1975) generations to those of the nineteenth (1966–1995) and twentieth (1986–2015) generations.

The Nineteenth and Twentieth Generations of the Youths

The nineteenth (1966–1995) and twentieth (1986–2015) generations, those born between 1966 and 2015, will carry a great responsibility. This commentary assigns upon them a great challenge, perhaps the ultimate challenge. For it is during their watch, their generational terms, that the black American community must achieve socioeconomic parity.

The seventeenth (1926–1955) and eighteenth (1946–1975) generations have made great strides in increasing the numbers of black Americans currently enjoying middle and upper class status, However, socioeconomic estate of black Americans and the per-capita socioeconomic estates of the nations ethnic groups as a whole are still seriously disproportionate. The key to the successes experienced by the seventeenth (1926–1955) and eighteenth (1946–1975) generations came about primarily as the result of increased levels of education. Therefore, further advancement of the black American community toward full parity hinges upon the nineteenth (1966–1995) and twentieth (1986–2015) generations' significantly advancing their level of education. This is why the charge rests so firmly upon them. Their generations must consign themselves to the achievement of greater levels of academic success if they hope to achieve socioeconomic parity. They are the generations of promise. If they perform well, the hopes and aspirations of a long history of black America will finally be realized. Socioeconomic parity is an achievement all black Americans, and particularly those of the tasked generations, owe the whole of our African and American ancestry. The debt falls heavily upon those of the nineteenth (1966–1995) and twentieth (1986–2015) generations because they enjoy more freedom and are the best educated of all black Americans since 1619. They have neither the constraints of enslavement nor the life-threatening intimidation of white supremacist terrorism to contend with. Validation of the merits of this approach to solving the problems that currently afflict Americans of African ancestry rests in this generation's willingness and ability to successfully commit itself to the disciplining influence of the following seven fundamental assertions regarding the black American community. Having achieved that, it is important to educate and integrate each member of this generation into the mainstream of American life.

Seven Fundamental Assertions Regarding Black Americans

1. That enslavement of the Africans was carried out in response to the New World's demand for an additional source of labor.

2. That enslavement of the Africans as a labor source was attributable more to the fact that they were politically, militarily, and strategically accessible than because their skin color was black or that they were Africans.

3. That enslavement of the Africans as a labor source did not, of itself, constitute a unique event in history. And that, until abolished, largely on the merits of the African immigrants themselves, slavery had been a socially and politically endorsed system of labor distribution for more than six thousand years.

4. That the socioeconomic disparities that presently exist between the Americans of African ancestry and the Americans of European ancestry is not attributable to race but to the elements of repression and hostility within the socioeconomic environment.

5. That recovery from such a socioeconomic disparity is achievable via the rules of formal education, social integration and the economic disciplines.

6. That black Americans, those Americans of African ancestry, must purge their own social ethos of the rhetoric and behavior of self-rejection.

7. That black Americans acknowledge the reality of their American inheritance, both of substance and heritage. And that their "heir ship" in the substance of America and their heritage in the history of America be embraced as the natural legacy of their ancestry.

The Generational Sexpartite

The movie *An Officer and A Gentlemen* featured a gunnery sergeant named P.T. Foley. Sgt. Foley was a Marine drill instructor, a "DI." As such, he had the unenviable task of taking newly-arrived civilians—some of whom were immature, physically underdeveloped, and mentally unfocused—and turning these raw recruits into mature, well-developed, disciplined, and focused Navy fighter pilots.

The movie also showed that as soon as Sgt. Foley had successfully completed the process of turning the first rambunctious assortment of civilians into a company of Navy aviators, a new assortment of equally rambunctious civilians would arrive. He would then begin the entire process all over again. The next batch of recruits, as illustrated in the movie, were more or less subjected to the exact same training regimen that Sgt. Foley had successfully applied to the previous of recruits. Consequently, the second company of Navy aviators would characteristically be the same as the companies of naval aviators that had graduated before them.

As it was with Sgt. Foley, so it is essentially with the culture of a people. Each new generation of children born into a society begins as one of Sgt. Foley's immature, underdeveloped, and undisciplined batches of civilian recruits. It is the task of the parental generation to take that generation of children and, being mentors of their society's social and cultural values, turn them into mature and socially acceptable men and women. Each successive parental generation must assume the responsibility to assure that, like the new recruits, each new generation undergoes a process of training in the social and cultural values held dear by society. And as illustrated in the movie, if the parental generation is successful, then each new generation will graduate into adulthood fully vested in the values and behaviors of the social and cultural estate of their parents.

Generally speaking, and within the scope of this commentary, a human generation is considered to extend over a thirty-year period. And, as mentioned earlier, generations tend to occur on average about every twenty years. A generation, as presented in this commentary, consists of the birth, growth to maturity, the production of a successor generation, and ultimately the death of that generation. The process continues with their descendent begetting descendents, and so on *ad infinitum*. The sequence of generations can be seen as a sort of punctuation in the erstwhile continuous flow of a family's procreation line. It is as if the entire history of a nation or people consisted of a non-stop relay race. The generational intervals occur as each runner hands off the baton of this generation to the runner for the succeeding generation as illustrated in the following sequence of generational figures. In the course of structuring the generations of the black American community, the first thirty years of the black American presence in the United States have been designated as the *generation of the 1619 Africans*, so called because those twenty African immigrants who arrived onboard a Dutch Man o' Warre are to be considered in no lesser fashion nor esteem than the 102 European immigrants who a year later arrived aboard the *Mayflower*. Thus, since the men and women of the *Mayflower* have been enshrined in American folklore as Pilgrims, then it also seems fitting also that the brave men and women of the Dutch Man o' Warre be equally enshrined in the folklore of America, not as "slaves," but as equals of *Mayflower* Pilgrims, both tilling the soil of a new morality.

For our purposes, the 396–year period from the arrival of the 1619 Africans in Jamestown until the year 2015 have been divided into twenty 30-year generational periods. They are defined as 30-year periods even though each of the 30-year generational periods overlaps by ten years the previous and succeeding generational periods. One of these periods has been designated for each of the twenty generations of black Americans who have lived in America since the arrival of the 1619 Africans. It should be noted here that although these Africans are depicted as the first generation (1606–1635), they were not the first Africans to have immigrated to America. Prior to 1619, a number of Africans from an assortment of sources had already made their homes in America. The reason why the Africans who arrived in 1619 are used as the referent generation here is not because they were first but because this commentary focuses upon the black American community as the unfortunate heirs of the legacy of enslavement of the African immigrants.

The over laps of the thirty-year generational periods means that at any given time, a six-span, or some number of up to six continuous generations of black Americans, can be alive. Members of the twentieth (1986–2015) generation's first tripartite (1986–1995), at this writing, are about sixteen years old. This group of children is unique within the child-rearing process because, generally speaking, they represent those most influenced by grandparents. The main reason they can be considered unique is because they are products of a phenomenon that occurs only once every generation, or every twenty years as the case might be. These children, whom I have designated as the first tripartite of a generation, are more than likely, representatives of the first children born to a set of parents. Two unique circumstances accompany children born into this particular niche. The first—being the oldest child—is adequately described in most psychological and sociological media that addresses the phenomenon of sibling birth orders. Most writings or research regarding the order of birth assign certain specific and distinct characteristics to the siblings, based upon the order of their birth.

Among the conclusions drawn from these studies is the contention that certain particular behavioral traits are to be associated with the first, middle, and last child. However, the role that the grandparents play within the lives of these children is another feature that must be given significant play. While grandparents play a role in the child-rearing lives of all children regardless of birth order, the oldest children are characteristically more affected than those born later on. There are undoubtedly other reasons for the disproportionate attention, but one very apparent reason is that grandparents are alive and active during the first years of the older children's lives, By the time children of the third tripartite of the generation are born, the grandparents may have become too inactive to play a meaningful role in the children's lives or are perhaps not longer living.

Over the years, I have had the opportunity to speak with a number of parents who had migrated to this country from other countries. And I have noticed that when I ask them if their children can speak their native language, those with grandparents in the home have almost always said "yes," while those without grandparents in the home, or in close proximity, will either say "no" or that the children can speak only a few words. The reality is that in the order of things, most black American parents—most parents in general, for that matter—tend to be fully engaged in the "now" aspects of their lives, and expend very little effort in teaching their children about the past. And since this is the case, black American children or any other children will learn only about those traditional values that have managed to align themselves with the "now" in their parents lives. And since, as contended by this commentary, grandparents represents the greater share of the socio-cultural resource of the black American community—and again this would apply to any ethnic community—the children born first tend to be more favored by learning traditional or socio-cultural values from their grandparents. Conversely, children born in subsequent birth orders will arrive too late to be directly engaged in any child-rearing activities with their grandparents. However, it should be noted that by the time these later children are born, their parents will have for the most part come to grip with their own values, and thus these children are reared under these socio-cultural values.

Distribution of the thirty-five or so, million black Americans that currently resides in the United States is as follows: approximately two million are of sixteenth generation (1906–1935); approximately four million are of the seventeenth generation (1926–1955); approximately fifteen million are of the eighteenth generation (1946–1975). Of the remaining two generations, approximately eight million are of the nineteenth generation

(1966–1995), and the remainder, approximately six million are of the twentieth generation (1986–2015). Consistent with the somewhat progressive nature of generational growth, each of these twenty generations undoubtedly contain significant components of the entire social and cultural estate of the black American community. In a scenario similar to that where the more successful businesses of the black American community are reportedly now amassing something in the order of billions of dollars in annual receipts, the black American community must affect sustained growth in its own social and cultural estates. And as it is with the black American community's economic estate, so it is, and should be, with the distribution of its socio-cultural estate. Obviously, not all of the billions of dollars of the economic estate are attributable to any one person, or company, nor should any one-generation be expected to carry the total burden of the community's socio-cultural estate.

We can begin an assessment of that socio cultural estates by first considering the care and attention shown by all successive generations for the remaining members of the fifteenth generation (1896–1915) as a measure of the character of those generations, and thus the character of the black American community as a whole. Members of the sixteenth generation (1906–1935) are most assuredly vested with the wise counsel of their age. Therefore, members of the sixteenth generation (1906–1935) should be called upon for their sage wisdom. The two million members of the sixteenth generation (1906–1935), by virtue of their place in the social and economic strata of the country, are principal holders of the black American community's economic resources. As such, members of the seventeenth generation (1926–1955) should further enhance their contribution to the black American community by focusing more of their attention and resources on at least some of the following items:

1. Additional funding for civil rights organizations such as the NAACP and the National Urban League, for example and other effective organizations.

2. Should increase volunteer service in charitable and civic organizations.

3. Increased financial support for effective local churches

4. Made additional sacrifices to assist in funding the education of their children and grandchildren

5. Increased financial support for charitable organizations

6. Become better informed in the full spectrum of politics. Get more involved in making political contributions in support of their choice of political candidates.

7. Overall backup financial support for their children and grandchildren

8. Become more active in adopting black American children

9. Establishment and maintenance of membership in the NAACP organization

10. Establishment and maintenance of membership in local PTA organizations

11. As members of social organizations, establishment of scholarship funds to aid in the education of black American youths

12. Buy and own real property

13. Become counselors for the eighteenth generation (1946–1975) and submit themselves to be counseled by the seventeenth generation (1926–1955).

14. Make reading and discussing books with children an active cultural enterprise.

15. Take trips to as many foreign countries, and as frequently as possible.

16. An increased focus on organizing and hosting family reunions on a regular basis

17. Assurance that a hospitable environment is available for senior citizens in all rest homes, senior centers, and other care facilities where members of the fourteenth, fifteenth, sixteenth, and perhaps some members of the seventeenth generation (1926–1955) are resides

18. A concerted effort to join, and participate in, other community organizations such as the Red Cross, the United Way, American Legion, and any other civic and Rotary club organizations

19. The black American community needs to revive its former faith in the edicts and merits of Judeo-Christian values.

The approximately eight million members of the nineteenth generation (1966–1995), by virtue of their having had access to considerably enhanced educational opportunities, constitute by far the most educated of all the previous generations of black Americans. As such, this generation is tasked with an obligation to hand off the baton of academic achievement to the twentieth generation (1986–2015), as Sgt. Foley was obliged to do. Though generations come and go, it is the accomplishments achieved between their comings and goings that history records as the measures of their contribution. While the teenage members of the nineteenth generation (1966–1995) and later on, the twentieth generation (1986–2015), may perceive the difficulties and obstacles in their lives as unique to them and their generation, the truth of the matter is they are not. The younger members of the eighteenth (1946–1975), nineteenth generations (1966–1995), and the generations of their parents, all have, or will face similar difficulties and obstacles. Basically, the only difference between the problems today's teenagers faces and those faced by their parents are primarily in the descriptions and metaphors by which such challenges are referred rather than by the emotional or psychological trauma engaged.

To test the validity of this premise, one need only to reflect upon the simple fact that members of both the nineteenth (1966–1995) and twentieth generations (1986–2015), like each generation before them, began as babies. And through the process of time they grew into adolescent teenagers, mature adults, and finally to old age. This trek through the years is, of course, true of all generations. It is a cycle wherein generations move through the various periods of life. The event is akin to watching an assortment of floats in a New Year's Day parade. From our vantage point, we can only see five or at the very most six generations at a time. The five or possibly six generation viewing range, or vantage point equates to a life expectancy of from 88 to approximately 108 years. After that, they pass around the corner beyond our line of sight. However, from the vantage point of history, all generations are viewed as having passed in continuous sequence along the very same route. Each generation, as indeed with each float in a New Year's Day parade, encounters and experiences the same bumps and potholes in the road as they move along the parade route. To better emphasize this point, let's consider yet another analogy. When the Native American peoples migrated into the Americas, they developed trails, primarily footpaths since horses and wagons had not yet been introduced into North America. Those trails or footpaths were in later years used for riding horses. And still later, the same trails that had been adapted to riding horses were utilized as roads for driving wagons. And in current times, those same trails and footpaths, established thousands of years ago are known to us as the Mohawk Trail, the Santa Fe Trail, the Overland Trail, and the Natchez Trace. Vistas along these paved multi-lane trails are now viewed from air-conditioned and computer-monitored Fords, Chevrolets, and Chrysler cars and SUVs.

The point of this illustration is to draw attention to the fact that countless people have traveled these footpaths or trails from the times of the Mohawk Chief Thayendandgea to the time of Commander-in-Chief George W. Bush. Yet the fundamental vistas of the trails remained unchanged. It is the same with the vistas of life. Although you may come along twenty to forty years after your parents, the fundamental elements of your life's experiences are unchanged from the time of your parents. In a way you can think of it as though each successive generation is simply a metaphor for the generation that preceded it. The repeated recycling of these same trails from Mohawk Trail, the Santa Fe Trail, the Overland Trail, and the Natchez Trace to riding trails, to wagon roads, and on to interstate thoroughfares, turnpikes, and freeways, provides additional clues that the life experiences of one generation mimics that of the previous one. While no essential change in the purpose or direction of the footpaths occurred, the words used to describe the footpaths appear to change with the flow of generations. Each succeeding generation restates their environment in a language consistent with the circumstances and facilities of their times.

The times of the native American footpaths have thus given way to those of modernity, and the footpaths have become known to contemporary travelers as Interstate 95, Interstate 40, Interstate 80, and Interstate 20. And still, as noted earlier, the essential origin and destination of these interstates—the footpaths—have changed very little since their founding thousands of years ago. This situation is akin to the anthropologist whose description of a native people notes that their diet includes wild grain and the roots of certain plants native to the area. This description takes on a totally different context when to the anthropologist has on his, or her dinner plate, a serving of rice pilaf and carrots.

Other examples of the cultural expression between generations reveal similar parallels. In politics, music, the arts, literature, and dance the similarities of the social expression are evident. In dance, the energy of the cake walk of the 1890s that excited members of the fourteenth generation (1866–1895), that of the 1920s Charleston which crazed the minds of the fifteenth (1886–1915) and sixteenth (1906–1935) generations. And the 1950s jitterbug rock that taunted the seventeenth generation

(1926–1955) teenagers of the James Dean era are no different than the energies that spurred the Dance Fever craze of the 1980s nineteenth generation (1966–1995). Social movements like the gilded-age of the 1890s that excited the industry of the fourteenth generation (1866–1895), the Roaring Twenties that teased and tantalized the fifteenth (1886–1915) and sixteenth (1906–1935) generations, and the war protests of the baby-boomers of the seventeenth generation (1926–1955) are fundamentally the same cultural expressions that emerged under the guise of dissident "rap" expressions and break dances of the 1980s nineteenth generation (1966–1995). Therefore, it would appear that the youths of each succeeding generation are wired to the energies of the previous generation by the almost-unalterable dictates of the maturation process.

Whereas the thirteenth generation (1846–1875), disenchanted with their government's handling of slavery in the 1850s, left the city streets and went to war to end it, their descendent generation—the eighteenth generation (1946–1975)—disenchanted with the government's handling of a war, left the war and went into the streets to end it, a century later. These are all cultural expressions, or paradigms, of the respective generations, and reflect the same generational energy communicated from one age group to the other. Therefore, members of the nineteenth and twentieth generation (1826–1855) must pledge themselves to the teaching and counsel of their three layers of parents, for they are the predecessor generations who have already traveled the path upon which the current generation now embarks upon.

6

THE LEGACY OF NINETEEN GENERATIONS

THE FIRST-GENERATION OF THE 1619 AFRICANS (1606–25)

In 1620 the great conflict in Europe between the Protestants and the Catholics had just begun. It lasted until 1648 and is known as the Thirty Years' War.

In 1620, the Mayflower left Leyden, Holland, and set sail for Virginia, but instead of arriving in Virginia, the ship docked at Cape Cod in what is now Massachusetts. Her passengers, men, women and children, were religious Separatists fleeing the religious persecution in Europe and seeking a place of their own where they could live and worship God according to their beliefs.

In 1624, Antony and Isabella, two of the original twenty African immigrants, became the parents of William Tucker, the first of the 1619 Africans to be born in English America. In the same year, eleven Africans were in the party that, after a long and stormy voyage over the Atlantic, established a trading post on Manhattan Island, which they named the New Netherlands.

THE SECOND GENERATION (1626–55)

In 1633, Francisco Negro incorporated the village of Bushwick in Brooklyn. And the next year, three black men—Francisco Peres, Mathias DeSousa, and John Price—were with the party that first settled the area, which later became the state of Maryland.

In 1641, Mathias DeSousa served in the Virginia General Assembly, which met in March of that year. (Over one hundred years later, from 1769 to 1774, Thomas Jefferson would also serve in the Virginia General Assembly.)

On May 27, 1643, the first land grant in the section of Brooklyn known as Gravesend was issued to Antonie Jansen Van Salee, and on December 15, 1644, a Dutch land grant was issued to Lucas Santomee, the "physician" son of Pieter Santomee, a free black American.

THE THIRD GENERATION (1646–75)

In 1661, actual statutory slavery was legitimized in Virginia. The statute did not apply to those black Americans who were already serving under indentured servants agreements, but to all future Africans who would be brought into the colony.

In 1662, Virginia legislated that black American children born in Virginia would be free or enslaved according to the social status of the mother.

In 1663, a large number of black Americans enslaved in Virginia conspired to revolt.

THE FOURTH GENERATION (1666–95)

In 1671, the Virginia legislature declared that conversion to Christianity would not affect the status of a slave. Also, Pere Jacques Marquette, a

Jesuit missionary, founded the mission of St. Ignatius, at Mackinac. In 1672, the Royal African Company was chartered to capture, enslave, and transport Africans to the Virginia Colony.

THE FIFTH GENERATION (1686–1715)

In 1687, a planned rebellion, by black Americans was discovered and crushed by Virginian authorities. In 1694, black Americans in Virginia had become so ungovernable that the governor of Virginia requested stricter enforcement of the codes governing the behavior of Virginia's enslaved persons.

THE SIXTH GENERATION (1706–36)

In 1712, black Americans of New York revolted against their enslavement.

In 1721, Onesimus, a black American, earned his freedom after suggesting to Cotton Mather, a noted clergyman and scientist, that a method of inoculation he learned in Africa would prevent an existing smallpox epidemic. The inoculation method, although it preceded Edward Jenner's article on the same subject by some sixty-eight years, was successful in stopping the epidemic.

In 1723, the black Americans enslaved by Massachusetts were charged with industrial sabotage.

THE SEVENTH GENERATION (1726–55)

In 1730, black Americans who were enslaved in Virginia revolted.

In 1739, black Americans enslaved in Stono, South Carolina, revolted, and in 1741, black Americans enslaved in New York were charged with industrial sabotage. Rumors of rebellions by enslaved black Americans were commonplace

THE EIGHTH GENERATION (1746–75)

In 1750, Kunta Kinte was born in Gambia, West Africa, and in America, Crispus Attucks escaped from slavery.

By 1756, there were 120,156 black Americans in the Virginia Colony.

In 1761, an eight-year-old girl, who was later to become the poetess, Phyllis Wheatley, arrived from the coast of African and was sold to a Boston tailor named John Wheatley. In the same year, Jupiter Hammon published *An Evening Thought: Salvation by Christ with Penitential Cries.*

In 1765, Jean Baptiste Pointe du Sable arrived in America from Paris, France. He established a trading post at the mouth of the Chicago River around the year 1779. His trading post enterprise eventually became the city of Chicago.

THE NINTH GENERATION (1766–95)

During this generation, large numbers of black Americans fought in the Revolutionary War.

On September 29, 1767, Kunta Kinte arrived in America.

In 1769, Phyllis Wheatley published her first book of poetry, and published her poem, *On The Death of Reverend George Whitefield* in 1770.

In 1770, Crispus Attucks, a black American of the sixth generation (1706–1736), became the first person to die in the American Revolutionary War.

In 1773, black Americans enslaved in state of Massachusetts petitioned the state legislature for their freedom. Also in 1773, black Americans founded the First Baptist church of Silver Bluff, South Carolina.

On April 19, 1775, Prince Estabrooks, Cuff Whittemore, and Cato Wood of the Arlington Company, and Cato Stedman and Cato Bordman of the Captain Samuel Thatcher Company of Cambridge fought with Captain Parker and the Lexington Company at the battle of Lexington.

In 1776, the black Americans of Virginia formed a Baptist church at Petersburg, and on December 7, 1776, Prince Whipple accompanied George Washington when he crossed the Delaware River into Pennsylvania.

In 1777, the state of Vermont abolished slavery.

In 1778, Jupiter Hammon published a twenty-one-stanza poem titled *To Miss Phillis Wheatley*. Black Americans asked the city of Boston for a separate school, but the city fathers refused.

It was, perhaps, during this generation that the Africans became Americanized. This conversion is reflected in the heroic declaration of James Forten, the fourteen-year-old black American who served as powder attendant on board the Royal Louis vessel. When captured by the British and offered freedom in England, he replied, "I am here a prisoner for the liberties of my country, I shall never, never prove a traitor to her interest." Also, a black American soldier in Captain Pelton's company of the Second New York Regiment, Phillip Field of Duchess County, New York, died at Valley Forge during the bitter winter.

In 1779, George Liele, a black American, founded a Baptist church in Savannah, Georgia.

In 1780, black Americans established a school in Boston and employed two Harvard men as instructors. The school flourished for many years until preempted by another school built by the city of Boston, and the black Americans of Virginia formed another Baptist church, this time at Richmond, and the state of Pennsylvania abolished slavery

In 1781, a party made up of Native Americans and black Americans founded the City of the Angels—Los Angeles, California.

In 1783, the state of Massachusetts abolished slavery.

In 1784, the state of New Hampshire abolished slavery, and Prince Hall applied to the Grand Lodge of England and was granted a warrant to establish a chapter of "Negro" Masons. The chapter became African Lodge No. 459 in Boston, Massachusetts. In the same year, the states of Connecticut and Rhode Island abolished slavery.

In 1785, the black Americans of Virginia started a Baptist church in Williamsburg.

THE TENTH GENERATION (1786–1815)

In 1787, Jupiter Hammon published An Address to the Negroes of the State of New York, and Richard Allen and Absalom Jones organized the Philadelphia Free African Society.

On August 16, 1788, Native Americans on the shores of Tillamook Bay murdered Markus Lopeus a crewmember of the sloop Lady Washington. The ship's captain, Robert Gray, named the place Murderer's Harbor in memory to the black American sailor. It is so named until this day.

In 1789, Gustavus Vassa, a former slave, born in Benin, West Africa, published The Interesting Narrative of the Life of Oloudah Equiano, or Gustavus Vassa.

Benjamin Benneker became a recognized as authority in astronomy.

In 1790, the black American population in the United States was slightly more than 750,000, or approximately nineteen percent of the total population. Most of the black Americans were, of course confined to the Southern states. There were 641,691 people enslaved in the South Atlantic states, as well as 32,048 freedmen. There were 304,000 Africans enslaved in Virginia.

In September 1790, Kunta Kinte's wife, Bell, gave birth to his first American-born child, a girl.

In 1791 Benjamin Benneker began publishing his Poor Richard almanac and James Derham, a distinguished contemporary of Benjamin Banneker was regarded as the American's first African-born, physician.

In 1792, Joshua Bishop, a black American, was named pastor of the First Baptist Church (for white Americans) of Portsmouth, Virginia. Also in 1792, Benjamin Benneker, a friend of Thomas Jefferson, was commissioned to survey a location to build the White House.

In 1794, Richard Allen organized the first African Methodist Episcopalian Church in America.

In 1796, a party of forty-four black Americans organized the African Society. The organization did much to help sustain black American unity. Also in 1796, a black American named George Washington founded Centralia, Washington.

In 1797, black Americans petitioned the U.S. Congress to abolish slavery. At same time, the state of New York was initiating action to abolish slavery.

In 1800, Gabriel and other black Americans enslaved in Virginia planned a revolt. Also, the black American population in the United States during that time reached 1,002,037.

In 1803, Congress resolved to investigate the "expediency" of allowing black Americans to serve in the Army, Navy, and Marines. Also during

1803, George York, an enslaved black American, accompanied Louis and Clark on their famous expedition and earned his freedom as the result of the services he rendered.

In 1804, the state of New Jersey abolished slavery.

ELEVENTH GENERATION (1806–35)

In 1807, the royal man of war "Leopard" at Norfolk, Virginia took prisoner three sailors aboard the Chesapeake, a United States naval vessel. They were later released after proving that they were "Americans."

In 1809, Rev Thomas Paul organized the first black American Baptist church in Boston and assisted in starting the church in New York City that would later become the Abyssinian Baptist Church.

On August 6, 1810, the black American population of the U.S. was 1,378,000.

In 1811, black Americans in New Orleans, Louisiana revolted against their enslavement.

Black Americans of the tenth generation (1786–1815) fought in the War of 1812.

On January 8, 1815, the battle of New Orleans witnessed the largest gathering of black American troops ever assembled on American soil. It consisted of the troops from both the LaCoste and the Daquin Savary battalions. A white American soldier from one of the other battalions wrote in a letter to the Niles Register that the "New Orleans colored regiment was so anxious for glory that they could not be prevented from advancing from over our breastworks and exposing themselves. The eager black American militiamen of LaCoste and Daquin battalions chafed at the inactivity before their position at the center of the line. Finally, their impatience became so great that their officers could not longer restrain them and the soldiers began leaving the ranks to make unauthorized sorties against the British troops."

On June 1, 1820, the black American population of the United States was 1,772,000. Eighty-six black Americans returned to Africa subsequently establishing the country of Liberia.

In 1822, Denmark Vesey and thousands of other black Americans held in slavery in South Carolina, planned a massive revolt.

THE TWELFTH GENERATION (1826–55)

In 1826, John Russwurm became the first black American to graduate from college when he received his degree from Bowdoin.

In 1827, the first black American Newspaper, Freedom's Journal, was published and the state of New York abolished slavery.

In 1829, black Americans enslaved in Cincinnati, Ohio, rioted, and approximately one thousand black Americans migrated to Canada the same year.

In 1830, the black American population of America was 2,328,642, and Alcorn University of Lorman, Mississippi, was founded.

In August of 1831, Nat Turner led a rebellion of black Americans enslaved in Southampton County, Virginia. The rebellion became the benchmark of the black American's disgust toward the being enslaved. In the same year Boston's William Lloyd Garrison began publishing a weekly newspaper.

In 1833, Philadelphian black Americans, working with liberal white Americans, founded the American Anti-Slavery Society.

In 1835, a black American convention in Philadelphia advised black Americans to remove the word "African" from the names of their institutions and organizations.

In 1837, the Cheyney State College located in Cheyney, Pennsylvania was founded.

On September 3, 1838, Frederick Douglass escaped from slavery.

In 1838, the Mirror of Liberty became the first black American magazine.

In 1839, Cinque of Manis, Mendis, on the West Coast of Africa and a boat load of other Africans seized control of the their slave ship and sailed it into the Boston Harbor.

In the 1840s, Hiram Young, operating a factory of some fifty men and twenty-five forges out of Independence, Missouri, became a well-known builder of the famous Conestoga wagons used by early-American pioneers to settle the western United States.

In 1843, in Africa, Charlie Smith (?) was born. He is alleged to have lived for 134 years. He was brought to the Americas in 1853, and was sold into slavery when he was ten years old.

In 1844, Reverend B.W. Arnett, pastor of a church in Ohio, was refused admittance to the International Sunday School Convention in Atlanta, Georgia.

In 1845, Macon B. Allen, became the first black American to be admitted to the bar and Frederick Douglass published an autobiography. In the same year he made a lecture tour of England.

THE THIRTEENTH GENERATION (1846–75)

On December 10, 1846, Norbert Rillieux received a patent for an improved method of processing sugar.

In 1847, Frederick Douglass began publishing *The North Star* (later on called, *The Frederick Douglas Paper*), a newspaper that advocated the abolition of slavery.

Also in 1847, Joseph Jenkins Roberts, a black American Virginia native declared Liberia an independent republic.

In 1849 Harriet Tubman began her underground railroad. During its duration, she assisted and conveyed over three hundred black Americans from slavery to freedom in the northern states and Canada. Benjamin Roberts filed the first school integration suit in the Massachusetts school system. Massachusetts integrated its schools in 1855.

In 1850, the Baptist Churches had a black American membership of 150,000; and the black American population in the United States was 3,638,808, or 15.7 percent.

Although black Americans were enslaved, they still retained minimal access to formal communication media, they kept abreast of all information relating to the progress the abolitionists were making. Every success of the Federal armies and defeat of the Confederate forces was watched with the keenest and most intense interest. Often; the black Americans got knowledge of the result of great battles before the white American community received it.

In 1850, slavery had cultivated a negative attitude among southern white Americans toward performing labor-intensive jobs. The legacy of this attitude may account for the poverty still existing in many southern states.

In 1851, a black American abolitionist staged a Boston Massachusetts courtroom rescue of a fugitive slave.

In 1852, Harriet Beecher Stowe published *Uncle Tom's Cabin*.

In 1853, William Wells Brown published *Clotel*, the first novel written by a black American.

In 1854, Ashmum Institute was founded in Chester County, Pennsylvania.. It was the first black American college in the country. It later was to become the Lincoln University.

In 1855, James Augustine Healy became the first black American Roman Catholic bishop.

In 1855, Charlie Smith (?) arrived in America at the age of twelve and was sold into slavery.

In 1855, James Mercer Langston of Lorain County, Ohio, became the first black American elected to public office.

In 1856, the African Methodist Episcopal Church membership was 20,000 and Wilberforce University was founded.

In 1857, the U.S. Supreme Court handed down the Dred Scott decision.

In 1858, *Escape* became the first play published by a black American.

In 1859, the ship *Clothilde*, the last slave ship used to transport Africans to the Americas, made its final delivery of Africans to an American port.

In 1859, Clara Brown opened her own business in Central City, Colorado. Her many acts of charity prompted the city to dedicate a chair in the Opera House to her memory.

A young black American, John A. Copeland, left the security of the Oberlin College campus and the friendship of the nonviolent abolitionists to join the revolutionary John Brown in Maryland at the Kennedy farm. He was arrested with John Brown, tried for insurrection and murder and was sentenced to death. A short time before he was led off to the gallows, Copeland had penned these words to a friend, "I am not terrified be the gallows, which I see staring me in the face, and upon which I am soon to stand and suffer death for doing what George Washington was made a hero for doing. Washington entered the field for the freedom of the American people—not for the white man alone, but for both black and white."

In the 1860s, two Pony Express riders, George Monroe and William Robinson, manned Pony Express routes. Monroe rode from Merced to Marysosa, California, and Williams rode from Stockton out to the gold mining area.

From 1861 to 1862, eleven Southern states seceded from the United States including Alabama, Arkansas, Florida, Georgia, Louisiana, Mississippi, North Carolina, South Carolina, Tennessee, Texas, and Virginia.

On April 12, 1861, forces of the Southern Confederacy fired on Fort Sumter, Charleston, South Carolina.

On September 22, 1862, President Lincoln issued a preliminary emancipation proclamation, declaring that on January 1, 1863, all enslaved persons living in those states still in rebellion were to be liberated.

On March 2, 1863, Frederick Douglass wrote, "Men of Color, To Arms! I urge you to fly to arms and smite with death the power that would bury the government and your liberty in the same hopeless grave."

Following that call, more than 186,000 black Americans, freedmen and runaways, enrolled in the Union Army. The majority of the soldiers fought in one of the 166 all-black units that served the Union. The United States "Colored" Troops included 145 regiments of infantry, seven cavalry regiments, and one of engineers.

From 1863 to 1865, spearheaded by the thirteenth generation (1846–1875), four percent of the black American people fought the most noble battle of them all—the "War of Liberation" for the abolition of slavery, the American Civil War.

Of the black American soldiers, Colonel Higginson wrote in his diary, "The key to successful prosecution of this war lies in the unlimited employment of black troops. Their superiority lies simply in the fact that they know the country while white troops do not, and moreover, that they have peculiarities of temperament, position, and motive which belongs to them alone. Instead of leaving their homes and families to fight, they are fighting for their homes and families and they show the resolution and sagacity which a personal purpose gives."

In addition to those who served in the Union military, more than 250,000 black American men and women supported the military effort through civilian jobs such as teamsters, cooks, nurses, pilots construction workers, and security guards.

On January 1, 1863, President Lincoln issued the Emancipation Proclamation.

On December 18, 1865, the Thirteenth Amendment to the United States Constitution was ratified, abolishing slavery in the United States of America. In 1865, the U.S. Congress created the Freedmen's Bureau to provide humanitarian services for those previously enslaved.

THE FOURTEENTH GENERATION (1866–95)

In 1866, membership in the African Methodist Episcopal Church increased to 75,000.

On June 16,1866, the Fourteenth Amendment to the Constitution was ratified, declaring that all persons born in the United States or that were naturalized were citizens of the United States.

In 1866, the country's first Civil Rights Bill was passed, the Lincoln University opened in Jefferson City, Missouri, and black Americans Edward G. Walker and Charles Mitchell were elected to the Massachusetts House of Representatives.

In 1866, the Ku Klux Klan, the Knights of the White Camellia, the White Brotherhood, the Pale Faces, the '76 Association, and the Mississippi Plan began campaigns of terrorism to close the paths of socioeconomic mobility of black Americans. The terrorist campaign—which included lynching, shootings, murders, beatings, plundering, and other forms of intimidation—was utilized throughout the southern states. According to ads placed by the NAACP in the November 23, 1922, editions of the New York Times and the Atlanta Constitution newspapers, the campaign of terrorism cost the lives of as many as 3,436 black Americans during the years 1889 through 1922. Through such acts of barbarous intimidation, racist groups throughout the southern states and across the nation succeeded in denying black Americans access to their legal rights and other benefits accorded them by virtue of their citizenship, and further stipulated by the Emancipation Proclamation, Thirteenth, Fourteenth, and Fifteenth Amendments to the U.S. Constitution.

So vicious was their campaign of terrorism that even though congressional legislation in May of 1870 and again in February and April of 1871 sought to impose heavy penalties upon the perpetrators, neither had any effect. The legacy of their terrorist influence spread even farther and affected the treatment of more and more black Americans throughout the nation.

In 1867, Fisk University located in Nashville, Tennessee was founded.

In 1867, the Howard University, of Washington D.C. was founded.

The fourteenth generation (1866–1895) of black Americans participated in the U.S. military campaigns or battles in the Native American wars, and went on to fight in Europe during World War I.

In 1867, Morehouse College in Atlanta, Georgia, began operations; Morgan State University in Baltimore, Maryland, was founded; and membership in the African Methodist Episcopal Church increased to 200,000. Also, following Emancipation, large numbers of previously enslaved black Americans left the farms and moved into the local towns and cities. Where engaging in new and more technical skills, their number grew and soon outnumbered the white American artisans by five to one.

In 1867, the Johnson C. Smith University of Charlotte, North Carolina, was founded; the United States government implemented the Southern Reconstruction program; and the Bowie State College of Bowie, Maryland, was founded.

Between 1868 and 1876, black American Senators Hiram R. Revels and Blanche K. Bruce of Mississippi were elected to the United States Senate, and Congressman Richard H. Cain of South Carolina, John R. Lynch of Mississippi, and James T. Rapier of Alabama were elected to the U.S. Congress. Also, the black American legislators of the southern states of Alabama, Arkansas, Florida, Georgia, Louisiana, Mississippi, North Carolina, South Carolina, and Virginia were influential in making three major contributions: they re-established democratic governments, they made significant contributions toward the development of the free public school system, and they instituted social programs to support the establishment of charitable institutions.

In 1868, the Philander-Smith College of Little Rock, Arkansas was founded; Oscar J. Dun became the lieutenant governor of Louisiana; Hampton University, of Hampton, Virginia, was founded; and black American legislators participated in the writing of the constitutions for the states of Arkansas, Louisiana, Alabama, Mississippi, Florida, and South Carolina.

By 1869, the Freedmen Bureau had begun to close down and the land reform programs were a dead issue. For the most part, the formally enslaved black Americans were on their own only five years after gaining their freedom.

In 1869, Dillard University was founded in New Orleans, Louisiana, three black Americans were elected to the U.S. Congress and black American legislators participated in the writing of the constitution of North Carolina. Ebenezer Don Carlos Bassett, a black American, was appointed minister to Haiti.

In March 30, 1870, the Fifteenth Amendment to the Constitution was ratified. Hiram Revels was elected U.S. Senator from Mississippi, membership in the Baptist Churches rose to more than half a million, and black Americans Michael Howard of Mississippi and James W. Smith of South Carolina were nominated for appointment to the West Point Military Academy.

In 1870, black American legislators were instrumental in writing the constitution of Virginia. Joseph Rainey of South Carolina became the first black American congressmen to serve in the House of Representatives, and Robert H. Wood became the mayor of Natchez, Mississippi.

On June 1, 1870, the black American population of the United States was 4,880,000.

On March 31, 1870, Thomas Mundy of Perth Amboy, New Jersey, became the first freedman to vote after ratification of the Fifteenth Amendment.

In 1871, the Fisk Jubilee Singers gave their first concert and began a series of world concert tours that would eventually make them world famous.

In 1871, Henry A. Naxier, of Tennessee was nominated for appointment to West Point Military Academy.

In 1872, Thomas Van R. Gibbs of Florida was nominated for appointment to West Point Military Academy, Charlotte E. Ray became the first American woman to graduate from law school, and P.B.S. Pinchback became acting governor of Louisiana.

In 1873, black American legislators were instrumental in writing the constitution for the states of Georgia, P.B.S. Pinchback was elected to the U.S. Senate from Louisiana and

Richard T. Greener became the first black American to graduate from Harvard University.

In 1874, Richard T. Greener was named professor of metaphysics at the University of South Carolina, the Alabama State University in Montgomery, Alabama, was founded and John W. Williams of Virginia was nominated for appointment to West Point Military Academy.

In 1875, the Knoxville College of Knoxville, Tennessee and the Alabama A&M University of Normal, Alabama were founded. Also, Congress passed a Civil Rights bill that had been introduced by Senator Charles Sumner and Blanche Kelso Bruce became the U.S. Senator from Mississippi.

In 1875, jockey Oliver Lewis won the Kentucky Derby riding Aristides.

In 1876, Chief Justice Morrison R. Waite, in *United States* v. *Cruikshank*, decided that the Fourteenth Amendment "adds nothing to the rights of one citizen as against another."

In 1876, Johnson C. Whittaker of South Carolina was nominated for appointment to West Point Military Academy.

By 1877 there were 571,506 black American children in school. The Fayetteville State University, located at Fayetteville, North Carolina, was founded as was Jackson State University in Jackson, Mississippi.

In 1877, Charles A. Minnie and Henry O. Flipper of New York were nominated for appointment to West Point Military Academy. Flipper passed the entrance exam and went on to receive a commission in the U.S. Army.

In 1877, jockey Billy Walkers won the Kentucky Derby riding Baden Baden.

During 1877, eleven years after the government implemented the Southern Reconstruction program, President Rutherford B. Hayes, while visiting Atlanta, Georgia, told the black Americans ex-slaves that their "rights and interests would be safer" if southern white Americans were "let alone" by the general government. Federal troops were withdrawn from the southern states.

In 1878, although deserted by their northern friends and abandoned by the federal government—and often coerced, intimidated, or defrauded—black Americans nevertheless continued to vote in large number for the next two decades.

The Compromise of 1877 signified the end of the Reconstruction program. United States Attorney General Edwards Pierrepont concluded that "the executive branch of the national government announced that it had decided that the reconstruction acts of congress were a failure."

In 1879, Prairie View A&M College of Prairie View, Texas, was founded.

On June 1, 1880, the black American population of the United States was 6,581,000.

In 1880, Samuel Lowery became the first black American attorney to practice before the U.S. Supreme Court. "Sharecropping," a modified version of slavery had replaced the institution of enslaved labor as the model of agrarian economics. Lewis Howard Latimer was employed by the United States Lighting Company, at Bridgeport, Connecticut. It was during this employment that Mr. Latimer successfully produced a method of making carbon filaments for the Maxim electric lamp, which he patented.

In 1881, Spellman College was founded in Atlanta, Georgia and Booker T. Washington in Tuskegee, Alabama founded Tuskegee Institute.

In 1881, Bishop College in Dallas, Texas, and Bishop State Junior College in Mobile, Alabama were founded.

In 1882, jockey Babe Hurd won the Kentucky Derby riding Apollo.

In 1883, the U.S. Supreme Court pronounced the Civil Rights Act of 1875 unconstitutional.

In 1883, black American, John H. Alexander of Ohio was nominated for appointment to West Point Military Academy. He passed the entrance exam and went on to receive a commission in the U.S. Army.

On February 5, 1884, W. Johnson received a patent for the eggbeater.

On August 9, 1884, M. C. Harney received a patent for the oil-burning Lantern.

On October 11, 1884, G. T. Woods received a patent for development of a steam boiler furnace.

In 1884, jockey Isaac Murphy won the Kentucky Derby riding Buchanan.

In 1884, Charles Young of Ohio was nominated for appointment to West Point Military Academy. He passed the entrance exam and went on to receive a commission in the U.S. Army.

In 1885, William A. Hare of Ohio and William T. Andrews of South Carolina were nominated for appointment to West Point Military Academy.

In 1885, jockey Enoch Henderson won the Kentucky Derby riding Joe Cotton.

On April 7, 1885, Lee S. Burridge and Newman R. Marshman of New York received a patent for a typewriting machine.

In 1885, Tuskegee Institute produced it first graduating class.

On April 7, 1885, G. T. Woods was issued a patent for the invention of an apparatus for transmission of messages by electricity.

THE FIFTEENTH GENERATION (1886–1915)

In 1886, Henry W. Holloway of South Carolina was nominated for appointment to West Point Military Academy, Oakwood College of Huntsville, Alabama, and the Kentucky State University of Frankfort, Kentucky were founded.

In 1886 black Americans farmers throughout the cotton-growing states formed the Colored Farmers' National Alliance and Cooperative Union with an estimated membership of 1,250,000.

In 1887, jockey Isaac Lewis won the Kentucky Derby riding Montrose.

In 1887, The Central State University of Wilberforce, Ohio, was founded.

On October 11, 1887, Granville T. Woods of Cincinnati, Ohio, received a patent for a telephone system and apparatus.

In 1887, the Florida A&M University in Tallahassee, Florida, was founded.

On January 7, 1890, William B. Purvis, of Philadelphia, Pennsylvania, patented the fountain pen.

On June 1, 1890, the black American population of the United States was 7,489,000.

On June 3, 1890, a patent was issued to H. L. Jones for his invention of the corn harvester.

In 1890, jockey Isaac Murphy won the Kentucky Derby riding Riley.

In 1891, Isaac Murphy won the Kentucky Derby riding Kingman. In this race, Murphy became the first jockey ever to win three Kentucky Derbys.

On September 27, 1892, J. T. White was issued a patent for invention of the squeegee window cleaner.

In 1891, the Delaware State College, located in Dover, Delaware and the Elizabeth City State University, at Elizabeth City, North Carolina were founded.

On July 10, 1891, at Washington Park, a racetrack in Chicago, a jockey named "Monk" Overton won six straight races.

On June 7, 1892, G. T. Sampson of Dayton, Ohio patented a clothes drier. Jockey Alfie Clayton won the Kentucky Derby riding Azra.

In July 1893, Dr. Daniel Hale Williams performed the world's first successful heart surgery at Providence Hospital and Nursing School.

In 1893, William H. Lewis, an All American, who played center for Harvard University, published his pamphlet "A Primer of College Football."

On August 7, 1894, a patent was issued to R. P. Scott for invention of a corn silker.

On January 14, 1895, a group of black Americans joined together and formed the National Steamship Company. It then acquired the excursion steamboat, *The George Leary*, which sailed between Washington and Norfolk, Virginia.

In 1895, Booker T. Washington delivered his Atlanta Compromise speech, the Fort Valley State College of Fort Valley, Georgia was founded, and jockey J. "Soup" Perkins won the Kentucky Derby riding Haima.

In 1896, jockey Willie Simms won the Kentucky Derby riding Ben Brush.

On August 4, 1896, W. S. Grant received a patent for a curtain rod support.

In 1896, The U.S. Supreme Court sanctioned segregation (*Plessy v. Ferguson*) by declaring "separate but equal" facilities were constitutional.

On March 17, 1896, C. B. Brooks received a patent for the invention of the street sweeper.

In 1896, George Walker and Bert Williams' highly successful vaudeville team premiered in New York.

On December 8, 1896, J. T. White received a patent for inventing a lemon-squeezing device.

In 1896, W. E. B. DuBois published his first book, *Suppression of the African Slave Trade to America*.

On October 5, 1897, a patent was granted to J. H. Evans for inventing the convertible settee and bed.

On November 23, 1897, a patent was granted to J. L. Love for the invention of a pencil sharpener.

On November 7, 1897, J. A. Sweeting was issued a patent for inventing a device for rolling cigarettes.

In 1897, the Langston University opened in Langston, Oklahoma.

On October 26, 1897, a patent was issued to G. W. Kelly for the invention of a steam table.

In 1897, Paul Lawrence Dunbar began his writing career.

On May 4, 1897, J. H. Smith received a patent for a lawn sprinkler system.

This generation of black Americans fought against the axis powers of Germany in WW I.

In 1898, the North Carolina Mutual Life Insurance Company of Durham, North Carolina, was founded.

On February 8, 1898, A. L. Rickman received a patent for developing the overshoe.

In 1898, the Pilgrim Health and Life Insurance Company were founded in Augusta, Georgia.

In 1898, jockey Willie Simms won the Kentucky Derby riding the horse Plaudit.

In 1898, the U.S. Supreme Court (*Williams* v. *Mississippi*) approved a Mississippi scheme that used the poll tax, literacy tests, and residency requirements in an effort to reduce the number of black American voters.

South Carolina followed in 1895 and within the next twelve years, all Southern states would enact similar restrictions.

On February 15, 1898, the battleship *Maine*, anchored in Havana Harbor, Cuba, exploded, twenty-two black American sailors were among the 260 Americans sailors who lost their lives.

In July 1898, black American troops of the U.S. Ninth and Tenth Calvary, as a contingent of the Roughriders invaded Cuba and engaged the Spanish military under the command of Colonel Theodore Roosevelt. The military battle that ensued, often referred to as the Battle of San Juan Hill, defeated the Spanish and liberated Cuba.

On September 13, 1898, A. E. Long and A. A. Jones received a patent for the invention of a cap for bottles and jars.

During 1898 through 1900, Marshal "Major" Taylor, the fastest bicycle rider in the world, toured Europe and Australia to meet and beat the best riders in what was then considered the most popular international sport.

In 1899, Scott Joplin published his first work, a group of songs titled "Original Rags."

In 1899, W. E .B. DuBois published his second book, *My Philadelphia Negro.*

On June 1, 1900, the black American population of the United States was 8,834,000.

In 1900, Henry O. Tanner, one of the world's outstanding painters won medals for his paintings at the Paris Exposition, and his paintings won additional medals at the Pan American Exposition.

On July 19, 1899, John F. Pickering of Gonaives, Haiti, patented an airship.

In 1900, black American, Wallace Saunders popularized the song Casey Jones about a white American locomotive engineer named John Jones, who, in classic folk-hero fashion, crashed head-on into another locomotive in Vaughn, Mississippi.

In 1900, Coppin State College was founded in Baltimore, Maryland.

In the 1900s, Bill Picket, who is now in the Cowboy Hall of Fame, in Oklahoma City, Oklahoma, invented the sport of bulldogging and was a star at the 101 Ranch show.

In the 1900s, Boise Ikard, a black American cattle herdsman, pioneered the use of the Goodnight Trail route for getting Texas cattle to market.

By 1900, all southern states had enacted Jim Crow railroad laws restricting seats and other accommodation that were available to black American passengers.

In 1901, Booker T. Washington published *Up From Slavery. The Gazetteer and Guide*, Vol. 1, No. 1, reported that free black Americans in the United States owned personal and real property valued at $100,000,000.

In 1901, jockey Jimmy Winkfield won the Kentucky Derby riding His Eminence.

In 1901, Grambling State University, Grambling, Louisiana, was founded and the last black American congressman to be elected from the South left Washington D.C.

In 1902, jockey Jimmy Winkfield won the Kentucky Derby riding Alan-a-Dale.

In 1903, W. E. B. DuBois published *The Souls Of Black Folk.*

In 1903, the Consolidated Bank and Trust Company of Richmond, Virginia, was founded.

In 1904, Henry O. Tanner's paintings won another medal at the St Louis Exposition.

In 1905, W. E. B. DuBois organized the Niagara Movement for the advancement of the black American people.

In 1905, the Atlanta Life Insurance Company of Atlanta, Georgia, was founded.

On July 18, 1905, G. T. and L. Woods, were issued a patent for a railway brake apparatus

THE SIXTEENTH GENERATION (1906–35)

In 1906, W. E. B. DuBois published the *Litany of Atlanta*, an artistic commentary from the emerging black American perspective as evidenced in the riot that occurred in Atlanta, Georgia, that year.

In 1906, black American troops shot up the anti-black American town of Brownsville, Texas.

In 1907, at the Churchill Downs racetrack in New York, the jockey Jimmy Lee won six straight races.

In 1908, the Mechanics and Farmers Bank of Durham, North Carolina, was founded.

In 1909, Matthew Henson and his party became the first explorers to reach the North Pole.

In 1909, W. E. B. DuBois organized the National Association for the Advancement of Colored People (NAACP).

In 1910, almost one-third of all black Americans in the United States were illiterate.

In 1910, the North Carolina Central University Durham, North Carolina, was organized.

On May 2, 1912, James Reese Europe and part of his Clef Club orchestra made musical history by performing at Carnegie Hall in New York City.

In 1915, the Mammoth Life and Accident Insurance Company of Louisville, Kentucky, was founded.

In 1915, Carter Woodson founded the Association for the study of Negro Life and History.

In 1916, the Journal of Negro History was founded.

Beginning in 1919 and after 300 years (1619–1919) of agrarian skills, thousands of black American families—some having to flee their share-crop-plantation owners in the dark of night—abandoned those skills and moved north, seeking better education for their children, better jobs for themselves, and a life free from the bigotry-infested communities they had endured for three centuries.

February 19–21, 1919, the first Pan African Congress organized by W. E. B. DuBois met at the Grand Hotel in Paris, France.

On August 1, 1919, Marcus Garvey held his first national convention at Liberty Hall in Harlem to inaugurate the Universal Improvement Association. The next night, Garvey addressed some 25,000 black Americans in Madison Square Garden.

On January 1, 1920, the black American population of the United States was 10,463,000.

During the 1920s, the Harlem Renaissance Movement served as a social and cultural birth channel through which all the values and frustrations of black Americans were synergistically fashioned into the character of black America that emerged in the 1960s.

Ph.D. degrees were awarded for the first time to black American women: Eva B. Dykes (English) from Radcliffe; Sadie T. Mossell (Economics) from the University of Pennsylvania; Georgia R. Simpson (German) from the University of Chicago.

On December 21, 1920, a patent was issued to W. H. Sammons for invention of the hot comb.

In 1921, the Citizen Trust Bank of Atlanta, Georgia; the Supreme Life Insurance Company of America in Chicago, Illinois; and the Mutual Savings and Loan Association of Durham, North Carolina, were founded.

In 1921, the U.S. Department of Labor estimated that over 500,000 black Americans had left the South during the previous year.

In 1922, The Association of Negro Publishers was founded.

In 1923, Josephine Baker made her theatrical debut in the Blake and Sissle production of "Chocolate Dandies."

In 1923, the Universal Life Insurance Company of Memphis, Tennessee, was founded.

In 1923, the Bethune-Cookman College of Daytona Beach, Florida, was founded.

By 1923, Marcus Garvey's Universal Negro Improvement Association had a membership of approximately 500,000 black Americans who were prepared to return to Africa, to escape from a society that denied them the dignity, opportunity, and personal safety.

In 1923, the Protective Industrial Insurance Company of Alabama, Inc. was established in Birmingham, Alabama.

In 1925, A Phillip Randolph organized the Brotherhood of Sleeping Car Porters and Maids.

In 1925, the Golden State Mutual Life Insurance Company of Los Angeles, California, was founded.

In 1925, the Mutual Federal Savings and Loan Association of Atlanta in Atlanta, Georgia, was founded.

THE SEVENTEENTH GENERATION (1926–55)

In 1926, F. Q. Morton, LL.B., became the City of New York's first black American City Commissioner.

On January 24, 1926, Louis Howard Latimer became one of the charter members and the only black American member of the Edison Pioneers.

In 1927, the Chicago Metropolitan Mutual Assurance Company of Chicago, Illinois, was founded.

In 1928, Marshal "Major" Taylor published his autobiography, *The Fastest Bicycle Rider in the World*.

The seventeenth generation (1926–1955) of black Americans fought America's enemies in Korea and Vietnam.

In 1930, President Hoover nominated Judge John J. Parker of North Carolina, as justice of the U.S. Supreme Court. The NAACP launched a nationwide campaign against his appointment. Judge Parker was not confirmed.

On April 1, 1930, the black American population of the United States was 11,891,000.

In 1932, the Booker T. Washington Insurance Company in Birmingham, Alabama, was founded.

In 1933, United Mutual Life Insurance Company of New York was founded.

In 1934, the Industrial Bank of Washington in Washington, D.C. was founded.

In 1934, the Illinois Service/Federal Savings and Loan Association of Chicago was founded.

In 1935, Marian Anderson, after being acclaimed in Europe by Toscanini and Sibelius as one of the great singers of the world, returned to America in a blaze of glory.

On December 5, 1935, the National Council of Negro Women was founded in New York City with Mary McCleod Bethune as its president.

In 1936, black American voters begun to shift from the Republican to the Democratic party in support of President Franklin D. Roosevelt.

In 1936, the Winnfield Life Insurance Company was founded in Natchitoches, Louisiana.

On August 9, 1936, Jesse Owens won four gold medals at the Olympics in Berlin.

In 1937, *The Negro History Bulletin* was first published.

On April 1, 1940, the black American population of the United States was 12,866,000.

In 1941, A. Phillip Randolph, president of the Brotherhood of Sleeping Car Porters, threatened a mass march on Washington. President Franklin D. Roosevelt issued Executive Order 8802 forbidding discrimination in hiring practices in defense industries and establishing the Fair Employment Practices Commission.

In 1942, John H. Johnson began the Johnson Publishing Company, in Chicago, Illinois. The publishing firm has now grown into a $252,187,000 enterprise, and employs more than 2,000 people.

In June 1943, a race riot in Detroit, Michigan, occurred in which over thirty black and white Americans lost their lives.

THE EIGHTEENTH GENERATION (1946-75)

In 1946, Camilla Williams sang the title role of Madame Butterfly with a group of New York artists and Ellabelle Davis was invited to sing Aida with the Mexican Grand Opera Company.

In 1946, the Broadway Federal Savings and Loan Association of Los Angeles, California, was founded.

In 1946, the Mississippi Valley State University at Itta Bena, Mississippi, was founded.

In 1946, the Tri-State Bank of Memphis, of Memphis, Tennessee, was founded.

In 1947, the Williams-Progressive Life and Accident Insurance Company was founded in Opelousas, Louisiana.

On September 22, 1947, John Hope Franklin published *From Slavery to Freedom*.

In 1948, President Truman introduced his Civil Rights bill

In 1949, President Truman abolished segregation within the government and armed services.

The 1948 U.S. Supreme Court decision (*Shelly* v. *Kraemer*) removed the government's sanction from restrictive covenants that had formerly prevented black Americans from buying houses in specific neighborhoods.

In 1948, the Carver Federal Savings Bank of New York City was founded.

In 1948, the Family Savings Bank of Los Angeles was founded.

1948, the U.S. Supreme Court rulings (*Sipuel* v. *University of Oklahoma*, 1948; and *Sweatt* v. *Painter*, 1950) required state educational institutions in the South to admit black Americans when training available to them in black American institutions was not demonstrably equal.

On April 1, 1950, the black American population of the United States was 15,045,000.

In 1951, the Parks Sausage Company was founded. The company, located in Baltimore, Maryland, is clear and present evidence that a black American-owned company can do business in mainstream products.

In 1952, the NAACP argued before the U.S. Supreme Court against state laws requiring the segregation of children in public education.

On May 17, 1954, in the case of *Brown v. Board of Education of Topeka*, the U.S. Supreme Court, speaking through Earl Warren, the new Chief Justice, responded with a unanimous decision reversing *Plessy v. Ferguson* and outlawing racial discrimination in public schools.

In 1954, Eric G. Johnson began the Johnson Products Company in Chicago, Illinois.

In December 1955, the black Americans of Montgomery, Alabama, inspired by Dr. Martin Luther King, boycotted the city's segregated bus system.

In 1955, the Ku Klux Klan was reinitiated as the White Citizens Council and spread throughout the southern states.

By 1956, black American singers such as Marian Anderson, Robert McFerrin, and Mattiwilda Dobbs had signed contracts with the Metropolitan Opera Association of New York.

By 1956, Leontyne Price and Lawrence Williams were singing operas on television with the New York City Opera Company.

In 1957, Congress established the Civil Rights Act of 1957 to investigate denial of voting rights or equal protection of the law because of race, color, national origin, or religion.

In 1957, the Citizens Federal Savings Bank of Birmingham, Alabama, was founded.

In 1957, the Advance Federal Savings and Loan Association, of Baltimore, Maryland, was founded.

On September 24, 1957, black American children integrated Central High School in Little Rock, Arkansas.

In 1958, Duke's Barber Shop opened for business in Santa Ana, California. It was the first in Orange County owned by and for the black American community.

In 1958, the Golden Circle Life Insurance Company was founded in Brownsville, Texas.

In 1960, Congress authorized the courts to appoint federal referees to safeguard black American voting rights.

In April 1, 1960, the black American population of the United States was 18,872,000.

In September 1960, 765 of the 6,676 schools districts in the South had been desegregated.

In 1960, Gloria Davey, Thurman Bailey, and Grace Bumbry became regular members of European opera companies.

In 1961 and again in 1966, Leontyne Price received the singular honor of singing the title role at the New York City Metropolitan Opera on its opening night.

In October, 1962, James Meredith became the first black American student to attend the University of Mississippi.

In 1963, the Civil Rights Commission reported that black American citizens had been shot, set upon by vicious dogs, beaten, and otherwise terrorized because they sought to vote.

In April, 1963, Dr. Martin Luther King began a campaign to end discrimination in shops, restaurants, and employment in Birmingham, Alabama.

On January 23, 1964, the Twenty-fourth Amendment to the Constitution was ratified outlawing the practice of southern states to use the poll tax as a device to deny black Americans access to voting.

In 1964, the Congress passed the Civil Rights Act of 1964 prohibiting discrimination in the use of federal funds and in places of public resort and establishing the Equal Employment Opportunity Commission to prevent discrimination in employment.

In 1965, Congress passed legislation that permitted the federal government to register voters when the state refused.

In August of 1965, an otherwise-routine stop for a traffic violation in South Central Los Angeles sparked the Watts riots. Over the following two years, similar riots occurred in Detroit and Newark.

In 1965, six percent of the black Americans in Mississippi were registered to vote.

THE NINETEENTH GENERATION (1966–95)

In 1966, the American Woodmen's Life Insurance Company in Denver, Colorado, was founded.

In 1967, Stokeley Carmichael of the Student Nonviolent Coordinating Committee, and Floyd McKissick of the Congress of Racial Equality, injected the philosophy of "Black Power" into the civil rights movement.

In 1966, thirty-three percent of the black Americans in Mississippi were registered to vote.

In 1966, numerous outstanding black Americans painters were receiving recognition for their work. Among them were Hale Woodruff of Atlanta University and New York University for his murals in the Talladega College Library, and Charles Alston of New York whose portraits, caricatures, and sculptures are on display in various American museums.

In the 1960s, other artists who received recognition for outstanding works included Lois Mailou Jones and James Porter of Howard University, Ernest Crichlow, Romare Bearden, and E. Simms Campbell of New York.

In 1966, the U.S. Congress rejected the effort to establish open-housing guarantees.

In 1967, in the South, racial barriers fell in restaurants, hotels, and other public places of resort.

In 1967, black Americans made up 66 percent of the population of Washington, D.C., 39 percent of Detroit, 37 percent of St Louis, and 30 percent each of Chicago and Philadelphia.

In 1967, 16 percent of the 3,000,000 black American students in the South were attending desegregated schools.

On April 1, 1970, the black American population was 22,581,000.

In 1972, the U.S. Navy launched the warship Dorie Miller in honor of the hero who, after shooting down several Japanese warplanes, lost his life in 1943 when the Liscombe Bay sank.

In November, 1974, Alex Haley book *Roots, The Saga of an American Family* was published by The Readers Digest.

In January, 1977, from 9:00 P.M. on Sunday, January 23, through 9:00 P.M. on Sunday, January 30, more than seventy-five million television viewers watched the saga of Alex Haley's *Roots* as presented by the ABC television network.

On April 1, 1980, the black American population of the U.S. was 26,683,000.

This generation fought in the invasion of Grenada in 1986, in the invasion of Panama in 1989 and in Operation Desert Storm in 1990.

THE TWENTIETH GENERATION (1986–2015)

In 1987, Reginald F. Lewis, a black American, purchased TLC Beatrice International Holdings, Inc. TLC Beatrice is a processor and distributor of food products, and with over a billion dollars in sales in 1990, it is to-date, the largest business owned by a black American.

On April 1, 1990, black Americans constituted 30,666,000, or twelve percent, of the population of the United States.

In November 1990, Congress passed the 1991 Civil Rights Bill designed to repair some of the enforcement damage done by previous Supreme Court decisions.

In 1991, Thurgood Marshall resigned from the Supreme Court.

In 1991, Clarence Thomas, a federal appeals court judge was confirmed to serve on the U.S. Supreme Court.

In June, 1991, of the top one hundred industrial/service companies featured in Black Enterprise magazine, 83 percent were less than twenty-five years old. This trend suggests that if the current growth rate were maintained for the remainder of the generation, the median annual sales of the current top one hundred of $19,339,000 would increase by six hundred percent, or would approximate $114 billion by the 2015 closure of the twentieth generation (1826–1855).

On November 20, 1991, the Los Angeles Times, citing U.S. Census Bureau data, reported that over the last three decades, the number of black Americans officially counted as middle class or affluent in the language of the Census Bureau had grown by almost four hundred percent. Thus, the number of middle-class black Americans has increased by a rate of growth more vigorous than that of any other racial or ethnic group in American society. More than one million black American households are listed by the Census Bureau as affluent, with incomes of $50,000 or more, and these groups are enjoying a middle-class lifestyle was far beyond the reach of the generations of their parents or grandparents. The actual number, which equates to about 14% percent of the nation's black American population, is up sharply from 1967 when only 266,000 black American households, or 5.8 percent of the total, were considered "affluent."

In 2000, President George W. Bush named the former Joint Chief of Staff general Colin Powell to become this nation's first Secretary of State.

In June 2001, Black Enterprise magazine listed the earning of its BE100 as 19.7 billion dollars. In the June 1983 issue the magazine listed the earnings as only 1.53 billion dollars.

From January 1, 1986, to date, there are approximately six million children already born into the twentieth generation (1986–2015) varying in age from birth to approximately sixteen years old.

7

SOCIO ECONOMIC PARITY

Now that black Americans have had 137 years of post-slavery recovery time (1865–2002), at least thirty-four years of which they have enjoyed with the additional benefits of numerous civil rights bills, where are they now? What are the current socioeconomic circumstances of the black American community? As we enter into the twenty-first century, how do black Americans as an American community stack up against white Americans as an American community? In response to these questions I have assembled an assortment of facts and figures, gathered from various publications of the U. S. Census Bureau and other sources, in an effort to put forth a comparative metric of black America's socioeconomic progress.

The occupational categories in Table I on the following pages indicates that even though black Americans have made relatively significant progress toward socioeconomic parity, a substantial disparity still exists between the professional, technical and entrepreneurial levels of the average black American versus that of the average white American. As the figures in the occupational categories show, there are a disproportionately large number of black Americans in occupations that have low skill requirements. As a result, large numbers of black American workers are employed in occupations that pay minimum to modest wages or salaries. Or they work on day-to-day jobs, which leaves the workers subject to frequent interruption in annual incomes. The damaging effects of this disproportionate distribution of the black American community's human resource undermine the black American community's capacity for equitable earnings. The millions of unemployed, or underemployed black Americans that results from this underutilization of resources go a long way toward explaining why the disparity exist between the gross annual incomes of black Americans and that of white Americans seen in Table II. While it is obvious that there are certain historical, social, and economic factors, which have played a major role in the development and maintenance of this disparity, there are remedies that can be implemented. The historical events that played a role are fixed in historical time and therefore are not subject to revisionist remedies. The social and economic factors are more fluid in their impact and for the most part continue to be a source not only where the disparity is expressed, but also an ongoing source of it.

Additional discussions relating to the disparities in the distribution of black Americans versus white Americans in the occupational categories will be addressed when we go into more details in Chapter 12, *Grading the Progress of the Black American Community.*

	Occupational Categories As Listed in The U.S. Census Bureau Report	Total Employed In The U.S.	BAC's Percentage of Total Employment (Parity =13%)	BAC's Percent of Parity
1	Managers, marketing, advertisement and public relation	419,000	0.90%	1%
2	Fishers, hunters, and trappers.	61,000	1.10%	8%
3	Farm operators and managers	1,359,000	1.40%	11%
4	Nuclear Engineers	10,791	1.80%	14%
5	Sales-related occupations	63,000	2.10%	16%
6	Secretary and financial services, sales	266,000	2.20%	17%
7	Real estate sales	659,000	2.30%	18%
8	Sales representatives, except retail	1,509,000	2.30%	18%
9	Extractive occupations	194,000	2.60%	20%
10	Natural scientists	76,000	2.90%	22%
11	Mechanical Engineers	176,333	3.00%	23%
12	Financial managers	394,000	3.10%	24%
13	Architects	130,000	3.10%	24%
14	Dentists	155,520	3.10%	24%
15	Civil Engineers	252,808	3.20%	25%

	Occupational Categories As Listed in The U.S. Census Bureau Report	Total Employed In The U.S.	BAC's Percentage of Total Employment (Parity =13%)	BAC's Percent of Parity
16	Aerospace Engineers	143,434	3.20%	25%
17	Lawyers and judges	671,000	3.30%	25%
18	Dental assistants	168,000	3.60%	28%
19	Physicians	586,716	3.70%	29%
20	Supervisors and proprietors	3,316,000	3.80%	29%
21	Teachers, college and university	643,000	3.90%	30%
22	Financial Managers	635,911	4.70%	36%
23	Electrical and electronic Engineers	467,023	4.00%	36%
24	Insurance sales	541,000	4.70%	36%
25	Bookkeepers, accounting, and clerks	2,037,000	4.70%	36%
26	Waiters and waitresses	1,367,000	4.70%	36%
27	Carpenters	1,259,000	4.80%	37%
28	Purchasing Managers	120,775	4.90%	38%
29	Post-secondary teachers, subject not specified	615,068	4.90%	38%
30	Bartender	324,000	4.90%	38%
31	Managers, properties and real estate	342,000	5.10%	39%
32	Scientists and urban planners	286,000	5.20%	40%
33	Computer systems analysts, scientists	359,000	5.50%	42%
34	Sales occupations	12,667,000	5.50%	42%
35	Financial records processing	2,503,000	5.50%	42%
36	Personnel and labor relations management	110,000	5.60%	43%
37	Mathematical and computer scientists	571,000	5.60%	43%
38	Accountants and auditors	1,263,000	5.90%	45%
39	Firefighting and fire prevention	209,000	5.90%	45%
40	Transportation occupations, except motor vehicles	208,000	5.80%	45%
41	Bank tellers	484,000	6.00%	46%
42	Librarians, archivists, and curators	215,000	6.10%	47%
43	Technicians (not health), engineering, science	1,026,000	6.20%	48%
44	Vehicle and mobile equipment mechanics and repairers	1,850,000	6.20%	48%
45	Engineering, related technologies	904,000	6.40%	49%
46	Computer programmers	534,000	6.40%	49%
47	Secretaries	4,059,000	6.50%	50%
48	Librarians	201,000	6.60%	51%
49	Psychologists	150,000	6.60%	51%
50	Receptionists	679,000	6.70%	52%
51	Construction trades	4,745,000	6.70%	52%
52	Mechanics and repairers	4,475,000	6.90%	53%
53	Therapists	257,000	7.20%	55%
54	Precision production, craft, and repairers	13,340,000	7.10%	55%

	Occupational Categories As Listed in The U.S. Census Bureau Report	Total Employed In The U.S.	BAC's Percentage of Total Employment (Parity =13%)	BAC's Percent of Parity
55	Construction trades, except supervisors.	4,143,000	7.20%	55%
56	Automobile and motorcycle mechanics	906,000	7.50%	58%
57	Farming, forestry, and fishing	3,470,000	7.80%	60%
58	Science technicians	211,000	8.10%	62%
59	Precision production occupations	3,926,000	8.10%	62%
60	Sales workers, retail, personal service	5,682,000	8.20%	63%
61	Electrical and electronic equipment repair	8,100	8.30%	64%
62	Information clerks	1,257,000	8.40%	65%
63	Officials and Administrators, public	462,000	8.70%	66%
64	Hairdressers and cosmetologists	707,000	8.20%	66%
65	Technicians and related support	3,255,000	8.90%	68%
66	Child care workers	399,000	8.90%	68%
67	Personnel and Labor Relation Managers	275,495	9.00%	69%
68	Registered nurses	1,885,129	8.90%	69%
69	Administrators, Protective Services	49,273	9.10%	70%
70	Electrical and electronic technicians	304,000	9.10%	70%
71	Telephone installers and repairers	229,000	9.10%	70%
72	Administrators, education, related field	480,000	9.40%	72%
73	Attendants, amusement and recreational facilities	125,000	9.30%	72%
74	Legislators	12,716	9.80%	75%
75	Food counter, fountain, and related occupations	333,000	10.00%	77%
76	Administrative support, clerical	7,309,000	10.40%	80%
77	Child care workers, except private households	738,000	10.60%	82%
78	Elementary school	1,360,000	11.10%	85%
79	Adjusters and investigators	723,000	11.20%	86%
80	Material recording, scheduling, and distributing clerks	1,669,000	11.60%	89%
81	Farm workers	993,000	11.60%	89%
82	Counselors, educational and vocation	177,000	11.70%	90%
83	Duplicating, mail and other office machine operators	65,000	11.70%	90%
84	Pre-kindergarten and kindergarten	329,000	11.90%	92%
85	General office clerks	694,000	12.00%	92%
86	Agricultural and related occupations	1,948,000	11.90%	92%
87	Administrators and Official, Public Administration	506,783	12.10%	93%
88	Cashiers	2,174,000	12.10%	93%
89	Waiters' and waitresses' assistants	350,000	12.20%	94%
90	Supervisors	712,000	12.30%	95%
91	Production inspectors, testers, samplers and weighers	815,000	12.50%	96%
92	School, recreation, religious workers	873,000	12.60%	97%
93	Barbers	91,000	12.90%	99%

	Occupational Categories As Listed in The U.S. Census Bureau Report	Total Employed In The U.S.	BAC's Percentage of Total Employment (Parity =13%)	BAC's Percent of Parity
94	Trucks, heavy and light	1,838,000	12.90%	99%
95	Public transportation attendants	65,000	13.20%	102%
96	Computer equipment operators	779,000	13.50%	104%
97	Computer operators	774,000	13.50%	104%
98	Police and detectives	652,000	13.50%	104%
99	Health technologists and technicians	1,115,000	13.60%	105%
100	Transportation and material moving occupations	4,535,000	13.70%	105%
101	Chief Executives and General Administrators	19,123	13.90%	106%
102	Material moving equipment operators	1,024,000	13.80%	106%
103	Records-processing occupations, except finances	842,000	14.10%	108%
104	Motor vehicle operators	3,303,000	14.10%	109%
105	Operators, fabricators, and laborers	16,816,000	14.70%	113%
106	Textile sewing machine operators	760,000	14.90%	115%
107	Typists	880,000	16.00%	123%
108	Laborers, except construction	1,066,000	16.30%	125%
109	Freight, stock, material handlers	1,594,000	17.00%	131%
110	File clerks	290,000	17.40%	134%
111	Social workers	438,000	17.60%	135%
112	Communications equipment operators	223,000	17.70%	136%
113	Teachers' aides	379,000	17.80%	137%
114	Health aides, except nursing	350,000	17.80%	137%
115	Telephone operators	215,000	17.90%	138%
116	Kitchen workers, food preparation	134,000	18.00%	138%
117	Forestry and logging occupations	101,000	17.90%	138%
118	Cooks, except short order	1,553,000	18.40%	142%
119	U. S. military services	2,137,400	18.90%	145%
120	Data-entry keyers	353,000	19.50%	150%
121	Licensed practical nurses	402,000	19.60%	151%
122	Mail & message distributing occupations	805,000	19.80%	152%
123	Guards	722,000	20.20%	155%
124	Short-order cooks	103,000	20.70%	159%
125	Industrial truck and tractor operators	398,000	20.90%	161%
126	Welfare service aides	82,000	23.30%	179%
127	Janitors and cleaners	2,049,000	24.00%	185%
128	Postal clerks, except mail carriers	258,000	26.10%	201%
129 130	Private household	1,006,000	28.90%	222%
128	Postal clerks, except mail carriers	258,000	26.10%	201%
129	Private household	1,006,000	28.90%	222%
130	Nursing aids, orderlies, and attendants	1,242,000	29.20%	225%

	Occupational Categories As Listed in The U.S. Census Bureau Report	Total Employed In The U.S.	BAC's Percentage of Total Employment (Parity =13%)	BAC's Percent of Parity
132	Maids and housemen	563,000	30.80%	237%
133	Unemployed Americans	8,142,000	17.8%	137.2%
134	Prison and Jail inmates	1,600,000	39.10%	301%

Table II

Data in the columns 1, 2 and 3 of this table are taken from the U. S. Census report as note below. The author tabulated the percentages in column 4 of this table.

EMPLOYED PERSONS, BY SEX, RACE AND OCCUPATION 1985

[For civilian non-institutional population 16 years old and older. Annual average of monthly figures. Based on current population survey; see text, section 1 and Appendix III.]
Source: U. S. Bureau of Labor Statistics Employment, January 1986

Except prison and inmate data contained in this table is taken from a report by the U. S. Department of Justice's Bureau of Justice Statistics report, Prison and Jail Inmates. 1995

In the area of education black American have made equally commendable advances. A review of the U. S. Commerce Department Census Bureau reports for 2000 show that 79% of the nineteenth generation (1966–1995), those black Americans that are 25 year old, had earned at least a high school diploma. And that 17% of the nineteenth generation (1966–1995) had earned a bachelor degree from college. As commendable as those figures are, black Americans still do not stack up very well against the achievements of white Americans. There is still a lot of work remaining to be done by the black American community if they are to attain socioeconomic parity by the end of the twentieth first generation (2006–2035). As can be seen in Table III below, black American high school students out performed their white American counter parts by a percentage of 35.2% for black Americans to 34.5% for white Americans. This means that according to the March 2000 report, as a percentage of the black American population 7/10% more black Americans students of the nineteenth generation (1966–1995) graduated from high school than did the percentage of white American students. While this figure quite justly deserves accolades from the black American community, the same table also shows that black Americans dropped out of high school, or receive less than a high school diploma, in considerably higher numbers than did white American students. 21.5% of black American students ended up with less than a high school diploma compared to only 11.8 % of white American students who did. Two other categories where black Americans need, and must make significant advances in education are in completing their bachelor degrees and in continuing their education beyond a bachelor degree. 11.4% of black American students earned bachelor degrees compared to 18.4% of white Americans who did so. Additionally, 28.5% of white American college students advance their education beyond the bachelor degree compared to only 16.5% of black American college students who do so. While it is unlikely that all of the discrepancies between black Americans and white American educational statistics, can be corrected over the next few years, but the bulk of the problem can be redressed by members of the nineteenth generation (1966–1995) over their thirty-year duration. That generation is being tasked to make every effort to raised the bar. Not only would their contribution help to narrow the gap, but it would also turn them into an effective role model for the twentieth generation (1986–2015) that follows them.

Educational Attainment (Numbers in thousands)	Total		Black Americans		White Americans	
	Number	Percent	Number	Percent	Number	Percent
Total Population	175,230	100.0	20,036	100.0	130,783	100.0
Less than 9th grade	12,179	7.0	1,417	7.1	5,534	4.3
9th to 12th grade (no diploma)	15,675	8.9	2,899	14.5	9,600	7.1
High school graduate	58,086	33.1	7,050	35.2	44,554	34.5
Some college, or associate degree	44,445	25.4	5,366	26.8	34,390	26.5
Bachelor degree	29,840	17.0	2,278	11.4	24,331	18.4
Advance degree	15,006	8.6	1,025	5.1	12,374	9.3
Less than high school diploma	27,853	15.9	4,316	21.5	15,134	11.8
High school degree or more	147,377	84.1	15,719	78.5	11,5649	88.0
Less than Bachelors degree	130,384	74.4	16,732	83.5	94,078	71.7
Bachelors degree or more	44,846	25.6	3,304	16.5	36,705	28.5

Table III

Educational Attainment of the Population of Black Americans and White Americans

25 years and older. Information extracted from data published by the U. S. Census Bureau's March 2000 Population Survey.

The education and occupational distribution of black Americans aside, it would be impossible to answer the question as to how well the black American community stacks up against the white American community without dealing directly with the issue of annual incomes. Even though in a more formal fashion, one's income is not necessarily the sole dictate of one socioeconomic standing. However, in reality, the key component of one's social standing is the amount of money he, or she earns. True it matters as to the source of the income, but the bottom line is still the amount of the income. And so, in black America's quest for socioeconomic parity, one could resort to that old, not so old saw, "it's the income stupid."

The statistically disproportionate numbers of black Americans that are employed in low skill, and thus low paying jobs, as noted earlier in this commentary, adversely affects the overall income of the black American community. In a report published in March 2000 by the U. S. Census Bureau Population Survey (Table II), black Americans were three times as likely to be employed in jobs that paid less than $2,499.00 per year. And when viewed at higher income levels the ratio switches rather dramatically in the other direction. At an annual income of $75,000.00 for instance, black Americans trail white Americans by only 3.7%. This 3.7% difference at the $75,000.00 income level actually points out the area in which black Americans income suffers the most. And that is the area of the low skills and low paying job occupations. The reason for this lies in the fact that large numbers of black Americans, 3.5 to 1.0 are in these occupational categories. According to information published by the U. S. Census Bureau, the number of black families earning between $35,000 and $70,000 annually doubled between 1970 and 1990, even though the number of black families earning less than $15,000 more than doubled during the same time frame.

The following information on education and potential lifetime income is presented in this section to illustrate the role that education plays in the gross annual income of the black American community. In 1968 there were 1.7 million members of the nineteenth generation (1966–1995), those under 35 years old enrolled in college. According to census data this figure represents a 50% increase in the number of members of the third tripartite (1946–1975) of the eighteenth generation (1946–1975) of the eighteenth generation (1946–1975) that were enrolled in college ten years earlier. The census data reports that over the adult working life of a high school graduate they will earn an average of $1.2 million dollars. If you have a bachelor degree the expected earnings go up to $2.1 million dollars. And members of the nineteenth generation (1966–1995) that go on to earn a master's degree can expect to earn as much as $2.5 million dollars over their working lives. Conversely, earnings for members of the nineteenth generation (1966–1995) that drop out of high school will plunge to about $25,900.00 per year.

Family type and money (Numbers in thousands)	Total Population Number	Percent	Black Americans Number	Percent	White Americans Number	Percent
Total families with money income 2/ 3/	72,031	100.0	8,664	100.0	53,071	100.0
$1 to 2,499 or loss	1,023	1.4	292	3.4	486	0.9
$2,500 to $9,999	717	1.0	251	2.9	303	0.6
$10,000 to $14,999	2,404	3.3	721	8.3	1,146	2.2
$15,000 to $19,999	3.485	4.8	793	9.1	1,887	3.6
$20,000 to 24,999	4,381	6.1	615	7.1	2,912	5.5
$25,000 to $34,999	8,550	11.9	1,176	13.6	5,932	11.2
$35,000 to $49,999	11,861	16.5	1,326	15.3	8,837	16.7
$50,000 to $74,999	15,236	21.2	1,369	15.8	12,150	22.9
$75,000 and over	20,076	27.9	1,354	15.6	16,783	31.6

Table IV

Total Money Income in 1999 of Families by Type, and Race of the Householder: March 2000

Source: U. S. Census Bureau, Current Population Survey, March 2000, Racial Statistic Population Division

During the course of this chapter, an attempt will be made to share with the readers some thoughts and concerns over the plight of black Americans. The word "plight" is specifically chosen here because the socioeconomic future of black Americans, and black American youths in particular, is so tenuous. Describing that future requires a word that suggests temporary avoidance of ultimate disaster. And to render some observations as to why the black American community in general has not yet achieved socioeconomic parity with other ethnic groups. If one were to seek answers to the three questions posed at the beginning of the chapter, they would probably receive the more or less standardized reply suggesting that the average black American does not really try, or care much about getting ahead. Asking the same questions of an equal number of black Americans and you will most likely get an equally standardized answers suggesting that the reason black Americans have been unable to succeed is because of American racism. I suppose that in some small way, each of the stereotypical responses can claim some evidence as to their respective merit but neither offer any clear relationship to the true cause of the disparity.

While there are obviously no simple answers to these questions, there are any number of explanations and circumstances that must be considered. Before one can hope to form any semblance of an informed opinion regarding the socioeconomic mobility of the black Americans, these circumstances and explanations must be considered. It is hoped that after reading this response, the reader does not still say, "Okay, okay, so I've read all that. Now tell me, why hasn't the black Americans succeeded in attaining socioeconomic parity? After all, other ethnic groups, and some who arrived in America well after the black Americans did, have succeeded in establishing socioeconomic parity." And such persons might still dare say, "And don't tell me it was because of slavery. There have been a fair number of other ethnic groups who have immigrated to America even after the end of slavery, and they've managed to get a generation of their children educated. Moreover, they have, for the most part, gone on to establish, and often exceed peer parity."

Now the question is, how will my answer or reasons for black America's delay stack up against these arguments? After all, the questioners would be making a salient point. After all, as stated before, black Americans have been in America for a very, very long time. Their 1619 arrival in colonial America makes them among the very first immigrants to arrive. And it is true that the black American community was already fully entrenched within the American cultural mindset, albeit skewed by the affliction of their enslavement when a number of the other immigrants arrived. And again while those immigrant groups were still speaking in their native languages, African immigrants, or their black American descendents were already English speaking. While the habits and customs of the newer immigrants were still clothed in the cultural fabric of their origins—Scandinavia, Germany, Italy, China, Poland and Ireland—black Americans had for the most part adapted to the cultural idioms, habits and customs of the American mind one to two centuries before.

In a manner of speaking, black Americans have been in America so long that, had they been so inclined, they could have trekked up the coast in 1620 to greet the Pilgrims as the Mayflower docked at Plymouth Rock. With this kind of residential resume, how then do we justify or interpret the fact that even though they were among the first immigrants to America, black Americans still enjoy less of America bountiful resources and have access to fewer opportunities than their white American counterpart—or even than the other ethnic groups, all of whom arrived after those twenty Africans John Rolfe wrote about. Revisiting the history of the black American in this country there are at least three significant and very primary reasons why parity between the black and white Americans has been delayed.

HISTORICAL HINDERANCES TO SOCIOECONOMIC PARITY

Slavery

The first and foremost reason for the delay was certainly the existence of slavery itself. In 1661, the Virginia legislature passed a statute legally instituting slavery in the Virginia colony. Although the statute did not apply to the 1619 Africans or to their immediate descendents, it applied to all future African immigrants. And so black Americans were officially enslaved in 1661. They remained so until the end of the Civil War in 1865, a total of 205 years or around thirteen generations. These 205 years were extremely expensive years for the black American community. In the absence of slavery and the discrimination that followed it, there is no, otherwise reason to think that the accomplishments of those thirteen generations of black Americans would have been proportionate, in all regards, to those political, social, and economic accomplishments the thirteen generations of their white American counterparts. One would to think that, had slavery not existed and had it, slavery not been the festering pool for the castigating stereotypes of black American inferiority that it did, any number of the thirteen generations of African descendents would have qualified for, and undoubtedly would have risen to, prominent position in the United States government. For instance, Abraham Lincoln, who was born February 12, 1809, would be a member of the eleventh generation (1806–1835). Without the subordinating effects of slavery, history might have written of America's sixteenth president not that he freed the African descendents from slavery but that he himself was an African descendent.

Might one be able to make the argument that had slavery and its denigrating stigma not stood in the way, a black American might have written, or participated in the writing of that good and noble document, the Declaration of Independence? The fact that the Africans were shanghaied and brought to America did not necessarily or in any degree mitigate their claim and rights, as Americans, to have participated in the founding of this country's government. Accordingly, any number of Englishmen were also shanghaied and brought to this country under the indenture programs. Since their indenture did not preclude their service in the organization of the new government, then neither should the black American's indenture service, or even slavery have been used to deny them access. Commensurate with that thought, it is worth noting that men and women who had been shanghaied and indentured also settled Australia, the "land down under." Yet those same persons have gone on to become, for the most part, the very core of the nation itself. Therefore, the failure of black Americans to have full participatory access to all phases of the development of America caused them to miss out on the opportunity to participate in the drafting of the Declaration of Independence, performing in the continental congress, drafting and approving the Constitution of the United States of America, and in all elections and other opportunities of service. Only by envisioning such an America can we hope to portray at least a modest picture of the damaging effects the institutionalization of slavery had upon the social and economic mobility of the black American community. It is important for the reader to recognize the lasting effects upon the black American community of having been enslaved for so many years.

For unlike, and drawing again upon the ancient Hebrews of Egyptian slavery, whereas upon their emancipation from Egyptian slavery immediately fled the country of their former slave masters, the black Americans were obliged particularly by logistical circumstances, to remain, not just in the same country of those who previously enslaved them, but more often than not, as the very neighbors, and even more probable, the very employees, of their former slave masters. A potential benefit the Hebrews enjoyed by leaving the land of their enslavement was the probable negative and prejudicial backlash of Egyptian society. Remaining in America after the emancipation of slavery meant that the black Americans continued to inter-act with those who had previously offended them: masters, field-bosses, nurslings, sex-abusers, plantation guards, and former slave-traders. They were obliged to disclaim relationships to white American fathers, brothers, sisters, and other relatives. These actions were deemed by the status quo as necessary to preserve the white American's social and politically correct views of that day that the African immigrants and their American descendents were inferior to white Americans of all stripes.

As we can see then, not only did they not leave but continued to live and submit themselves for more that a hundred additional years to a social and cultural environment bereft of any reasonable allowance of social or cultural nurturing. In fact, the very use of the concept of social and cultural nurture is an antithetical notion because not only were these elements absent in their environment, but just the opposite climate prevailed. The reality is that not only was their environment not nurturing but during the hundred-year period following emancipation from slavery—roughly the 1870s though the 1970s—that same social environment, through the use of a particularly vicious form of quasi-state sponsored terrorism continued to ravage the black American community. The campaign of terror lasted for a hundred years and was responsible for the death of over seventeen thousand black Americans citizens.

Thus the institutionalization of slavery did more than simply impound the black American community in bondage for 205 years. It was more than that. It had other, subtler, and more demeaning properties than the simple act of physical confinement. There was also emotional and spiritual confinement. Consider this. The West African people had a history and a tradition of political and social freedom. Their mindset was scarcely conditioned to inculcate the notion of slavery, particularly as being practiced by the Europeans. Slavery from the African's perspective did not contain all the dehumanizing aspects found in European-American slavery. To have been enslaved in ancient Ghana or Mali meant that one, the slave, belonged to and was obliged to work for his or her owner. It did not mean that the enslaved person had to forfeit his or her status as a morally redemptive and intelligent human being simply because of slavery. On the contrary, Africans enslaved in Africa, were like Joseph's enslavement in Egypt: permitted to exercise great power and respect while in their owners' employ. They could marry in and out of the ranks of slavery and could own and hold property. Perhaps the most significant difference between having been enslaved by Africans in Africa and of being enslaved in America by Americans that in Africa, the ones enslaving and the ones enslaved were all Africans. So the mindset of the African immigrants would have undergone a substantial culture shock as it struggled to adapt to the disemboweling rigors of the European-American system of African enslavement. Along with the abject lost of their physical freedom, enslavement also brought a dark cloud upon the African's basic rights as human beings. Those rights as stated in the Declaration of Independence and as articulated by the yearnings of mankind throughout the ages, are that; all men are inherently equal, and are fashioned by their creator with certain inalienable rights among which are life, liberty, and the right to live in a non-molesting social environment. Such freedoms are socially functional assets, and must be considered fundamentally significant to the estate of any structured social organization.

Harkening back to the original question of why black Americans continue to lag behind the socioeconomic achievements of white Americans, when all analysis are completed, it must be reckoned that enslavement of the Africans was inherently a degenerative process. It undermined all other social institutions and attacked the individual's self esteem like a destructive virus. Under American slavery, the beneficial components of such institutions as family, home, motherhood, fatherhood, and relatives were denied allegedly for the good of the institution.

Therefore, enslavement of the African immigrants had an effect similar to storing the family wardrobes in an unattended, leaky, moldy and moth-ridden warehouse for an extended period of time. In such an environment, the Africans' sense of self, their cultural estate, and their personhood were subject to deterioration. For two hundred years, the warehouse environment remained the same, except when it got worse. If fact, the concept of "storage" makes a very effective and appropriate metaphor for the environment that American slavery engendered. As in storage, when you place sufficient restraints upon a person or a people to deny them access to means of self-expressions, you in effect stymie their genius, their ability, and their initiative to create.

For example, suppose that you were taking an extended vacation and as a result, you place the family car in storage for a number of years. You or the storage company would first have to initially prepare for storage. Such preparation would be achieved either by checking or draining the crankcase and other fluids, packing the wheel bearings, and attending to an assortment of other details. And after your extended vacation was up, you could not just go to the storage yard and drive your car away. Just as it had to be prepared in order to put it into storage, it would equally have to be prepared to recover it from storage. This process is so essential that the United States government, an agency that stores thousands of pieces of equipment worth millions of dollars, has an elaborate publication or technical directive just to provide instructions for storing equipment and for recovering equipment from storage. The equipment storage analogy regarding the practices and technique of equipment storage and it's recovery from storage can provide much-needed insight into the skills and techniques necessary to effectively manage the black American community since the end of their enslavement. While all recognize that the black American community was not military equipment in storage. The analogy works to point out the fact that the consequence of stopping the black American community's free expressions from 1661 until the 1960s era of the civil rights movement and the legislation had a tremendous impact upon the forward mobility of the black American people.

The Department of Health, Education, and Welfare's minimum daily allowances of nutritional food content also makes an effective metaphor. American enslavement did not only seek physical confinement but also sought to confine and reformulate the model, the paradigmatic structure of the African's mind. Under an inhibiting social environment, one's mental faculties generally have an unlimited source of informational food to feed upon. However, as black Americans were under penal enslavement, their informational diet remained fixed; the dogma du jour, for example, remained constant for generations. Europeans or white Americans were declared to be "superior" and those that were African or black Americans were declared to be "inferior."

For those enslaved, the perimeter of the agricultural plantation was their operational boundary. They were required to live and die within it or if they did have the opportunity to relocate, it was simply from the boundaries of one plantation to the boundaries of another. Under the limits and intimidation of such boundaries, the only thing one generation could hand off to the next was that they were to be considered as "inferiors" who could exercise no rights or claims worthy of consideration by either the plantation owner, nor by the civil authorities. Cycling one generation after the other through such a demeaning social system as slavery would be like the fossil footprint of an ancient dinosaur destined to remain static.

To accomplish and sustain such an environment, the persons involved with the enslavement of black Americans deliberately indoctrinated them to accept as a fact that they were inferior beings. In his biography, Frederick Douglass tells of the lengths one plantation owner went to prevent the enslaved black Americans on his plantation from coming into contact with poor white Americans. His reasoning was that in order for the black Americans to accept as an emphatic truth that white Americans were superior; it was necessary that they not be permitted to see a white American living in poverty. Additionally, black Americans, under the restraints of their enslavement, were denied participation in normal social and family life. They were in a strange land among strange people with a strange language, forbidden to learn to read or write the language; being bought and sold as chattel; and being alienated from the right of personal expressions and denied the rights to life, liberty, and the pursuit of happiness; all of these, according to the authors and signers of the Declaration of Independence, are endowed by God and should have been treated as unalienable rights

Additionally Frederick Douglass spoke of how he witnessed the treatment of enslaved black Americans solely on the color of their skin. He feared being punished simply for inquiring as to the day and date he was born, and was denied the knowledge of who his parents were. He and other such children were separated from their mothers within the first year of their birth and had to experienced utter rejection by their white American fathers. They feared being savagely beaten simply for not being at work on time. They were not able to see their mothers, except by stealth, and then for only a few minutes a week in the dark of night. They were denied the privilege of going to their mothers' deathbeds, and were not permitted to attend their funerals. They never enjoyed a mother's soothing presence, or her tender and watchful care. They were fathered by men who owned their mothers as chattel property, were confined to a place where men own their own children as chattel property, witnessed vicious beatings of their mothers. They were completely outside of legal and civil protection of the law, were taught that they were outside the benevolence of God, and were rejected by local churches and church doctrine. They were unable to claim or control their own children, had no claim to their own wives or husbands. They were not permitted to own property, had no access to any political remedies, were absolutely denied any rights of protest, and received no recompense for their labor, being owned by another person. They were never responsible for anything, never permitted freedom, reminded daily of their enslavement. They were deprived of the smallest degree of life's comforts, had to sleep on the ground, witnessed white-skinned people enjoy all that was denied to them. They faced the constant threat of savage beatings, and were consigned to a place where the mere notion of escape meant a horrible and vicious beating. They were born into all the above, had to live their entire lives under the above debilitating conditions, and had to watch their friends and families live and die under the above circumstances;

How can such a historical environment best be characterized? Consider this approach. When the Greek philosopher Plato sought to describe transcendental reality to his students, he did so via an allegory. Plato spoke of men sitting within a dark cave watching their own shadows reflected against the cave's walls. Having no other source of knowledge, these cave-bound men believed that what they saw on the walls of the cave was what they themselves looked and behaved like. To them, the silhouettes against the wall constituted their reality. Under the circumstances of their confinement, they could never know the real truth about the images they were witnessing on the wall. Whereas Plato was obliged to make use of an allegory to emphasize his point, we have the painful reality of slavery itself to make ours. Our men in a dark cave may not actually be men in a cave, but when you consider the limiting and distorting effects that slavery had upon the perspective of the black Americans, is it any wonder that they emerged to a skewed perception of the real world upon their emancipation during the latter 1860s.

Frederick Douglass' characterization of the enslavement of black Americans shows them as destitute of reality as the men in Plato's allegory. Even though the enslaved black Americans were not physically chained face-forward, as were Plato's prisoners, their real chains were much more subtle. Their chains were in power of the constant threats of severe beatings and death. These devices, like Plato's chains, were more than adequate restraints to assure that the enslaved black Americans would keep their eyes and minds straight ahead. Of such men Plato declares that their, "truth would be literally nothing but the shadow of the images." It is as though Plato had the enslaved black Americans in mind when he says of the men in the dark cave, "And now look again, and see what will naturally follow if the prisoners are released and disabused of their error. At first, when any of them is liberated and compelled suddenly to stand up and turn his neck around and walk and look towards the light, he will suffer sharp pains; the glare will distress him, and he will be unable to see the realities of which in his former state he had seen the shadows." From this perspective, one can easily see why that after two hundred years of enslavement the former slaves' perception of reality would be distorted as were the men of Plato's cave. But even in Plato's allegorical cave reality, when the prisoners were released someone was there offering the former cavemen corrective therapy. After having been exposed only to the images on the cave wall since their youth, the prisoners could not have been expected to understand the new reality of the world around them. In a like manner, neither should those black Americans who had been enslaved all their lives, be expected to make sense of their new world without the benefit of Plato's "someone" being there to offer corrective therapy. Such a program was never implemented for the black Americans who were, for the first time in their lives, being released from brutal human enslavement. As a result, many of them their eyes being blinded, if you will, by the glare of their new freedom, returned to the cave reality of their old plantation home. Once back there, their reality, though fraudulent, was nevertheless negotiable. Others, also blinded by the same glare, wandered about the countryside aimlessly.

For 307 years, the black American community lived within the social, political, and economic shadows of American society, it was not until the 1960s that they began to emerge from those shadows. During the 1960s, the black American community literally freed itself from the Jim Crow restraints of white supremacist terrorism. That emergence meant an end to social and civil tyranny, social denial, legal indifference, and cultural rejection. Having experienced the wrenching agonies of slavery and tyranny, the black American community was expected, without benefit of any planned adjustment, to move directly from the caves to the playing field. And once there, to not only play the game, but to compete with those whose perception had never been distorted by the images on the cave's wall. Such expectation was unrealistic and could not be achieved. The black American community required time and therapy to recover from those 307 years of social, economic and political impoverishment. Since culturally, each generation—as with an individual parent-child relationship—attempts to pass on its entire cultural estate, mores, knowledge, habits, and religious values, to the next generation, the generations of black Americans were handed a legacy of abusive treatment and social disregard. The irony of it is the fact that because the parent generation had received a distorted image of itself, it would pass that same distorted image on to its children. Like the abusive parents who raises children that also turn out to be abusive to their children and so on. Or, like the relay runner ever handing the baton to the next runner, or the spiraling DNA helix, ever separating, and ever recreating itself. And so it was with each of the thirteen generations (1619–1865) of black Americans who list the institution of slavery as a line item in their résumé of American citizenship. Each succeeding generation having passed on the constituent properties of low self-esteemed to their own generational descendents. Unfortunately, this predicament is destined to continue as each generation hands off to the one that follows the same dysfunctional social attitudes and structures.

Recovery From Enslavement

And so the next question one might ask is how long does it take or should it take people like black Americans to recover from the effects of slavery? Let us look at some examples that might provide some elements for a case study scenario that would assist us in determining just how long it should it take before black Americans can free themselves of the effects of that peculiar institution. There at least two episodes from which we can use to draw some conclusions. The first and perhaps the closest analogy to the plight of the black Americans is the biblical record of the Hebrew people in Ancient Egypt. While living in the land of Ur, Abraham was told by God to leave and immigrate to a land that God would show him. Accordingly, he and his wife, Sarah and his nephew, Lot, left the land of their birth and moved to the place where God had told Abraham to settle. In their old age Abraham and Sarah had a son, which they named Isaac. When Isaac grew up, he married wife Rebekah. Two sons, Esau and Jacob were born to Isaac and Rebekah. Esau went on to become head of the Edomite people and Jacob, whose name was later changed to Israel, became the father and namesake of the Hebrew people who became known biblically as the Children of Israel. Jacob, or Israel, continued to live in Canaan until around 1780 B.C. when in time, and as the result of a devastating drought and famine in the land of the Canaanites, Jacob and his entire family were invited to move to Egypt by the Egyptian viceroy. The man next in line to the Egyptian Pharaoh was Joseph, one of Jacob's twelve sons. As a child, he had been beaten and sold into slavery by his envious older brothers. As life would have it, Joseph had fortuitously overcome his enslaved status and was subsequently elevated to viceroy of the entire Egyptian government by the pharaoh. For years, the Hebrews, or children of Israel, lived as guests of the Egyptian government. Many years later a pharaoh came to power that no longer respected the earlier "guest" status of the Hebrew people. The reigning pharaoh declared the Hebrew people *persona non grata*, withdrew all their rights as guests of the Egyptian government, and enslaved them. The Hebrew people remained in enslaved in Egypt for many years before finally being emancipated. Considering the dramatic way in which the Hebrews fled Egypt and their miraculous crossing of the Red Sea, one would think that their greatest obstacles would have been behind them. However, this was not necessarily the case. After having been enslaved for so many years, their social and political disorientation suggests they lacked certain basic components in the secular realm of self-government. Besides the basics of food, shelter, and water, they also lacked a definitive sociopolitical system. It is reasonable to allow that while in Egypt, the Hebrews had established secular forms of social and political affiliations sufficient to govern the behavior and conduct of the two million Hebrew inhabitants. Yet no matter how successful and whatever form of social and political systems they had utilized before their enslavement, they had apparently not survived their enslavement.

In the absence of the sociopolitical guidelines, a population of over two million people found themselves living in a social environment of holistic anarchy. A kind of cultural Machiavellianism in which every man did whatever he wanted, or at least whatever he could get away with. In terms of perspective, one can envision a nation of over two million people where each did as he wanted. The image that comes to mind is that of the American's wild west. In that environment, the person with the fastest draw pretty much had things his own way, whatever the description. with such a large assembly of people, their form of non-government amounted to a system of sociopolitical anarchy and economic chaos.

During Jacob's lifetime when the Children of Israel were a family, albeit an extended family, of seventy people, they had managed to govern and support themselves. It was only when their homeland, Palestine suffered what appears to have been a regional famine that they sought the external assistance of their next-door neighbor, Egypt. And even after being in Egypt for around four hundred years and they had become a nation of several million, they were apparently still able to take care of themselves socially, economically, and politically. Therefore, it is reasonable to conjecture that it was while under the denigrating influence of slavery that those systems apparently broke down. And break down they did. Apparently, so destructive were those years of slavery that it was not until the appearance of the judges, almost one hundred years later that some form of political structure and management was finally implemented. Even under the direct leadership of Moses, their emancipation from Egyptian slavery was just the beginning. Fleeing the pharaoh army and crossing the Red Sea, which has become a poignant and symbolic affirmation of freedom, should have meant something in terms of their unity but it did not. They still had to spend forty years of confusion and frustration wandering around in the Sinai desert. And after that, even after arriving in their "land of milk and honey" they spent another twelve and a half generations (1400 B.C.–1025 B.C.) before finally becoming established as a nation under the first monarchy of King Saul. Of those twelve and a half generations, the book of Judges notes that "there was no king in Israel in those days and every man did whatever he thought was right." In today's vernacular, such a condition would be considered politically as anarchy and would be comparable to what has been occurring in various African nations as they struggle against the past generation and a half against post-colonial disorientation.

	AREA OF RECOVERY PROGRAM FOCUS	SOCIOECONOMIC CIRCUMSTANCES	RECOVERY PERIOD
1	SOUTHERN RECONSTRUCTION PROGRAN	DESTRUCTIVE AFFECTS OF SLAVERY	1866 TO 1876
2	POST WWI GERMANY	TERMS OF THE TREATY OF VERSAILLE	1919 TO 1932
3	PRE-INDUSTRIALIZED JAPAN	POST-FEUDALISTIC SOCIETY/ECONOMY	1866 TO 1900
4	FORMER COMMUNISTIC EASTERN BLOC COUNTRIES	POST-MARXIXT ECONOMIES	1998 TO ???
5	EAST GERMANY	POST MARXIST ECONOMIES	1998 TO ???
6	WESTERN EUROPE	AFTER THE FALL OF THE ROMAN EMPIRE	AD 476 TO 1453
7	WESTERN EUROPE	AFTER THE SECOND WORLD WAR	1947 TO 1967

Table V

The author collected and assembled the information in this table.

Perhaps, to some extent at least, the reason it took the Children of Israel over three hundred years to establish a political structure sufficient to govern themselves is because, as stated earlier, enslavement of a community of people is degenerative, and robs them of their former self-esteem and self-worth.

How did the Hebrews manage to overcome the social, political, and economic disruption caused by years of Egyptian enslavement? Did it truly require more than three hundred years for them to become politically, socially, and economically stabilized? If it did take that long, then the question is, is slavery so degenerating that after emancipation of the Children of Israel their cultural order and economy had declined so much, that it took them many many years to recover?

This table shows the seven recovery programs that will be examined in the following pages in an effort to understand the time and commitment that must be involved in any large-scale recovery programs if they are provide the promise of success.

Southern Reconstruction Program

The southern states are good examples of what happens when the socio economics of a state, or region becomes depressed over long periods of time. For at least a hundred years after the end of the Civil War the southern states that once formed the confederacy remained victims of their devastated economies. The southern states reconstruction program that the federal government launched after the Civil War provided these states with no more of a vehicle for economic recovery than it did for the black Americans just emerging from enslavement. However even prior to the Civil War, the economy of the southern states was going nowhere. The very concept of a slave economy undermined the South's competitiveness against the more industrialized northern neighbors and competitive foreign countries. So in a way, the socioeconomic plight of the southern states was not too dissimilar from the socioeconomic plight of the millions of black Americans whom they had formally enslaved. While technological and economic growth flourished in the northern, and later on, in the western states, the southern states languished in a self-serving and deceptive economic malaise. After the Civil War, its lack of economic growth is a kinship analogy to what the length of recovery times could be when no formal recovery programs are in place. During the post-Civil War years, many of the southern states, in their efforts to suppress black Americans, implemented repressive programs and rejected progressive economic programs to the extent that their states remained in depressed economic and technological condition until the civil rights legislation of the 1960s freed their own industrial labor relation systems from the repressive philosophy of Jim Crow segregation. From the point of view of the black Americans just coming out of enslavement, the federal government's southern reconstruction program did too little and went away too quickly. What was need was a massive program of recovery, but what was applied was a program of appeasement.

The Southern Reconstruction Program, as designed was supposed to contain provisions to assist the previously enslaved black Americans in their efforts to reenter the civilian work force, but it suffered from a severe lack of adequate funding and political commitment. Both limited the amount and nature of the assistance and its duration to less than twelve years. If it was going to have any meaningful benefit in the lives of the millions of black American citizens now being discharged from years of enslavement, then it should have to have lasted long enough to have benefited both the thirteenth (1846–1875) and fourteenth (1866–1895) generations. What the former slaves desperately needed was a reconstruction program with benefits similar to those featured in Congress' 1944 Servicemen Readjustment Act.

That program, more familiarly known as the G.I. Bill of Rights contained well-funded provisions designed to assist former military men reenter the civilian work force. Some of the more popular provisions were; financial aid to discharged servicemen and their families; a bill that provided for low-cost home mortgages whereby ex-servicemen could buy homes at lower than market interest rates; and its most popular feature, the G.I. Bill's educational assistance program. Under this provision, veterans could receive tuition and sometimes living allowances to assist them in completing their education. Since it beginning in 1944, more than twenty million veterans have taken advantage of its tuition benefits to complete their college or trade school education. Such a program might have permitted the black American community to avoid the one hundred years of intimidation, lynching, and mayhem that followed. Another meaningful approach for providing an effective program of formerly enslaved black Americans repatriation was one that would ensure environmental hospitality. What the former slaves needed perhaps more than anything else was what I have referred to as environmental hospitality. That is, they needed a program designed around their particular emotional and psychological condition. The line in Moliere's *Le Misanthrope*, "Doubts are more cruel than the worst of truths" does a fine job of defining the fate of the Southern Reconstruction Program in the face of rising doubt in America over the future of the former slaves. The abrupt discontinuation of the program surely left millions of former slaves wholly unprepared to take on the realities of life off the plantation.

The black American community is a charter member of the original settlers of the United States. As such, it must diligently seek socioeconomic parity. In order to do so, it will be necessary to erase the negative effects caused by its impressions of the past three centuries of its American history and focus its energy and resources on its future generations. The black American community would have been well-served had there been a persistent and well-planned reconstruction-type program, if for nothing but to nurture the black American community's confidence in the brotherhood of its white American counterpart. Such a gesture would have gone a long way toward restoring confidence in the national blessing of American citizenship. Unfortunately no such program was ever implemented.

President Lyndon Johnson's Great Society attempted to address at least some of the more obvious failures of such programs. Conceptually and architecturally, the great society was structured in such a manner as to offer substantial environmental improvements. But whether it would have worked or would have just become another well-meaning social welfare program is academic. It is all too likely that such a program, as architecturally sound as it might have been, would have failed. Not because of external flaws, but because, as a direct government project it would undoubtedly have demonstrated an otherwise-proven fact that governments, by virtue of their bureaucracies, are not designed to render a nurturing environment. To nurture is not consistent with the nature of a bureaucracy. The impetus for programs where nurturing is an integral part must come from people who care or who have a personal stake in the program's successful outcome.

During the seven years of the Southern Reconstruction Program and the years immediately following and before the effects of the terrorist campaign were apparent, black Americans were enjoying what can only be characterized as extraordinary successes. In Mississippi, Blanche Kelso Bruce became a U.S. Senator; in Louisiana, Pinckney Benton Stewart Pinchback, became governor and his children were escorted to school daily by white American policemen; both Mississippi and Louisiana boasted black Americans as lieutenant governors; Florida's secretary of state was a black American; a black American sat on the supreme court in South Carolina; and black Americans routinely held positions such as superintendents of education, state treasurers, adjutant generals, solicitors generals, judges and major generals of the various state's militia. In Natchez, Mississippi, Robert Wood was mayor, and in Texas, Norris Wright Cuney was candidate for Galveston's mayor. There were seven black Americans in the Texas House of Representatives; schools and street-cars were integrated, and men and women married freely across racial lines; the Board of the University of South Carolina; was integrated; Richard T. Greener was professor of metaphysics at the University of South Carolina and Patrick Francis Healy was president of Georgetown University. Another significant advance occurred on the part of the black American community to assert themselves socially, economically, and educationally. Following the Civil War, and during the brief period of the Southern Reconstruction Program, large numbers of black American-oriented colleges and schools were founded. As noted above, major inroads into politics were achieved. However, all of these achievements were mediated by a reactionary southern backlash.

If the progress cited above is representative of what can occur under a program of environmental hospitality, one can only speculate on what the black American community might have achieved, had the Southern Reconstruction Program been allowed to continue for at least two generations. If on the basis of just seven years of the reconstruction program, the climate in the South—the presence of Union troops notwithstanding—was such that these numbers, meager when compared to the whole, were indices of the formula for success, then time is the only component of the formula that remains unknown. Under the tutorial custody of the Southern Reconstruction Program and the presence of the Union Army for at least full duration of the thirteenth (1846–1975) and fourteenth (1866–1895) generations, the black American community would have possibly emerged from the "caves" fit and able to hold their own in the market places of America.

While the Southern Reconstruction Program was too short to have been of lasting consequence in the lives of the black American community, there were, by 1872 potentially effective reconstruction programs that might have altered the socioeconomic landscape of the black American community forever. Unfortunately, the program, or programs got entangled in the throes a philosophical debate. The debate, more theoretical than substance, was between the eminent Dr. Booker Telifaro Washington and Dr. W. E. Burghardt DuBois and focused on the efforts then being made to enhance the socioeconomic conditions of black Americans. In a scenario similar to the political science debate that occurred between Thomas Jefferson and Alexander Hamilton three hundred years before, W. E. B. DuBois and Booker T. Washington were in conflict over the course and character of programs designed to elevate the formerly enslaved black American citizens. In the theory espoused by Booker T. Washington, skills development came first, and social mobility and social integration were slated to come along later after the formally enslaved black Americans learned sufficient living skills to be able to feed and clothe themselves. In opposition, Dr. Dubois' argument would have social mobility and social integration occurring concurrently, both as the result of classic liberal arts education. The ability to feed and clothe themselves would also occur naturally, as a product of their education. Perhaps if they had agreed on a planned course of action, it may well have influenced the national point of view, and had a meaningful and mitigating impact upon the country's response to the support base of the former slaves' reconstruction needs. Politically, the cost of the reconstruction program was being borne as a cost item by the national government

The reconstruction plans or theories outlined by Washington in his 1870 "compromise" may not have been appealing rhetorically and may have caused W. E. B. Dubois and his northern constituency some concern, but the salient point of what Booker T. Washington seem, with advantage of a hundred years of hindsight, to have had some merit. A defensive argument can be made that had, the Washington plan gained the support and the funding required, the socioeconomic plight of black Americans today would be much improved, and they would not have spent the last 100 years intimidated by terrorists and wandering around aimlessly in the desert of confusion and socioeconomic chaos. Furthermore, the legitimacy of the Washington plan can be confirmed by assessing the merits of its underpinning argument. That argument being, that the resources for achieving socioeconomic parity in America are vested in its majority white American community. And that the only means available to the formally enslaved black Americans for accessing those resources was through a process of "gratuitous concession." Gratuitous concession, as I am employing it means the mutually engaged in transfer of resources, technical knowledge or otherwise, from one to another, as opposed the forceful seizure of those resources. A simplified example would be what occurs when the chauffeur's daughter marries the son of her father's employer. As a feature of their marriage, the former working class daughter suddenly finds herself a full partner in the family resources and thus full socioeconomic parity. An example of the opposite of gratuitous concession would be the seizure, or attempted seizure of the Kuwaiti oil fields by Iraq's Saddam Hussein. Another example would be the efforts, or threats, on part of the Chinese government to seize, by force, the technologically advance island of Taiwan. Perhaps the best illustration of the benefits of gratuitous concession can be found in the technological concessions made to Japan by the U. S. following World War II. Through those concessions, Japan has succeeded in developing a technologically based economy that rivals the most advanced technological economy in the world.

Mr. Washington's successful founding and management of his school at Tuskegee Alabama was the results of concessions granted by his constituency of wealthy northern philanthropists. It is easy to assess that Mr. Washington had witnessed the process involved when resources are transferred through forceful seizure, albeit the Civil War. However, his logic for choosing the second approach can perhaps best be found in the man himself. He was a man born, as in the words of Charles Dickens' dilemma, in "the best of times and the worse of times." Additionally, being a black American, Washington had nothing to his credit but his personal inspiration to do better. The fact that he was able to do so occurred, not because of his ability to seize the resources of those who had them, but rather through the gratuitous concessions of those who had them. This he did with such success that during the years 1901 through 1913, he became an advisor to both President Theodore Roosevelt and to President William H. Taft.

National Depressions: The U.S. And Germany

In 1929 the stock market crashed signaling a depression that cost hundreds of thousands of jobs and swallowed up thousands of dollars in consumer savings. While the U. S. economy was teetering, half a world away Adolf Hitler was brewing up a war in Europe. Although President Franklin D. Roosevelt was busy creating government programs to aid the country in recovering from the worst depression in its history, the actual recovery plan was been set in place, not so much by Mr. Roosevelt's political maneuvering, but by Hitler's war machine.

Only a few years before Germany, Hitler own nation had become plagued by a great depression. Following WWI Germany had had its economic hands tied behind its back at the Treaty of Versailles in 1919. The peace terms that the treaty imposed on Germany left the country in a stifling depression. Anecdotally, it is said you needed a wheelbarrow full of marks just to buy a loaf of bread. By the time of the Second World War, Germany had recovered from its depression. The U. S. depressed economy recovered as the result of the U. S. efforts to supply the British with sufficient weapon systems to defeat Hitler's Germany. In these two disparate instances the recovery periods were as short as the ten to twenty years needed by the Germans to overcome the devastating consequences of World War I, and just the fifteen years needed by the United States to revive its economy after the Great Depression.

Pre-Industrialized Japan

Prior to the 1850s when the Japan opened its ports and markets up to trade with the West, the Japanese people had lived under a system of feudalism not too unlike a system of caste slavery, which was governed by various and often feuding warlords. In 1868, the Japanese government, after approximately twenty years of exposure to the industrial strength of the United States and of Great Britain, began to disengage itself from of medieval and feudalistic system of labor management. Its use of warlords declined, and a more central government evolved. The new government committed itself to developing Japanese industries and initiated an assortment of reconstruction programs to build industries comparable to those of the United States and Great Britain. That fiercely aggressive effort lasted for about forty years, and by the early 1900s, had succeeded in making Japan a world power comparable to the industrialized status of Great Britain.

The Japanese recovery time was forty years, but theirs was a government—sponsored recovery plan and it was not accomplished without severe exploitation of the Japanese citizenry. A glimpse into the tragic extent to which the Japanese were willing to go to achieve industrial parity is evident in the account of a coal mine referred to as "Battleship Island." The Japanese government, or at least the shipbuilding company that worked the mines on the island, confined thousands of Japanese citizens to work in what could only be classed, even at the turn of the century, as subhuman conditions. The island, located just off the coast of Nagasaki, was called "Battleship Island" because the coal it produced was used mainly to fuel Japan's shipbuilding industry. From the 1890s until late into the 1920s, Japanese miners labored like animals under impossible conditions in the tunnels that honeycombed the island. Because the tunnels were built too low to walk in the workers could only crawl. Often working in temperatures practically hot enough to fry an egg. Men, women, and children worked side-by-side for eighteen hours each day and subsisted on meager diets.

This was all done in an effort to fire up the Japanese industrial revolution. Virtually imprisoned in a hellhole that often reached temperatures as high as 130 degrees, they produced tons of fuel coal that helped sustain Japan's march toward industrialization. And if the abusive neglect of their working environments was not bad enough, the value of their lives was even less considered. When an outbreak of cholera spread among the island's inhabitants, the coal mining company, in an effort to stave off the epidemic, ordered the entire island, workers and structures, burned. The island and all its inhabitants were set afire.

In marshaling arguments for the recovery time required for the black American community, such extremes as those of the Battlefield Island are obviously not called for. But it is worth noting that such examples notwithstanding, the Japanese government moved its industrial might from being a nonentity to being comparable to the other industrialized nations of the world in just forty years.

Former Communist Eastern Bloc Countries

And, of course, the problems that the former Soviet Union is currently experiencing are an indicator of the approximate recovery times one can expect when the programs that are in place are ineffective. The inherent weaknesses of the Marxist economic system were primarily responsible for leaving the Soviet Bloc in virtual economic chaos since the Bolsheviks revolution of 1917. Eighty-five years later, the Russians are struggling to make any substantial gains in their ability to utilize the tools of modern industry in its efforts to achieve a stable and prosperous economy. Additionally, there are the examples of the recovery or reconstruction programs now being implemented in all the nations of the former Soviet Union and

Eastern Europe. Countries such as Poland, Hungary, Czech, Slovakia, the countries of the former Yugoslavia, East Germany, and the eleven countries (Confederation of Independent States) of the former Soviet Union are busily soliciting the technological, economic, and entrepreneurial assets of western nations in an effort overcome the negative effect of communism has had upon their economic systems relative to that of western nations, over the past forty to seventy years. Along with the fall of the communist regime, multitude of other examples can be cited to illustrate the apparent ill effects that dramatic socioeconomic changes such as Marxism can have upon the initiatives and confidence of a community of people. The lengthy time periods noted in this chapter, are indicators of the approximate amounts of time required for a nation or people to recover from repressive regimes or governments. These time periods were required, even when formal reconstruction programs were in place.

East Germany Recovery

Of particular interest are the circumstances of East Germany. When the Berlin wall came down, it showed how far East Germany lagged behind the West Germans technologically and economically. In just forty-odd years, two groups of the same people had become so varied in their cultural and socioeconomic perspective that one could exercise such dominance over the other. In an effort to correct that disparity the German government has committed itself to a ten-year reconstruction program in which it plans to spend at least $100 billion per year. While this ten-year plan is about the same as the eleven-year reconstruction program implemented by the United States government for the emancipated slaves, the $100 billion per year, even in 1866 dollars far exceeds the money expended by the government for reconstruction of the millions of U.S. citizens the country had enslaved for the previous 205 years. In spite of this massive and costly effort on the part of the German government, some economists estimate that it will still take roughly one and a half to two and a half generations—or thirty to fifty years—before the areas formerly under East German communism will attain full socioeconomic parity with the rest of the German economy.

Western Europe

Perhaps the greatest example of a regional, or continental recovery occurred in Western Europe after the collapse of the Roman Empire. The Germanic tribes—the Goths, Lombards, Franks, and the Vandals—were largely responsible for the fall of the Roman Empire and were in control of most of what remained of it during the Middle Ages. However, because of the fact that they were more inclined to eating, drinking, and fighting, they hadn't the slightest idea of what to do with the libraries, the books, and other tools of Greek and Roman enlightenment that had come into their possession. In a figurative way, it was as if multiple generations of cultural evolution had been excised right out of the heart of Europe. The libraries and books sustained the cultural predecessors to the Germans, the refined cultures of the Greeks and the Romans. But the Germanic tribes were ignorant of such things and showed no interest in them. They were essentially an unlearned, ignorant, and primitive people. In their culture they had no need of such refinements as the Greeks and Romans did. Because of their indifference, brought on by their limitations, Europe slipped into the period known in history as the Middle Ages or Dark Ages. However, before the ignorance of the Germans tribes could lay waste to the entire continent, Charlemagne, Charlemagne the Great, in an effort to avert a disaster, issued a decree to the Roman Catholic Church directing it to utilize its knowledge and familiarity with Latin, which was the language of the church services and also the language of the Romans, to teach not only church abbots and other officials, but also to teach the local children how to read and write. It was through this effort that the European Dark Ages did not continue beyond the period in history that it did.

Another substantial recovery that occurred in Western Europe was the U. S. sponsored Marshall Plan. Following the devastation of England, France and Germany in the aftermath of the Second World War Europe, the U. S. sought to restore the economic viability of Europe by lending, or perhaps word granting may be better, the three nations extremely large sum of money. The plan called for the investment of vast amounts of U. S. dollars into rebuilding the cities and industries in the aftermath of the war. The plan adopted was scheduled to last for 20 years and was called the Marshall Plan. The Marshall plan was an extremely successful recovery plans. Today the economies of Western Europe are strong and vigorous Europe's large and very modern industrial economy has made it one of the economic powerhouses of the world's economic systems. Next to Japan, the European Marshall Plan is perhaps the best illustration of the effectiveness of the concept of gratuitous concession.

Paraphrasing the above comments regarding the southern states, if the recovery periods can be as short as the ten to twenty years needed by the Germans, or the fifteen or so years needed by the U.S. economy after 1929, how do we contrast those time periods with the fact that the Black Americans, as an ethnic group, remained in a depressed economic and technological state for at least a hundred years after their 1865 emancipation from slavery? There is a certain irony in the fact that the problem, which plagued the black Americans in their quest for economic achievement and that that has been equally successful in depressing the economies of the southern states, is essentially the same. Even more obvious is the amount of time and resource apparently required to recover from such an experience. The point I am making is that when the other ethnic group arrived in America, they brought with them whatever assets or social advantages they had whether rich, poor, lawyers, doctor, bankers, merchants, along with other skills they possessed.

Finally, and after we have explored all the depreciating effects that slavery visits upon its victims, the fault, alas, does not lie in damaging attributes but in the institution itself. Slavery, particularly as it was practiced against Africans, was an inherent evil. It can be likened to the drug traffic. On the one hand, drug trafficking generates large incomes for the people and the countries that engage in it, but those incomes are not collected from the free purses of the consumers or its addicts, but rather from the misery drawn from otherwise happy parents and the despair drawn from an otherwise talented, ambitious, and aspiring young man or woman. Slavery was a similar taxing agency. The elaborate antebellum homes, the immaculately manicured estates, and the aristocratic lifestyle of the southern gentry were possible only via an institution vile enough to consume the humanity of its victims in exchange for its vain productivity.

Slavery, as instituted by the Europeans and sustained by Americans was quite possibly history's most formal and insidious form of human bondage. From its legalization in 1662, it continued unimpeded and unabated for 205 years. In its uninterrupted saga, it consumed or sacrificed lives, the free will and personal aspirations of over twelve generations of Africans and their American descendents. When it ended in 1865, it had impoverished the cultural and psychological estates of millions of black Americans. And before the nation finally arrived at a moral resolution, slavery had cost another 655,000 in Civil War battlefield deaths, injuries and the ruination of the economies of the southern states. From a given perspective, it is possible to see these painful losses as part of the price that human enslavement, that vile institution, demanded before being abolished in the United States of America, and thanks largely to efforts of the Americans, essentially banished as an institution of civilized societies. While it remained, though, it levied an exorbitant tax in human lives and human agony and plunged millions of black Americans in cultural and socioeconomic poverty for generations to come.

Normal Operation	Percentage Accessible To	
	Free People	Enslaved People
Need for social affiliation	90–100%	5–10%
Need for rights as citizens	90–100%	0–1%
Need for free moral agency	90–100%	0-5%
Need for family environment	90–100%	0–5%
Need for parental affection	85–100%	2–10%
Need for religious freedom	85–100%	0–5%
Need for personal responsibility	85–100%	0–1%
Need for life	100%	0–5%
Need for individuality	80–100%	0–5%
Need for personal freedom	80–100%	0–5%
Need for personal pride	80–100%	0–10%
Need for ego appreciation	75–100%	0–10%
Need for social status	75–100%	0–15%
Need for operational ethics	75–100%	0–5%
Need for respect	80–100%	0–5%
Need for personal relationships	75–100%	10–15%
Need for personal privacy	70–100%	0–5%
Need for intellectual demand	90–100%	10–30%
Need for display of courage	65–100%	5–10%
Need for safety	75–100%	10–20%
Need for security	80–100%	0–5%
Need for belongingness	75–100%	10–15%
Need for affection	90–100%	10–20%
Need for self-respect	80–100%	10–30%
Need for self-actualization	80–100%	5–10%

Table VI
(For illustration purposes only)

Whereas classical psychologists and social scientists might codify the estates of basic human needs via a lexicon skewed to their field of expertise, it is possible to speak of such needs in pedantic and practical terms. The table below is an illustrated attempt to depict the basic emotions and psychological needs or components required in the estate of any self-actualized person. Table V attempts to match the attributes of an erstwhile socially and culturally healthy person against the injurious, and destructive impact that the institution of slavery might have had upon the emotional, cultural, and psychological health of those enslaved. Although the table draws loosely upon Maslow's characterization of the basic needs, basic human emotions, and basic human capacities of a psychologically healthy person, it by no means intends to invoke Maslow as an authority for the conclusions drawn.

The black American community, as an operationally effective social unit, had its cultural and psychological estate depleted, or bankrupted by the institution of slavery. In his book *Toward a Psychology of Being*, Abraham Maslow states, "the state of being without a system of values is psychopathogenic. The human being needs a frame work of values, a philosophy of life, a religion, or religious surrogate, to live by and understand by, in about the same sense that he needs sunlight, calcium or love. This condition is referred to as the cognitive need to understand. The value—illnesses which results from valueless ness are called variously anhedonia, anomie, apathy, amorality hopelessness, cynicism, etc. and can become somata illness as well. If the projected assessments are valid, then the Maslow diagnosis is that the enslaved black Americans were vulnerable to an assortment of psychological traumas. These are the deficits four million formerly enslaved black Americans had to contend with as the emancipation proclamation was signed into law. Although the proclamation meant freedom from the bonds of physical slavery, it did nothing to arrest or undo the emotional and psychological damage that occurred over the previous eleven generations—discounting the first (1606–1635) and second (1626–1655) generations. Under current-day insight, any person victim of a substantial trauma such as the schoolmates of victims of a tragedy, employees of a company which has experienced an office shooting, survivors or family member airplane crashes, or victims of various types of molestation, are now almost always administered some form of counseling.

Yet no such programs were offered to the victims of what could only be described as the most vicious trauma-sustaining environment ever visited upon so large a community of people for so long a period of time. As tyrannical as communism was and considering the number of people it affected, it lasted for only three and a half generations, or seventy years, even in Russia. Slavery embraced eight million to ten million people and lasted for over two centuries—seven continuous generations. Consequently, and as mentioned above, each generation, consistent with its role to transfer its respective cultural and social estates to succeeding generations, has continued to transfer the impoverished estates of 205 years of slavery from one generation to the next.

Even though the tabulations in Table V are strictly intuitive, they can be utilized to exemplify the plight of the enslaved black American in much the same manner a fictional fable or novel can be utilized to illustrate a particular moral point or value. In this instance, these fictional tabulations are being used to illustrate by analogy a hypothetical and comparative analysis. The table draws its strength from a Euclidean-like premise. The column labeled *Free People* list those attributes that are generally accepted as the necessary components of a healthy community. The column labeled *Enslaved People* on the other hand, shows the probable diminished estates that would more than likely have represented the black American environment during the period of their enslavement.

One Hundred Years Of Terrorism: 1865 To 1968

The Terrorism Prevention Branch of the Vienna-based UN Office for Drug Control and Crime Prevention (ODCCP) has issued the following *Academic Consensus Definition* for terrorism.

"Terrorism is an anxiety-inspiring method of repeated violent action, employed by (semi-) clandestine individual, group or state actors, for idiosyncratic, criminal or political reasons, whereby—in contrast to assassination—the direct targets of violence are not the main targets. The immediate human victims of violence are generally chosen randomly (targets of opportunity) or selectively (representative or symbolic targets) from a target population, and serve as message generators. Threat-and violence-based communication processes between terrorist (organization), (imperiled) victims, and main targets are used to manipulate the main target (audience(s)), turning it into a target of terror, a target of demands, or a target of attention, depending on whether intimidation, coercion, or propaganda is primarily sought"

The second reason for the extensive delay in black American socioeconomic parity can be attributed to dehumanizing effects of the one-hundred-year terrorist campaign (1876 – 1970s) against them. It is a repugnant notion, but for one hundred years, citizens of the southern states engaged in a de facto state-sponsored campaign of vicious terrorism. We refer to it as de facto state-sponsored terrorism because the legal system that was constitutionally and morally charged with the responsibility for the welfare of its citizens, failed to own up to such responsibility. Further, it was because of the wanton and vicious aspects of terrorist tactics that socioeconomic progress in the black American community, particularly in the southern states but generally in the entire country, was virtually pinned down by terrorist threats. The villainy of the terrorists, combined with their obvious supportive backing by the judicial process, the Dred Scott decision for example, and local law enforcement officials made them next to impossible to dislodge and defeat. For roughly a hundred years, from 1876s to the 1970s, terrorists roamed the southern states with virtual legal impunity. While the 1970s are shown as the end of the 100 years of terrorism, it more specifically alludes to the years in which such terrorist groups operated with at least some fear of prosecution. We know that terrorist's activities continues even though now codified as *hate crimes*. Formal definitions of terrorism characterizes it as a "sustained clandestine use of violence—murder, kidnapping, hijacking, bombing—to achieve a political purpose."

For the past 127 years—the six generations since the emancipation proclamation—the black American community has had to deal with the emotional and physical agonies of white supremacist terrorism and the presence of post-enslavement social disorientation. It is the remaining stigma of European-American enslavement. The psychological and sociological effects of such a brutal repression would severely depress the motives and initiatives of any civilized community. During that 127-year period, the non-nurturing environment of the black Americans was dictated by a set of hideous and brutalizing Jim Crow laws, used to intimidate, maim, and deny the rights and privileges of United States citizenship to the nation's more than fifteen million black Americans citizens. It is, therefore obvious that the formerly enslaved black Americans did not enter into a nurturing environment after their emancipation. The trauma of slavery and the terrorism that followed it have, in fact, done just the opposite of what one's cultural environment is wont to do. The consequence of such a self-denigrating environment has been injurious to the social and emotional lives of black Americans.

The United States Intelligence and Surveillance Act of 1979, and the United Kingdom Prevention of Terrorism Act of 1976 both emphasize that organizations that use violence to coerce or intimidate the civilian population with a view to affecting government policy are terrorists. On the world scene, terrorist groups have utilized some of the most inhuman tactics known to civilized man in their attempt to put forth their agendas.

Among the tools of their trade are murders, bombings, assassinations, kidnapping, and willful destruction of property.

In 1990, a terrorist group placed a cleverly concealed bomb inside a portable radio on board Pan Am airline Flight 103, a commercial airline carrying 269 passengers. The flight, originating in Germany was scheduled to fly to London, England, and then on to New York. As Flight 103 was flying over Lockerbie, Scotland, the bomb exploded. The airplane disintegrated into a thousand jagged fragments. Pieces of airplane amid human bodies and personal items plummeted to the ground around the town of Lockerbie. The explosion and resulting crash killed all passengers and the crew, plus a number of people on the ground. That same terrorist group is also believed to have been responsible for the bombings of the U.S. embassy in Beirut, Lebanon, in April 1983, the U.S. and French military compounds at the Beirut Airport in October 1983, and the U.S. embassy in Kuwait in December 1983; for the assassination of Malcolm Kerr, President of the American University in Beirut in January 1984; and for the September 1984 bombing of the U.S. embassy annex in Beirut.

Another terrorist group, the Irish Republican Army (IRA), was founded in 1919 as a radical movement against the British troops and the Protestant religious community of Ireland. The group of terrorists was persistent for at least seventy-five years in pursuit of their objective, an independent and united Ireland. Perhaps most notorious among their terrorist acts was the 1979 assassination of Lord Mountbatten. Additionally the IRA has been involved in numerous bombings, killings, and assassinations, both in Ireland and in England. Over the seventy-odd years of its terrorist activities, thousands have died as a result of the IRA's relentless villainy.

And finally, perhaps the most notorious terrorist group, before emergence of the terrorist group Al Qaeda, are the terrorist wings Hamas and other allegedly associated with the Palestine Liberation Organization (PLO). Over the past twenty years, the terrorist wing of the organization has dedicated itself to the destruction of the state of Israel. To that goal, they have engaged in some of the modern world's most wretched acts of terrorism. Among the atrocities committed, and credited to the PLO are the willful murder of the helpless athletes at the 1972 Olympic games in Munich, Germany; the mid-air destruction of civilian airliners; the 1985 hijacking of the Italian cruise ship *Achille Lauro* off the Egyptian coast and the murders of countless civilians living in and around the Jewish state of Israel. In response to the need to counter the activities of such terrorist groups, the international community met in Tokyo in 1963, in Montreal in 1971, at The Hague in 1973, and at The Hague again in 1979.

In 1986, after the United States, under then-President Ronald Reagan, launched a bombing raid in response to charges that Libya's Colonel Muammar al-Qaddafi was actively engaged in the funding and training of terrorists, the world community including the U.S., Canada, Japan, Germany, Great Britain, Italy, and France committed themselves to the task of eradicating terrorism. An added note is in order here. For the first ninety or so of those 102 years, terrorist groups aimed at disenfranchising black Americans were permitted to terrorize by bombings, pillage, and murder with virtual judicial impunity.

From the beginning of the terrorist campaign in 1876 until the heightened civil rights activities of the late 1950s and early 1960s, America launched no such programs to eradicate those activities.

Perhaps the most notorious terrorist group to date is Al Qaeda terrorist groups ostensibly out of Afghanistan, but as we have come to realize, is distributed throughout the nations of the world. Their acts of terrorist villainy are so horrific and so current no additional commentary is warranted. However, we must not be persuaded to think that the terrorist groups that perpetrated the 100-year terrorist campaign against the black American community are to be defined by any other definition than that which defines Al Qaeda. They differ only in their historical time period, and of course by the magnitude of their terrorist's acts. The bottom line is that they are all terrorists whether they are Al Qaeda, or KKK.

In 1866, following passage of the Thirteenth Amendment to the U.S. Constitution (1865), creation of the Freedmen Bureau (1865), and passage of the Fourteenth Amendment (1866), the social climate in the states of the former confederacy reacted with an animal-like thirst for violence. Over the next 102 years, the various hate groups that emerged out of that social reaction would leave a path of murders—over twenty thousand dead, assassinations, bombings, and other atrocities that rival the record of the present-day Hamas terrorist group. Rising out of this reactionary movement were such terrorist groups as the Ku Klux Klan (KKK), the Knights of the White Camellia, the White Brotherhood, the Pale Faces, the '76 Organization, and the Mississippi Plan. The confederate states, which had suffered enormous military losses during the Civil War and cultural, political, and social humiliation in what it saw as an unforgiving government and Northern press, sought through terrorism what it had been unable to achieve by military force. These organizations began a unilateral campaign of terrorist activities that began in 1866 with their infamous hooded raids and included the April 4, 1968, assassination of Dr. Martin Luther King, Jr. in Memphis. Tennessee. During this period, such groups as the ones named above and smaller, less organized ones were responsible for an average of 180 to 200 black American deaths per year for each of the 102 years of the terrorist campaign. Drawing upon the racist sentiment of bigots throughout the United States, the terrorist movement operated openly in the southern states and went underground in the northern states. It also remained relatively underground in the western states. Reaching its peak during 1915, the KKK and its subordinate terrorist organizations are estimated to have operated with a membership of as many as four million members. With such a large membership, the organization had one terrorist for every 2.5 of the roughly ten million black Americans citizens living in the United States in 1915. In that capacity they were responsible for an assortment of terrorist acts among which were

- A race riot in Memphis, Tennessee, in May of 1866 that cost the lives of forty-six black Americans

- The July 1866 racial incident in New Orleans, Louisiana, in which more than thirty-five black Americans were killed and another one hundred were injured

- The tactic of using murder, intimidation, and beatings from the 1870s trough the 1960s to prevent black Americans from voting in national and other elections

- The Colfax massacre in Grant Parish, Louisiana, on Easter morning in 1873, in which sixty black Americans were killed

- The sixteen black Americans that were taken from a Tennessee jail by hooded men and shot to death on August 26, 1874

- The July 1917 incident in which up to two hundred black Americans in East St. Louis, Illinois, were killed

- The December 25, 1952, bombing of the Miami, Florida, home of NAACP official Harry T. Moore in which he was killed and his wife injured

- The August 28, 1954, death of fourteen-year-old Emmett Till, kidnapped and lynched in Money, Mississippi

- The June 12,1963 assassination of NAACP field secretary Medger Evers in Jackson, Mississippi

- The September 15, bombing of the Sixteenth Street Baptist Church of Birmingham, Alabama, in which four young girls were killed

- The June 21,1964, murder of three young civil rights workers in Philadelphia, Mississippi

- The April 4,1968, assassination of Dr. Martin Luther King, Jr., in Memphis, Tennessee

Thousands of other terrorist acts, whether carried out in the streets of our cities, or underground in the boardrooms and courtrooms of our nation are simply too numerous to catalog in this book.

Since the KKK, the Knights of the White Camellia, the White Brotherhood, the Pale Faces, the '76 Organization, the Mississippi Plan, and of other groups with less published names did in fact routinely engage in acts of violence against black American citizens. They did so to intimidate those citizens and to thwart the U.S. government policies toward those citizens as expressed in the Thirteenth, Fourteenth, and Fifteenth Amendments to the U.S. Constitution. By the definitions of both the United States and of the United Kingdom, these groups were terrorists' organizations. And since they ran rampant over the legal rights of the black American citizens from 1866 until at least the 1968 Civil Rights Bill, then any reasonable person can clearly see and should concur that the black American community has endured 102 years of terrorism.

Terrorist organizations do not terrorize simply for the sport of it. Generally, they have political agendas. However, in the case of the black American community, there was not so much a political, but a racist's agenda. Which was to sufficiently intimidate the black Americans community to effectively remove them from any degree of social, political, or economic competition. To accomplish this these groups formed units staffed by people who were motivated by hatred. Since the primary focus of any terrorist organization is to create a pathway to its objective by killing those who stand in its path and intimidating those who oppose from the sidelines, the 102-year terrorist campaign of the southern states can be characterized as ruthless. Its successes though murders, assassinations, and mayhem, cost the black American community dearly. For the most part, each of the approximately twenty thousand black Americans who died perished as individuals and not en masse as would have occurred in a battlefield environment for instance. The effect of this difference is that instead of the grief coming as the result of the casualties of a single battle, the emotional and social impact for each death upon the affected family and community was registered as twenty thousand separate applications of grief and terror. The result would akin to the concept of the Chinese water torture where the victim is continually beset by individual drops of water. The 1915 population of black Americans in the United States was ten million; which meant that on a statistical average, the terrorists had managed to murder one in every five hundred black Americans citizens then living. As the results of their terrorism, the black American voters were driven from the polling booths and their political candidates gunned down in the street. The activities of the terrorist organizations had the entire social and political fabric of the country, particularly in the South, under a siege mentality. Even if you were a white American, your behavior toward black Americans had to comply with certain politically correct expectations, or you too would also be targeted. Yet, amidst all the death, destruction, and intimidation, black Americans, still struggling to cope with the bewildering burden of 205 years of abject slavery, received no legal or judicial assistance from either the state, or the federal government. And if the circumstances here illustrated appear to describe an environment of near intolerable hostility, then the description is valid because these were the conditions that faced the black American community for up to a hundred years even after the Civil War and the emancipation proclamation.

Recovery From The 100-Year Terrorist Campaign

The second major effort occurred when thousands of black Americans abandoned their sharecrop fields in the South and began what I have termed the plow-to-computer migration because farming with the plow was the most prominent skill that black Americans of that era possessed. And when they abandoned the South for the northern factories, they set the stage for their children and descendents to become initiated into the computer age. But whatever the consequence, they went north after literally fleeing in the middle of the night in an effort to improve the social and economic circumstances of their lives and that of their children. The movement, which involved the northern migration of as many as two million black Americans, began in early 1910 and gradually slowed to a more moderate pace during the civil rights movement of the late 1950s and 1960s. During that period, farmers from the rural South, fed up with lynching, beatings, and other acts of terrorism and perhaps sensing that the future of the country was in industrialization rather than in agriculture, abandoned their sharecropper farms and fled to the north's major cities. They left behind over three hundred years of skills as farmers and farm hands in search of the jobs and job training the industrial revolution offered.

Men who, although gratified at the improvements in their earning power and living standards were for the most part only seeking to escape from terrorist attacks of the various white supremacist organizations characterized the migration. The women, the lesser targets of terrorist violence, were relieved that their living condition and the quality of life they and their families would be improved. Finally, they might have contemplated, the opportunity to share some of the social and economic amenities that, as Americans, they had a right to expect. It is conceivable that the net results of the migration to improve their lives and that of their children may have included a social feature that tended to undermine their anticipated benefits from a northern migration. That is, the family structure of most black American families consisted of nuclear and extended families that meant that, generally speaking, black American children were often raised beneath the umbrella of the generational sexpartite. In the rural farming environment in which most black Americans then lived, it would not be uncommon to see families of three or four generations living in homes arranged within a communal pattern only a few miles apart. Since the family home would most likely be located in or near the center of the communal pattern, children were in frequent relationship with varying layers of parental authority.

In that residential structure, there were parents, grandparents, great-grandparents, and sometimes-even great-great-great-grandparents, and a host of other family members, and neighbors around to provide additional layers of parental care. And in this case parental authority rested not only with the actual parents but also, according to the social structure of the communities and it kinship system, also with all adult members of the family. Neighborhood or community actually assumed parental responsibility and thus became additional layers of parental authority. Considering the nature of the generational movement, children of that time and circumstance had easy access to their entire cultural estate. Their whole living heritage was accessible to them, not during annual visits but, if not daily, then weekly, or at least monthly. That meant that for the most part, each child was under the tutorial guidance of at least three and sometimes five, generations of parents, grandparents, and great-through-great-great-great grandparents.

Therefore, when the children of these migrating parents arrived in Boston, New York, Chicago, St Louis, and Detroit, most of them were effectively orphaned by the lost of numerous layers of parental authority. Even those whose extended family unit survived the migration intact, at least one layer or one-half of their parental authority was still displaced when the father went outside the family environment to work. And if this wasn't undermining enough, it got worse.

Soon after their arrival, especially those that arrived during the 1950s and early 1960s, these families quickly learned that the world had changed from the days of their parents. In the first place, modern innovations in the homes had already begun to lessen the hours mothers traditionally needed to maintain her home and family. Also, they were equally quick to discover that it took more than one income to supply the needs of the family. The result was that the mother, who traditionally carries the major portion of child-rearing responsibilities, now had to take a job outside of the home. Prior to the migration, mothers, even when they worked—especially if they worked on the family farm—worked either alongside their children, or if the children were too small to work, within visual distance of their children. However, the effect of the diminished role of the mother's influence upon the children, resulting from her job away from home was the loss of at least another layer of their parental authority. In a sense, I think a serious and inadvertent oversight occurred at this juncture in the lives of the black Americans that had a profound effect upon the community, even today. When black American mothers came to the northern cities, particularly during the latter part of the 1950s and in the 1960s, they went outside the home to work. It can be acknowledged that some of the impetus do so was prompted by simple economic demands. On the other hand, additional motivation came from the fact that laborsaving devices had substantially reduced the amount of hours customarily needed by homemakers to maintain a home.

Of the two circumstances that prompted homemakers to seek employment outside the home—economics and convenience—neither apparently took into consideration the mother's role as sentry of the family's success and welfare. In previous years and all during her traditional homemaker role, the mother had successfully and seamlessly integrated her homemaker's activities into her role as sentry. And when the demand or opportunity to go outside the home and work presented itself, little thought of the sentry role was considered. After all, the functional aspects of sentry duty are not nearly as obvious as the functional aspects role of the person who cooks the meals, does the laundry, or cleans the house. And so, since laborsaving devices made it possible to do the laundry quicker, prepare dinner faster, and vacuum the floor in a breeze, what need was there for Mom to remain in the house where the work that was "never done" could now be accomplished in a few hours? The problem with this kind of approach is that the removal of "Mom-as-sentry" from the child-rearing formula has apparently had some rather devastating consequences upon the lives of the youths of the eighteenth, nineteenth and possibly upon the lives of the youth of the twentieth generation (1986–2015).

The children of these parents, all of the eighteenth (1946–1975) and nineteenth (1966–1995) generations, suffered as the result of this damaging depletion in parental authority. The undermining attribute of all this may be found in the phenomenal rise in juvenile delinquency—166 percent between the years 1960 and 1978—a period which coincides with the arrival of children born to parents during the more aggressive phase of the great migration that occurred between 1940 and 1958. Although the children did find better-quality education and improved educational opportunities, the sociological price paid by the migrating families and by the youths of the twentieth generation (1986–2015) may yet prove to be extremely costly. At the current rate of homicide among young black American males, the cost in human lives versus the benefits of the migration may yet be subject to challenge.

While a true analysis and description of the actual sociological circumstances that occurred during this period will have to await inquiry from other, more adept practitioners in this venue than me, my current level of understanding leaves me with only questions and possibilities. Some are as follows. Is it possible that migrating black American parents, themselves, reared in an environment buffeted by the threats and violence of white supremacist terrorists, are able to develop new child-rearing strategies, or practices to accommodate the environment they encountered in the cities of the North? The question may at first sound a bit out of place, but you must remember who these migrating parents were. They were people who had been reared in an environment that, for three or four generations, had been able to buffer their child-rearing strategies or practices against the imminent life-threatening environment of Jim Crow segregation. While at home in the South, Jim Crow segregation, with all its dangers and threats, had become their child-rearing "boogey man." It had been necessary to inculcate the threat of this dangerous environment into their child-rearing practices. They themselves had been reared against the backdrop of the deadly environment of terrorism as perpetrated by an assortment of white supremacist terrorist groups. The erstwhile, non-engaging task of simply keeping their children alive and out of harm's way was for these black American parents a daily and major feature of their child-rearing strategies.

And so, the question would appear to have merit. Could it be that after migrating to the various cities of the North, and finding jobs and homes, they suddenly found themselves in need of new child rearing strategies? Having perhaps relaxed their own religious and church affiliations and thus distanced themselves from another of traditional child-rearing disciplines, could those parents have found themselves in new settings where the old rules failed to work effectively? With the decline of the influence of their church life and the "boogey man" component of their child-rearing formula no longer a salient feature, it would appear that the child-rearing strategies and practices of those black American parents would have become seriously impaired. The effect of the removal of such parameters of behavioral management would be tantamount to the complete and sudden removing of a wall a person was leaning against. The obvious effect of such action would be to cause the person to stumble and fall.

Other examples that can be used to affirm that Americans, and particularly American families, depend upon the application of external environmental phenomena in their child-rearing and discipline-invoking practices. Such an application can be detected in the environment of scarcity that surrounded families of the Great Depression era. During that period, one that roughly covers the years from 1929 to the late 1940s. Following the 1929 stock market crash, the nation's economy took a nosedive and did not recover until after America began production of military equipment for WW II. And even after the war began, the scarcity continued. Whatever lessening of economic scarcity brought on by the increased economic activity was quickly countered by the rationing of components considered essential to the war effort. Parents who had gone through this period of scarcity employed it as their "boogey man" for shaping the behavior of their children. The result of this child-rearing discipline produced in their children's children the collective anti-materialism movement expressed by the 1960s cultural reawakening commonly referred to as the "hippie" movement.

The idea that Jim Crow segregation might have played a role in the formulation of the child-rearing practices of southern black American parents is distasteful, but before one rushes out and disavows the probability, I implore you to ask yourself if we are not taking the very same approach in our current handling of sexual promiscuity and AIDS. Parents, educators, public health officials, and some religious leaders are telling children not to have sex because they could contract the HIV virus or AIDS, thus setting themselves up for the same letdown that occurred with the black American parents of the great migration. Attempting to control sexual promiscuity by frightening people can only advance its cause. True enough, this "boogey man" approach can produce some positive results, but on the other hand, it will produce a far greater assault on promiscuity. For when a cure for the AIDS virus is found—and by all reasonable accounts, it will be the social hold on promiscuity will disappear along with the AIDS and it will then be too late to attempt to re-impose morality as a basis for countering promiscuity. Consequently, with the risk of AIDS gone, promiscuity will run rampant and the "boogey man" approach will have suffered another abysmal loss. And so, with the child-rearing buffering component of Jim Crow segregation behind them and with diminished layers of parental authority with them, children of the migration produced a baby-boomer generation that lacked the personal motivation and moral foundation their grandparents had left behind in their efforts to secure a better and more rewarding life for their children and grandchildren. In spite of the difficulties the parents of these youths might have had with child-rearing techniques, the children of the great migration did arrive in communities where educational opportunities were greater than those they had.

However, even though the school systems were superior, they had also come into a social environment that spoke an almost-entirely different cultural language than that spoken by them, or their parents. Since language acquisition and the acquisition of cultural values are very similar in their processes, a connection can easily be made between the children of the great migration and the children of immigrant families, which is particularly true of immigrants from the poorer countries. The immigrants who come to the United States from poorer countries and the black Americans families who migrated north during the great migration possibly share more commonalities than differences. For the most part, they both migrated from places of extreme poverty and were introduced to a language and culture that varied considerably from those in their previous and native environments.

While it is easy to accept the fact that non-English-speaking immigrants would encounter language difficulties upon their arrival in the United States, it is not so easy to accept the fact that black Americans entering northern cities would experience a similar transition. However, one must remember that during the period of the great migration, black Americans were not only leaving a region of the country whose own economy consistently operated at or below what would have been the national poverty level, had there been one, but one in which they had been confined by Jim Crow legislation to occupy only the lower rungs of that impoverished economy. And at that poverty-ridden, almost apartheid-like environment, black Americans were also accustomed to habits, customs, and to a great extent, a language that was considerably different than the one they encountered in the northern, eastern and western cities. Thus being poor, uninformed, and unlearned, black Americans of the great migration, as with the foreign immigrants, were only marginally able to articulate the requirements of the more sophisticated cultures and languages of the cities of their destination. This analogy points to the fact that the children of the migrating parents applied a "broken" cultural understanding in much the same manner in which recent immigrants and foreigners speak in broken English. Upon arriving in places like Chicago, St. Louis, New York's Harlem, and many other like them they took steel mill jobs, auto assembly line jobs, housekeeping jobs, any jobs so long as they were paying jobs. They were hungry for any opportunity to trade in their old agrarian skills for almost any industrial skill. Sometimes, they ended up settling for jobs that were barely more substantial than those that had been left behind except in pay.

That the second effort did not succeed to its full expectation, can, to a great extent, be attributed to the terrorist threatening influences that made most opportunities for real socioeconomic growth, even in the northern cities, still closed to the black American. All was not lost of; course, and the migration northward did produce some notable successes. Among them were the advances made by black Americans in professional sports, music, and in entertainment. Some of the largest salaries received by black Americans today are in these three fields. And these inroads can be attributed directly to the efforts of black Americans who traveled north via the great migration.

The Undermining Effects Of Bigotry

The third cause of the setback among the black American community and the effect that, in my opinion dealt the most damaging blow to its self-image, began during the period of the enslavement of the Africans and continued at least until the civil rights movement of the 1960s. That was the deficit effects that the racial climate of America had upon the mindset of the black American community.

A self-image is akin to the degree of wholesomeness one feels about oneself. When this state of wholesomeness is not present, the ability of a person to function efficiently and effectively is impaired. The condition would persist as long as the negative self-image remained lodged in the person's psyche. To put it a different way, consider that the physical wellness of a person. If he or she were deprived of the nutritional nourishment necessary for physical wellness for a sustained period of time, that person's state of wellness would obviously be adversely affected. Under such a condition, the person would be unable to function as effectively or efficiently as someone who had not endured such deprivation. Needless to say, the condition of the starving person would not improve until the nutritional and nurturing environment were revived.

Even if the starving person were suddenly given all the nutritional nourishment necessary, this person would still require time to recover from the effects of his or her prior condition. The image that people have of themselves is as dependent upon the nurture and nourishment of their social and cultural environment as the body is dependent upon nutritional nurture. The Food and Nutrition Board of the National Research Council has researched the nutritional needs of the human body and have, for the past fifty years, published a brochure detailing the recommended dietary allowances for a healthy and nutritional diet. In that brochure, the Food and Nutrition Board provides specific mineral and vitamin requirements necessary to maintain one's health. Unfortunately, there are no such national agencies publishing brochures explicitly defining the mental and emotional counterpart for recommended dietary allowances to assure a healthy self-image. However, supposition itself is sufficient to accord us with sufficient knowledge and insight to know that demeaning cultural and social stereotypes are not conducive to a healthy self-image. And extreme deprivation of the most basic civil and legal rights is sufficient to provoke a state of social anomie, if not downright anarchy.

Summary

The result of all this was to give the black American community the impression that America belonged only to white Americans and that black Americans were more or less here at the discretion of the white Americans. Nothing could be further from the truth. Yet the institution of slavery, terrorism and the national scheme of bigotry that followed have gone a long way to convince the black American community that is in fact the case. Such disinformation suppresses the appreciation that black Americans young, and old, should have for the land their forefathers fought and died for; a land wrestled from the wilderness so that their children and grandchildren could enjoy its beauty and resources.

I think it extremely unfortunate that the Jamestown version of America has persisted so long. Based on Thomas Jefferson belief that the Britain's King George was responsible for the sustaining slavery, and the fact that slavery was of European origin, then it would appear to a reasonable conclusion that America as a nation, and even as the Mayflower Colony, was never pre-disposed to engage in the enslavement of the Africans. It simply inherited the institution from it colonial authorities. Had Americans intended to be a nation of slavery, they could most assuredly have written slavery into the constitution just as the white South Africans wrote the terms of apartheid into their constitution. Yet, they did not. The action of the Continental Congress in 1776, the same year America celebrated its independence from England, supports this premise when it decreed that no additional enslaved Africans were to be brought into the country. Additionally, eight of the original thirteen colonies voted to emancipate those enslaved black Americans within their borders (Vermont in 1777; Pennsylvania in 1780; Massachusetts and New Hampshire in 1783; Connecticut and Rhode Island in 1784; New York in 1799; and New Jersey in 1804). The colonies that took no action regarding emancipation were Delaware, Maryland, Virginia, South Carolina, and North Carolina—the same colonies that had developed agrarian economies based upon the use of indentured-servant and enslaved labor. After wrestling with its own conscience for the better part of a hundred years, they reckoned slavery too immoral and inconsistent with either the Declaration of Independence or the Constitution to continue.

Finally, the nation, in an act akin to the Apostle Paul's characterization of the warfare between man's two natures, declared war against itself. When it was all over, the price of a consistent morality had cost the young nation the lives of six hundred thousand men and women, both enslaved and free. It would appear the conscience of America had not reconciled itself to the immorality of maintaining a system of human enslavement. However, America had apparently and undoubtedly grown accustomed to the benefits of its peculiar institution, but time and its own conscience could not reconcile themselves with the inherent immorality associated with enslavement of the African people. And in time national politics, churches, the people, families, the military, and the nation split all in an effort to expunge itself of its self-induced trauma, its canker sore of immorality. That uprising of the American people and the war that followed demonstrate that America's ownership is vested in the morality of its people. This tend to make the final argument on behalf of the ethical, social, and moral philosophy of the 1620 settlers of Plymouth Rock over the more mercantile philosophy and aspirations of the British Government's 1619 settlement at Jamestown, Virginia. That is, whereas the 1620 settlers at Plymouth Rock represented the morality of the church, the settlement at Jamestown was strictly mercantile, and having little if any inclination in this regards.

The civil rights laws of 1968 and later years have provided an opportunity for black Americans to make up for the thirteen generations (from 1619 until 1865) the institution of slavery cost, as well as for the deficits in progress suffered by the fourteenth (1866–1895), fifteenth (1886–1915), sixteenth (1906–1935), seventeenth (1926–1955), and eighteenth (1946–1975) generations attributable to the hundred years of terrorism.

But black America should take heart in the fact that they can still attain, or exceed parity. Traditionally, the image that has portrayed the contest between the black American and the white American has been the analogy of two runners, one analogous to the black American community and the other to the white American community. They are depicted as being engaged in a foot race. One runner is handicapped by having weights symbolic of the many years of black American disenfranchisement attached to his shoes whereas the other runner runs free and unencumbered. The application of this analogy is that, without special catch-up programs, the black American community is destined to lag behind the white American community indefinitely. This would probably be correct if this analogy were paradigmatically true, for then socioeconomic parity between the two groups would truly be unlikely; that is, unless the white American community were prepared to take itself out of the socioeconomic race for eighteen generations and allow the black American community time to make up for eighteen generations of disproportionate market access. That would be necessary if the analogy of the two runners were true. The problem is that the analogy contends the runners are in a foot race forever, or that the prize or parity is awarded to one of the runners, based upon who arrives at the finish line first. This is definitely not the situation. The analogy contains a fundamental flaw by presuming that the runners black Americans and white Americans get wealthier the farther they run. While this argument may have some peripheral truths associated with it, the good news for the black Americans is that not all white Americans get progressively wealthier and wealthier. When you consider that a hundred years ago, the bulk of the wealth of this nation was in the hands of around five percent of the population that really hasn't changed. The current figures hold that the top three to five percent of the population controls a substantial portion of the country's wealth. What this means for black Americans is that white Americans do not necessarily get richer and richer but rather, that they achieve middle-class status and then stop. Envision, if you will a herd of Texas longhorns on a cattle drive. It is true that the longhorns in the front may indeed get to the watering hole first, but if those that are, for whatever reasons, eight or ten rows back persevere, they will inevitably get to the same watering hole.

Combine these three features into the mix that is the mindset of the black American community, and you can readily understand, and perhaps sympathize with the plight of the black American community. It has sufficient resources to free itself from this predicament but it must be motivated from within to do so. Unfortunately no amount of government money can provide this stimulus. The black American community still suffers from the effects of the past 305 years of social and cultural abuse of their self-image. Restoration of a positive self-image, present when the Africans were free, must be achieved. Some political leaders, perhaps over-imbued with a sense of self-righteousness have attempted some solutions. However, either for lack of understanding or convictions, their most frequent problem-solving technique has been something along the lines of a "greenback applique." The practice of applying more and more money in an effort to solve more and more problems has proven non-effective. While I believe the government can solve social problems, I am convinced that in this instance, its first task is to convince members of the black American community that America is no longer hostile to their interest and social welfare. Achieving that objective, though difficult, is essential if any other government-funded programs are to be effective.

President Lincoln came very close to confronting this problem when he gave his Gettysburg address. Soon after the Civil War was won, the federal government initiated the Southern Reconstruction Program to repatriate the southern states and assist in enfranchising those black Americans who had been enslaved. Even though that program was short lived those formerly enslaved black Americans did make substantial progress educationally, politically and as entrepreneurs. One must not forget that they possessed practically all the technical skills present in the South at that time.

These three tragic circumstances in the history of the black Americans—the institution of slavery, the white supremacist terrorist campaign that followed it, and the social pathology of that terrorism—have set them back at least eighteen generations. It was not until 1968 when events happened that would have significant impact on the course of black American socioeconomic progress. In fact, it is a reasonable argument that such progress should actually be measured only from 1968, or from the nineteenth generation (1966–1995). The twenty-six years since 1968 represent the only period of time in which the black American community has had relatively access to the market places of America.

The initial drive for black American socioeconomic parity was inaugurated by members of the fifteenth (1886–1915) and sixteenth (1906–1935) generations and increased in intensity through members of the seventeenth (1926–1955) generation. The movement, which involved the migration northward of thousands of black Americans, began in earnest, during the early 1920s and continued for at least forty years. During that period, farmers from the rural south, fed up with the denial of their rights, sharecropping, the lack of grow opportunities, and an assortment of terrorist activities abandoned their sharecrops and headed north in search of a better life for themselves and their families and better education opportunities for their children.

This commentary is written in the hope that it might assist in inspiring black American people to "jump start" the nineteenth (1966–1995) and twentieth (1986–2015) generations. And that black Americans will work diligently to build a basis for self-esteem and confidence throughout those generations, both for those already born and for the future benefit of those not yet born. With such a foundation of self-esteem and high morale, they will put in place the under girding structure necessary for attaining socioeconomic parity. To be effective, such a structure shall include a program to develop marketable skills and an influential peerage—the latter attainable only by accomplishing a sufficient degree of social integration and the assimilation of the tenets of the American dream. These will enable black Americans to access the socioeconomic resources associated with the bountiful lifestyle Americans so frequently enjoy.

The black American community can began the process of building self-esteem by establishing means to pay tributes, or memorial appreciation to the 1619 Africans, and a solemn commitment of respect to all subsequent generations. All generations of the black American community should be esteemed, for all have suffered. The Kunta Kinte generation, is only one among them, who are distinguished by the fact that they were permitted no rights of personal expressions, and were committed to chattel slavery with no viable options. Even so, they managed to sustain the pride and courage of their heritage and to successfully plant those values within the hearts of all succeeding generations of black American people. And a special debt of gratitude to those of the fourteenth (1866–1895), fifteenth (1886–1915) and sixteenth (1906–1935) generations, who, without the benefit of "law and order" or of civil or judicial support, took on the Ku Klux Klan, the lynch mobs, and white supremacist groups and took to the streets in an effort to secure for black Americans rights due them by virtue of their American citizenship.

Utilizing the U.S. Census Bureau data, estimates can be made that suggest that, all things being equal, slavery and the terrorism that followed it, has cost the seventeenth (1926–1955), eighteenth (1946–1975), and nineteenth (1966–1995) generations of the black American community parity in the following occupations. As we used the socioeconomic impact of the baby boomer generation (the beginnings of which coincide with the time periods of the seventeenth (1926–1955) and eighteenth (1946–1975) generations) previously to illustrate the nineteenth (1966–1995) and twentieth (1986–2015) generations' progression to socioeconomic parity. We utilize them here again to illustrate the negative socioeconomic impact of the nation having undereducated the seventeenth (1926–1955) and eighteenth (1946–1975) generations of black

Americans. Like the age-based movement of the 1945–1950 baby boomer generation's movement, the black Americans' seventeenth, and eighteenth generations (1926–1975 also shaped the nation's socioeconomic demography. The difference is that where the baby boomers' movement promoted growth and increased productivity, the movement of the seventeenth (1926–1955) and eighteenth generations, being less educated and thus less productive, affected the nation socioeconomic demography by absorbing increasingly greater portions of the nation's ongoing growth and productivity. Unfortunately, wherein the 1945–1950 baby boomers motivated by the "American Dream," became well educated, this was not the case with the seventeenth (1926–1955) and eighteenth (1946–1975) generations of black Americans.

The motivating effects of Dr. Martin Luther King's 1963 Civil Rights March on Washington's "I Have a Dream" speech and the dreams inspired by the 1964 Civil Rights Bill that followed it, motivated black Americans for a brief period of time, but the momentum did not last. However, as brief as the dream lasted, the response was almost awe-inspiring. Between 1964 and 1978, such a brief period of time that it constitutes only a moment in historical reckoning, record numbers of black American high school students went on to enroll in various colleges throughout the nation. Large numbers of black Americans, who had previously become disenchanted with the American dream and had opted instead for the dreams of the inner-city street hustler, picked themselves up, brushed themselves off, and went back to college. Neither the motivation inspired by the dream of Dr. King, nor the incentive wrought from the passage of the 1964 Civil Rights bill were sufficient to sustain the momentum.

In 1868, the nation ratified the Fourteenth Amendment. Section 1 of that amendment validated the rights of those emancipated from slavery to American citizenship. In fact, it is reasonable to assume that the black Americans of 1870 esteemed the Fourteenth Amendment more than any other document. Looking back, I surmise that the Fourteenth

Amendment was viewed by those black Americans who had known nothing but enslavement as their passport to the American dream. I dare say that when they owned a copy of the Fourteenth Amendment, it was undoubtedly kept in a place reserved only for the most special and precious documents—where their family Bibles were kept—and would have been the source of their hope and the basis for their aspiration. However, the dream was to be short-lived. Even before the Fourteenth Amendment was ratified, white supremacists groups across the nation were already federating themselves into terrorist organizations. And by 1877, all the dreams promised or implied by the Fourteenth Amendment died under the violent intimidation and threats of white supremacist terrorists. For almost one hundred years, the black American community functioned without any hope to access the same American dream that had inspired and motivated every other American.

Again, the boogey man came and took away the dream. In 1978, the same nation that had written Section 1 of the Fourteenth Amendment to ensure black Americans as legitimate heirs to the American dream used that precious document to disallow them that place in the line assured them just fourteen years earlier. Black American's flirtatious relationship with first one civil right bill and then another reflects their constant pursuit of access into the nation's market places. In 1968, Congress passed, and the president signed, another civil rights bill, and the saga began all over again. Then the politics of the 1980s, playing the boogey man, came and took away that dream.

One can see that black Americans have taken jobs in occupations that would hire them and, having limited skills and limited education, most of those jobs were in the low-paying occupations. The movement of those black Americans who went to college just after the 1964 Civil Rights Bill has already begun to have an affect upon the nation's socioeconomic demography. Data for 1987 indicates that they have already increased the ranks of the black America's middle class considerably. Beyond that, black

America's movement through the nation's socioeconomic system did not really start until the beginning of the nineteenth generation (1966–1995). The first child of that generation was born just two years before the 1968 Civil Rights bill was passed. Obviously this does not mean there were no socioeconomic accomplishments by black Americans prior to that time. There were, of course. Even beyond the 1964 college rally, black Americans have maintained an ongoing interest in entrepreneurial ventures. And even though access to most socioeconomic ventures were closed or extremely limited for black Americans, a number of them did succeed and established successful businesses and other enterprises. Much credit must be paid to those black Americans who succeeded against all odds. That alone is sufficient to validate the legacy of the black American community to not only survive but to engage the competition and succeed. Of all the socioeconomic avenues that were closed, there remained a few were, for the most part, that were always open. Those positions were preachers, morticians, beauty salons operators, barbers, and burial insurance agents. Other major fields of opportunity substantially open before the Civil Rights movements were sports and musical entertainment.

In these two examples, the logic and practicality for the "watering hole" solution as expressed earlier is borne true. For even though the black American community did not arrive at the metaphoric watering holes, those engaged in sports and music, even though these fields were already fully occupied by others, were still able to reach the watering hole and become amply rewarded. In response to this, some black American magazine or other publication should create an annual man—or woman-of-the-next-generation perspective. Such a characterization would be a model for young black Americans to emulate in the next generation. During the past twenty generations, the black American community withstood 114 years of enslavement under authority of the British government and an additional ninety years of enslavement under authority of the American government. For the following 103 years, white supremacist terrorists terrorized these generations of black Americans.

With so much historical trauma, is it any wonder that the nineteenth generation (1966–1995) of black Americans, the first post-Jim Crow generation, appears frustrated in their socioeconomic direction? Those black Americans born of this generation were the first born into a post-Jim Crow period. Their sociological circumstances are similar to the fourteenth generation of black Americans (1866–1895) the first generation born into the post-enslavement period. In 1964, in the middle of the civil right movement, the United States Congress passed and the president signed, the 1964 Civil Rights Bill. This bill was supposed to guarantee black Americans, access to the place of dreams and also ensure they would have a place in the line, even though two-hundred years of enslavement had delayed their arrival. It was this simple implication that for fourteen years prompted black Americans to go to and remain in college. In lieu of the Horace Greeley cry of "Go West, young man," the era was energized with black Americans urging young people to stay in school and get an education, the argument being that "no matter what happens, you are better off with an education than without one."

8

RACIAL SLURS:
WITHIN AND WITHOUT THE BLACK AMERICAN
COMMUNITY

Racial slurs are words, deeds, images, or behaviors that when communicated to another either voluntarily or involuntarily, have the effect of negating or denigrating the race of another person. The effective property of a racial slur is harassment and it is used against individuals as well as against entire ethnic, or racial groups. In the current climate of sensitivity, racial slurs are more likely to be used by individuals rather than by groups or a collective of individuals. An individual may consciously resort to the use of a racial slur in an effort to accentuate his, or her own sense of self-esteem. Or a person may engage in racial slurs when they are a community that endorses racial slurs as a corporate act. In such a case, the individual employs such slurs as statement of social conformity. The intent and purpose of this chapter is to desensitize those who are more commonly the victims of racial slurs and to cause those who are apt to use them to become more sensitive to their injurious effects.

The chapter provides detailed illustrations for an assortment of racial slurs and suggests as many as three different possible responses. The suggested responses are intended to cause a moment of reflection before reacting to a racial slur. And, the chapter provides three optional responses, or suggestions. The intent is to direct the reader toward an appropriate respond to each incident. The objective of this approach is to limit the emotional trauma that could readily accompany exposure to such slurs. The offensive effect is present regardless as to whether the user of such slurs did so with the intent to offend or his intention was benign. Since, as far into the future as one can reasonably envision, it is extremely likely that racial slurs will continued to be a part of black America's social environment, it is therefore essential that black Americans be provided coping techniques to enable them to deal successfully with this a phenomenon. There is legal recourse for a number of racial slurs, but for the most part, legally prohibited acts of racism or racial indifference constitutes only a small percentage of the racially motivated acts of harassment most black Americans experiences.

This "handbook" of racial slurs should hopefully provide you with a brief and simple codebook of what you should do and should not do. Codifying the kind of responses that are appropriate will enable a black American to safely navigate such offensive, and sometimes painful, incidences such as ethnic jokes that seem to pop up suddenly among your white American associates. Or they will enable one to cope with the predicament of arriving at a restaurant first—or perhaps be already seated—yet see white American patrons who arrived or were seated after you served before you. There are also occasions when you are in the company of white Americans business associates, classmates, friends, or co-workers and hear them make a racially denigrating statement against another black American. Some examples are discussed below.

A RACIAL SLUR

While reading the evening newspaper you encounter an article regarding two young fourth-graders. The two are classmates. One white American and the other is black American. The newspaper article talks about the two girls' friendship, but after its commentary the article quotes the young white American girl as saying, "I don't care about her skin color. I treat her the same as I do my white American friends." It is possible that some might ask where the racial slur in such an innocent comment is? They might even be prepared to comment upon the beauty of a relationship between fourth graders where skin color apparently makes no difference.

The problem with such a statement is that it contains an element of deference that implies, however subtly, that there is something about the white American child that renders her more whole, more qualified, than the black American child. The question is, upon what basis would a fourth grader feel that the skin color of the other fourth grader is something that is within her prerogative to care about? Is there a suggestion that she feels the eligibility of the black American child is hers to dispense?

Would it be the same if the black American child had been quoted as saying of the white American child, "I don't care about her skin color, and I treat her the same as I do my black American friends"?

What Should You Do?

Option 1 – Ignore the whole thing as lacking merit.

Option 2 – Write to the newspaper and express your complaint.

Option 3 – Become more active in civic organizations that would enable you to help shape and influence the way in which other ethnic groups see black Americans.

A RACIAL SLUR

You are passed over for a promotion. You personally believe that the only reason you did not get the promotion is because you are a black American.

What Should You Do?

Option 1 – Commit yourself to work harder and put forth a greater effort the next time.

Option 2 – Become depressed, sullen and resentful.

Option 3 – Initiate action to seek legal redress.

A RACIAL SLUR

You are contemplating a business venture. Accordingly you apply at your local bank for a start-up loan. After some time, the bank loan officer informs you that your loan has been declined. You then learn that the same bank has approved a loan for a white American associate of yours. You are puzzled because you know that his loan application package is not better—and perhaps not as good—as yours.

What Should You Do?

Option 1 – Curse out the bank's loan officer.

Option 2 – File suit against the bank for racial discrimination.

Option 3 – Work to improve your loan package. You should do so while at the same time have a serious talk with your bank loan officer. However, the fault may not lay more with your statistical profile than it does with the bank.

To understand what I mean by statistical profile, let assume that a person, who is an acquaintance of yours, asked you to loan them a particular sum of money. Even if the sum asked for was relatively modest, you would of course be concerned with the person's intention of paying you back. You would want to have confidence that the person borrowing your money would pay you back, or at least have the good intentions of paying you back. On that premise, if you had the money that the person sought, you would probably be willing to make the loan. However, if you had fore knowledge that this particular person had a reputation of borrowing money and not paying it back, you would be less inclined to add your name to such a person's list of creditors.

While this is an extremely simplified version of what this racial slur is all about, it essentially negotiates the same principle. And that principle is, that your reputation as a poor risk has traveled before you. When your bank's loan officer checks the statistical probabilities that you would be able to pay the loan back is when the loan officer rejects your loan application. It essentially has nothing to do with you the person, but rather with you the socioeconomic profile. And that socioeconomic profile said that the bank will be taking a greater risk lending you the money than it would if it loan the same money to almost any other ethnic group. That's because, statistically speaking, as a black American your business failure rate is considerably higher than the business failure rate for almost any other ethnic groups.

A RACIAL SLUR

A racial slur is the use of any denigrating remark by a black American to another black American.

What Should You Do?

Option 1 – Ignore the remark.

Option 2 – Realize that racial slurs from one black American are acceptable and therefore do not be offended.

Option 3 – Treat the person using the racial slur in the same way that you would any other person acting in that fashion. Just because the person using the offensive slur happens to be a black American does not lessen its negative effects. In fact, as stated elsewhere, the uninhibited use of racial slurs within the black American community constitutes a greater danger, primarily because its usage is so widespread and tolerated. The fact of the matter is that it really doesn't matter what the ethnicity of the person using the racial slurs is. The injurious effects of the slur alone are sufficient to warrant its discontinuance. The idea that because racial slurs are being used by fellow black Americans, they are non-injurious, is as fallacious as concluding that friendly fire on a battlefield is somehow not as lethal as hostile fire. Racial slurs should not be tolerated from any source, friend or foe.

A RACIAL SLUR

You are in the bathroom of the place where you work. While sitting on the toilet, you notice various and assorted racial and ethnic slurs. Some of them refer to black Americans but a number of them are in reference to other ethnic groups.

What Should You Do?

Option 1 – Protest the ones that refer to black Americans and leave the others for someone else to protest.

Option 2 – Do nothing. After all, you don't know who wrote the slurs on the wall in the first place.

Option 3 – Report the racial slurs to you company's personnel, human resources, or other department that has cognizance over such issues. Make them aware that you are noting the time and date of your notification and that you expect the offensive slurs to be removed, or painted over.

A RACIAL SLUR

You are reading a newspaper article in the local black American newspaper and you come across this paragraph: "While blacks had lower overall cancer rates, the rates were higher for blacks when age was taken into account."

Option 1 – Take no action because you do not perceive that the paragraph contains racial slurs.

Option 2 – Recognize that the use of the lone and sole word "blacks" to designate black Americans is tantamount to a racial slur. Its use tends to de-personalize rather than describe. Generally, the use of "black

Americans," or black person as a generic designator of black Americans simply represents an effort to designate black Americans but the use of the word "blacks" says something altogether different.

Option 3 – Write to the editor of the newspaper and express your concern that the newspaper is perpetrating a slur against the black American community.

A RACIAL SLUR

For example, let's say that you are listening to the news on your radio when the news reporter makes an announcement that refers to "homosexuals and minorities" as occupying some particular category in a survey.

What Should You Do?

Option 1 – Take no offense, particularly since black Americans were not specifically mentioned in the news account.

Option 2 – Take no notice of it.

Option 3 – Reject any news account as a racial slur in which black Americans are categorized with, or along any morally deficit group of people. The fact that black Americans are not specifically mentioned is irrelevant, anytime the terms "minority" or "minorities" are used in America, the black American community is picked up in the implication. Persons who engage in acts of homosexuality do so at their own choosing, and run the risk of impairing their social acceptance. Although homosexual acts in America have, for the most part, been decriminalized, most Americans still view acts of homosexuality as morally repugnant behavior. Additionally, homosexual behavior, though historically persistent, has nevertheless been traditionally rejected as not contributing to the human agenda and injurious to society as a whole. Consequently then, for a government agency, a news network, or a news broadcast, to have put black Americans, as a minority, in the same category as homosexuals is to cast the black American community via an offensive imagery. Rapists who prey upon women, and murderers who inhabits death row are also, denotatively speaking, minorities. Should black Americans be cast in statistical categories alongside the rapist and the murderer?

In my opinion, this type of negligence on the part of the affected government agencies, news networks and broadcast media, and any other such media constitutes one of the most offensive racial slurs.

A RACIAL SLUR

You are in a party of people, mostly white Americans, and one of them tells an offensive racial joke.

What Should You Do?

Option 1 – Ask him, "Why do you think that was funny?"

Option 2 – Laugh like everyone else.

Option 3 – Tell the joke teller that you don't like racial or ethnic jokes.

A RACIAL SLUR

You and your family are awaiting seating in a restaurant. Then you notice that people who apparently arrived after you and your family are being seated.

What Should You Do?

Option 1 – Compare the number of people in your party to number of people that are in the parties that are being seated. If they are different, do nothing.

Option 2 – If the number of people are the same, then you should ask the maître d' or the seating coordinator for an explanation.

Option 3 – Discretely slip the maître d' or seating coordinator a tip.

A RACIAL SLUR

A fellow employee on your job calls you a racially offensive name.

What Should You Do?

Option 1 – Fight him.

Option 2 – Report the incident to company management.

Option 3 – Ignore the incident altogether.

A RACIAL SLUR

You are seated in a restaurant and notice that people who apparently came in after you are already being served.

What Should You Do?

Option 1 – Pay no particular attention to it.

Option 2 – Inquire of the person assigned to your table as to the circumstances of the apparent discrepancy.

Option 3 – Inform the person assigned to your table that you and your party are leaving because of their lack of attention given you and your party. You should also write the restaurant management.

A RACIAL SLUR

You, a black American, are on a company business trip with a number of fellow employees. You are the only black American. While discussing plans for dinner on a particular evening, a member of the group makes the comment, more or less directed at you, that he had noticed a "soul food" restaurant along the street to the hotel.

What Should You Do?

Option 1 – Thank him for the information, but otherwise ignore it.

Option 2 – Ask if he was interest for himself, or did he presume that you were interest.

Option 3 – Should you become angry and depressed over the incident?

A RACIAL SLUR

You are in a staff meeting and another member of the staff asks you, who are sitting across the table from him, for your opinion regarding some social issue, or media coverage that involved black American issues.

What Should You Do?

Option 1 – Pretend that you didn't hear him/her.

Option 2 – Lie about not having heard the news account.

Option 3 – Freely discuss the issue with him and any others that express interest in it.

A RACIAL SLUR

It's break time. You are sitting in the company cafeteria. A white American female, who works in the same office as you, comes into the cafeteria. Finally, additional people, all white Americans and all of who work in the same office area as you, comes into the cafeteria for their break time. Although you feel that you and the rest of the people in the office have a good relationship, the group coming into the cafeteria all go to the table where the female employee is sitting.

What Should You Do?

Option 1 – Just continue your break where you are sitting.

Option 2 – Go over to the table where they are sitting and join them.

Option 3 – Just observe how racist rednecks are.

A RACIAL SLUR

There are ten to fifteen people, about as many women as men, working in the same department where you work. It's your understanding that all of you get along quite well together. You take breaks together; generally sit around the same tables at lunchtime and, generally, your family and theirs sit together during the annual company picnic.

However, today at break-time Mike, one of the guys in the department, asked you if you were planning to attend the Carol's, one of the female office worker's, up coming wedding. You knew that Carol was getting married, but since you hadn't received an invitation you weren't sure of the date. Mike says that the wedding is this coming Saturday and as far as he knows, everybody in the department had already received their invitations.

What Should You Do?

Option 1 – Do you ask Carol about your invitation?

Option 2 – Ignore it.

Option 3 – Get angry with Carol and the rest of the people in the department for leaving you out.

A RACIAL SLUR

You are standing in the cashier line at the grocery store. The people ahead of you appear to be moving through the register at a more or less regular pace. The cashier is routinely approving the checks that are being writing by the shoppers ahead of you. However, when you arrive at the register and present your check, the value of which is same as the price of items you're buying, the cashier summons the store manager to approve your check. Without any significant delay though, he arrives and courteously approves your check.

What Should You Do?

Option 1 – Just ignore it.

Option 2 – Discuss the issue with the cashier.

Option 3 – Give the cashier and the store manager a piece of your mind.

A RACIAL SLUR

There are ten to fifteen people working in the same department where you work. It's your understanding that all of you get along quite well together. You take breaks together, and generally sit around the same tables at lunchtime. However, during break-time one Monday, you over hear two of the guys you work with, discussing some of the antics that occurred, on the previous Friday, at one of the employees' nearby watering holes. After a few well-placed and discreet questions, you learn that most of the guys in the office were at this particular place on the previous Friday after work. You were not told about the plans to meet up there.

What Should You Do?

Option 1 – Should you ask why they didn't bother to tell you that they were going out on that Friday evening.

Option 2 – Should you simply invite yourself the next time.

Option 3 – Get angry and tell a few of them off.

A RACIAL SLUR

You work in an office with five other people. You are the only black American in the office. On this particularly Tuesday morning, two of the women, Vickie and Ellie, are discussing problems they are having with their respective cars. Vickie says that she would put her car in the shop if she had a way to get to work. You and Vickie live in the same general area. Sometimes when you have been coming to work in the morning, you and Vickie have greeted each other while you waited for a traffic signal.

What Should You Do?

Option 1 – Ignore the conversation.

Option 2 – Offer to give Vickie a ride.

Option 3 – Assume that Vickie doesn't want to ride with you because she is obviously a redneck racist.

A RACIAL SLUR

On Monday morning, everybody in the office in back from a long weekend. In discussions about the weekend, one of the guys remarks about the great tan one of the ladies in the office has. She acknowledges his comment and says, "If I'd stayed on the beach any longer, I would have been almost as dark as Michele," referring to you.

What Should You Do?

Option 1 – Ignore her remark.

Option 2 – Tell her how beautiful she would have been become.

Option 3 – Consider it a redneck racist remark, and make her aware that you resented it.

A RACIAL SLUR

You and two other guys from the office are on an out-of-town business trip. After picking up your bags in the airport, the three of you go over to the rental car agency. The group manager picks up the rental car and will be the driver. As you and the other employee approach the car, you notice that it has only two seats in the front.

What Should You Do?

Option 1 – Walk faster so that you can sit in the remaining front seat.

Option 2 – Have absolutely no concern as to whether you sit in the front or back seat.

Option 3 – Make a humorous comment as to how you don't sit in the back anymore, and rush to sit in the front.

A RACIAL SLUR

You are on an out-of-town business trip with three other guys, none of whom are black Americans. You meet with your customer's representatives in the company's conference room. One of the members of the other party is also black American. Do you make any effort to engage the black American in any outside conversation?

What Should You Do?

Option 1 – Yes, it would be appropriate.

Option 2 – No, it would not be appropriate.

Option 3 – Yes, if the occasion warrants it.

A RACIAL SLUR

You are on break with the guys from your office. As you approach the table with a cup of coffee, one of the guys, is berating the department's boss. Among the things he says are that the boss is stupid and that he only got the job because of affirmative action. The boss, with whom you feel you work well, is also a black American.

What Should You Do?

Option 1 – Join in with your fellow employee in berating the boss.

Option 2 – Challenge your fellow employee to stop talking like that.

Option 3 – Nothing.

A RACIAL SLUR

You are talking to one of the guys in the office and he casually mentions that he has become a new grandfather. As you and he continue talking, he takes out his wallet to show you a picture of his new grandchild. As he displays the child's pictures, he identifies other peoples pictures and when he identifies his wife, you are struck by the fact that she is a black American.

What Should You Do?

Option 1 – Do you display any sign that you recognize that she's a black American.

Option 2 – Do you ignore it as though you didn't notice.

Option 3 – Do you inquire about why he married a black American woman?

A RACIAL SLUR

You are sitting a table with a number of white American co-workers. At the next table, are two black American women and one of them is telling the other, in a rather loud voice, about the date she had had the night before. The people at your could over hear her saying things like, "...girl, I told that nigger that...," etc."

What Should You Do?

Option 1 – Pretend to ignore the conversation.

Option 2 – Politely ask her to tone down her voice.

Option 3 – Move your party to another table.

A RACIAL SLUR

You and some your co-workers, all white Americans, are having your pictures taken at the company's annual picnic. You realize that the lady taking the snapshot probably has the exposure set for the white American guys and thus will show you as dark and featureless.

What Should You Do?

Option 1 – Do you tell her to change the exposure.

Option 2 – Do you do nothing, and let nature takes its course.

Option 3 – Do you refuse to have your snapshot taken.

A RACIAL SLUR

You are sitting in a meeting in which a fellow worker, who is also a black American, is being berated in a rather unkind manner by his supervisor. Some of the supervisor's comments come awfully close to racial harassment.

What Should You Do?

Option 1 – Leave the matter to the person being berated.

Option 2 – Meet with the supervisor after the meeting and suggest to him that, in your opinion, you think he went a bit too far in his remarks.

Option 3 – Meet with the employee being berated and counsel him regarding his rights.

A RACIAL SLUR

You are in the presence of several of your co-workers, one of whom is telling the other about a litter of puppies that his dog gave birth to. In the course of the conversation, he mentioned that three of the puppies have spots and two of them are brownish and black American. And then he says, "One of them is just as pretty as he can be, and he's just as black as Johnny over there (motioning to you)."

What Should You Do?

Option 1 – Ignore him.

Option 2 – Not be offended by the comment.

Option 3 – Report him to management for making an offensive racial comment.

A RACIAL SLUR

As two people approach you they are discussing a black cat that apparently crossed their path while they were returning from lunch. As they approach your workstation, one of them, says, here's another "black cat," obviously applying the slang interpretation of the word "cat" to you.

What Should You Do?

Option 1 – Ignore them.

Option 2 – Consider that the remark does not warrant a response.

Option 3 – Report them for making an offensive racial comment.

A RACIAL SLUR

You are in an office in which a potluck luncheon is being planned. As the list of what to bring goes around the office and when it arrives at you desk, the only remaining item is for a watermelon.

What Should You Do?

Option 1 – Bring a watermelon.

Option 2 – Refuse to bring anything.

Option 3 – Trade with someone else.

A RACIAL SLUR

A group of your fellow employees are in your office discussing the plans for a potluck luncheon. As the discussion come to a close one of the participants says, more or less jokingly, "I vote that John (which is you) bring in the watermelon.

What Should You Do?

Option 1 – Bring a watermelon.

Option 2 – Simply ignore the remark.

Option 3 – Challenge the individual for the remark.

A RACIAL SLUR

During a meeting in the office, it is determined that a couple of people need to visit one of you company's suppliers. But because the supplier's factory is located in South Los Angeles, in an area of the city that has a reportedly high incident of gang shootings. Someone in the meeting suggest that you be selected to visit that site.

What Should You Do?

Option 1 – Decline his suggestion.

Option 2 – Ignore his suggestion.

Option 3 – Report his comment to his supervisor.

A RACIAL SLUR

You are a student in a particular class. When you arrive, there are only a few people in the classroom; however, as other students arrive, they all sit around and away from you in such a manner that you are isolated in the middle of the classroom.

What Should You Do?

Option 1 – Move into an area when other students are sitting.

Option 2 – Stay where you are.

Option 3 – Consider that the students are all racist rednecks and drop the class.

A RACIAL SLUR

You are a student, and the teacher asks the class to assemble into small groups for a special project. While all the students are picking and selecting their group, no one is coming to ask you to join their group.

What Should You Do?

Option 1 – Move around and seek to join someone's group.

Option 2 – Stay alone and see who will come to you.

Option 3 – Consider that the students are all racists rednecks and drop the class.

A RACIAL SLUR

You are approximately the fifth person in line at the school cafeteria. Suddenly a white American ahead of you allows two other white Americans to enter the line ahead of you.

What Should You Do?

Option 1 – Ignore them.

Option 2 – Concentrate more on the class you'll attend after lunch break.

Option 3 – Make a fuss about what happened.

A RACIAL SLUR

You are in the registration line at the local college. While in line, you notice that the person at the window makes a considerable effort to assist those students who have problems with their registration papers. However, when you arrive at the window, she takes a quick look at your papers, smiles at you, and informs you that your documents are not in order and that you will have to go back to your last station to get your papers corrected. You are not sure, but you're almost certain that the person ahead of you had the exact same problem but had the difficulty resolved at her window.

What Should You Do?

Option 1 – Demand to know why she's sending you back when she assisted your predecessor.

Option 2 – Ignore your suspicions and return to the previous station to have your documents corrected.

Option 3 – Consider the registrar to have been a bigot and drop out of the school.

A RACIAL SLUR

Your child is seven years old. He informs you that one of his schoolmates who is a white American, asks if she could feel his hair.

What Should You Do?

Option 1 – Tell your seven-year-old that it's okay for his classmate to feel his hair.

Option 2 – Tell your seven-year-old to tell her that people don't go around feeling other people's hair.

Option 3 – Should you become so emotional over the incident such that you confront your child's teacher, and perhaps the classmate's parents, over what you consider a racial issue?

A RACIAL SLUR

Your ten-year-old daughter informs you that one of her classmates, who are white Americans, asks why she wears her hair braided up all the time?

What Should You Do?

Option 1 – Tell your ten-year-old to tell her classmate anything she wants.

Option 2 – Tell your ten-year-old to tell her that braids are a common hairstyle among black Americans.

Option 3 – Initially, become angry over the little girl's question. Then, become concerned over your daughter's personal feelings about being perceived as different and toward fitting in with the other girls in her class, a large number of whom have straight hair. However, reflecting over the nature of situation, you arrive at a solution: You will tell your daughter to tell her nosy classmate that, however she wears her hair, it is none of her business. Or perhaps you suddenly become conscious of the fact that this question, or thousands or perhaps millions like it, has probably confronted every black American child at one time or another. And, that every black American parent has had to provide some kind of an answer for his or her children. It occurs to you that, with all the hair care products on the market and with the wide availability of professional beauty salons, it isn't necessary to answer that question. So, even with the increased expenses and extra effort on your part, you will begin taking your daughter to the beauty salon.

A RACIAL SLUR

You child is eight years old. She informs you that one of her white American classmate asked her, "Are you black all over?"

What Should You Do?

Option 1 – Tell your eight-year-old to tell the classmate, yes.

Option 2 – Ignore your eight-year-old.

Option 3 – Tell your eight-year-old to ask her classmate if she's white all over.

A RACIAL SLUR

Your child is seven years old. One evening she mentions to you that, one of her classmates had asked her if she were a "nigger."

What Should You Do?

Option 1 – Go to the school and speak with the teacher regarding the incident.

Option 2 – Ignore your seven-year-old.

Option 3 – Contact the child's parents.

A RACIAL SLUR

Your child is nine years old. Their drama class is presenting play for the end of the semester. One evening, your nine-year-old informs you that the teacher has asked her to play the role of the maid in the play. She will be the only black American in the play.

What Should You Do?

Option 1 – Inform your nine-year-old that it's okay.

Option 2 – Tell your nine-year-old not to do so.

Option 3 – Meet with the teacher to discus the issue.

A RACIAL SLUR

Your daughter is in an all-white American class. She is thirteen years old and complained to you that when her class has dances none of the white American boys dance with her.

What Should You Do?

Option 1 – Take her out of the school.

Option 2 – Provide a dancing partner for her.

Option 3 – Explain the extent that racism is prevalent in this country.

A RACIAL SLUR

You child is twelve years old. Her class project is putting on an ethnic lunch. What do you do for her.

What Should You Do?

Option 1 – Prepare a sweet potato pie.

Option 2 – Submit no dish.

Option 3 – Prepare a dish of black-eyed peas.

A RACIAL SLUR

You share an office cubicle with two other co-workers. You have noticed that they frequently refer to each other as "boy."

What Should You Do?

Option 1 – Nothing.

Option 2 – Become upset over their antics

Option 3 – Ask them to discontinue the practice.

A RACIAL SLUR

One of your co-workers seems to make it a habit to use street language whenever he addresses you. (Other than that, you feel confident that the employee is sincere and does not mean to be offensive.)

What Should You Do?

Option 1 – Play along with him.

Option 2 – Inform him that you do not appreciate what he does.

Option 3 – Should you become angry and depressed?

A RACIAL SLUR

Fellow workers discussing their weekend are talking about what they did. One of the employees spent considerable time on the beach, and it is apparent in the deeply browned suntan that she has. One of the other workers comments that she is almost as dark as you (a black American) are.

What Should You Do?

Option 1 – Disregard her comment.

Option 2 – Enter into the humor of the remark.

Option 3 – Become offended and depressed that they are all racists rednecks.

A RACIAL SLUR

You are sitting in the conference room with a number of other people while waiting for a meeting to begin. While waiting, one of the guys around the table asks, "Chuck, tell that joke to Steve that you told us yesterday!" Chuck and Steve are both white Americans, you are the only black American in the group. When asked to repeat the joke, Chuck looks directly at you and remarks that you might not appreciate the joke.

What Should You Do?

Option 1 – Insist that he tell the joke anyway.

Option 2 – Affirm the fact that you would not like to hear the joke.

Option 3 – Become angry and leave the conference room.

A RACIAL SLUR

You are driving to or from work. You happen to interfere with a car carrying several people. Although the incident is not entirely your fault, one of the passengers in the other car yells "Can't you see, nigger?" While you didn't recognize them, as the car pulls away from you, you remember that you have seen the personalized license plates parked in the company parking lot where you work.

What Should You Do?

Option 1 – Ignore the incident.

Option 2 – Personally confront the offenders.

Option 3 – Report them to their boss.

A RACIAL SLUR

Oftentimes, at the place where you work, the conversation comes around to the issue of civil rights. Usually when this occurs, one of the guys will ask, "what do you people want from us?"

What Should You Do?

Option 1 – Tell him what black Americans want from him.

Option 2 – Placate him with some nonsensical reply.

Option 3 – Ignore him.

A RACIAL SLUR

Your child is seven years old. On a particular day, she wore her hair in braids. During play period, the braids became loosened and rather disorderly. In response to that, she tells you that one of her classmates told her that she looked like the "Our Gang" character Buckwheat.

What Should You Do?

Option 1 – Tell your seven-year-old to ignore the incident.

Option 2 – Don't answer your seven-year-old.

Option 3 – Tell you seven-year-old to act as though she doesn't know who Buckwheat was.

A RACIAL SLUR

You child is nine years old. She told you that one of her classmates, a nine-year-old white American student, asked her if she were a Black Muslim.

What Should You Do?

Option 1 – Tell your nine-year-old to answer the child yes, if she is a Black Muslim. And tell her to answer no, if she is not.

Option 2 – Tell your nine-year-old to ignore the student.

Option 3 – Direct your nine-year-old to say that she doesn't know what a Black Muslim is.

A RACIAL SLUR

Your seventeen-year-old daughter has been using a skin bleaching cream.

What Should You Do?

Option 1 – Nothing.

Option 2 – Caution her regarding any chemical side effects.

Option 3 – Tell her that to bleach her skin is to reject her race.

A RACIAL SLUR

You learn that your seventeen-year-old son is dating a white American girlfriend.

What Should You Do?

Option 1 – Nothing.

Option 2 – Discourage him.

Option 3 – Encourage him.

A RACIAL SLUR

Your fifteen-old-son has asked if its okay for him to get his hair permed.

What Should You Do?

Option 1 – Give him permission to do so (at his expense).

Option 2 – Advise him against it.

Option 3 – Tell him that to perm his hair is to reject his race.

A RACIAL SLUR

Your are the department manager. Your secretary has just shown a customer representative into your office. At the time that they entered, you were in a discussion with one of your subordinates. However, before the secretary could introduce the representative to you, he made the assumption that your subordinate, who is a white American, is the department manager and proceeded to introduce himself.

What Should You Do?

Option 1 – Get angry and depressed over the incident.

Option 2 – Ignore the incident (perhaps getting a good chuckle over the representative's subsequent embarrassment).

Option 3 – Accuse the representative of racism and report him/her to his company.

A RACIAL SLUR

You routinely buy expensive clothes and you dress accordingly. However, the people in the office where you work, your own boss included, do not give much consideration to the clothes they wear. They tend to wear regular, less expensive clothing.

What Should You Do?

Option 1 – Should you dress down so as not to appear different?

Option 2 – Continue to dress in the same fashion that you've always dressed.

Option 3 – Attempt to shame the others into improving their dress fashions.

A RACIAL SLUR

Your co-worker and officemate is talking on the telephone. Although you are not particularly listening to him, you overhead him on the phone saying "I don't care how you fix it, I just don't want to have to deal with that 'black bastard' again."

What Should You Do?

Option 1 – Ignore what you heard and make no response.

Option 2 – Ask the co-worker not to use such words in your presence.

Option 3 – Tell him that you consider that to have been an offensive remark.

A RACIAL SLUR

You are twenty-seven years old and unmarried. You work in a relatively small company. Often the boss's twenty-two-year-old daughter comes into the office to help with some of the filing. You are sure that she is making subtle passes at you.

What Should You Do?

Option 1 – Ignore her.

Option 2 – Pursue her advances.

Option 3 – Ask her to refrain from making such suggestive advances.

A RACIAL SLUR

Two co-workers are engaged in a conversation near your desk. As you sit at your desk, your back is toward them but you can easily hear their conversation. One of the men says to the other, "Look man, since I started to work here, there's one thing I've learned. If you want to get ahead in this company, you have got to kiss ass." Then, engaging you into the conversation, he says to you, "Tyrone, I'd shine my bosses shoes to get ahead, wouldn't you?" He then mimics a "Yessir, boss" kind of routine.

What Should You Do?

Option 1 – Make no reply, just ignore him.

Option 2 – Answer him as to whether you would shine your bosses shoes.

Option 3 – Inform him that you consider his remarks to be offensive.

A RACIAL SLUR

A woman in your office mentions that she wishes she had a big butt like a black American woman has

What Should You Do?

Option 1 – Ignore the remark.

Option 2 – Agree with her that it would be good.

Option 3 – Disagree with her that it would be good.

A RACIAL SLUR

You go into Bob Bowers office to retrieve some papers that he has instructed you to pickup. While you are at his desk, Guy Danforth comes into the office and says, "Bob you sure have changed since the last time I saw you."

What Should You Do?

Option 1 – Ignore his remark. But follow up with a remark such as, "Oh, Guy, I'm glad you're here, I need to see you about those work orders."

Option 2 – Ignore him and make no reply.

Option 3 – Make some rhetorical remark like, "Yes, we all change as we get wiser."

A RACIAL SLUR

You go into Frank Spenser, a white American co-worker's office to retrieve some papers that you'd loaned him. Frank is not there, but while you are gathering up your documents from his desk, Howard Menks, who is also white American and is one of your co-workers, comes into the office. In a faked mistaken identity manner, Howard says to you, "Frank, you've got to stay out of the sun, good buddy—you're way too tan already."

What Should You Do?

Option 1 – Ignore his remark and go on to discuss things of official interest.

Option 2 – Give him a piece of your mind.

Option 3 – Engage the joke, and reply in words like, "Yeah, you're right, good buddy. I'm going to have to do just that."

A RACIAL SLUR

It's Monday morning. You and other co-workers are called into a meeting with the department manager. When he enters the room, he glances around briefly and declares, "Damn, it looks like you guys got a better tan than I did this weekend. I stayed out in the sun so long, I thought I'd bake."

What Should You Do?

Option 1 – Hear his remarks, but otherwise have no particular thoughts about them.

Option 2 – Ignore his remarks.

Option 3 – Be offended by his remarks.

A RACIAL SLUR

You are walking along the street and as a particular car passes you, someone in the car yells out, "Hurry up, nigger."

What Should You Do?

Option 1 – Ignore them.

Option 2 – Yell back at them.

Option 3 – Should you become angry and depressed over the incident?

A RACIAL SLUR

You've purchased a new car. You are in the process of describing it to some of the guys at work. As you mention that the car is black with a black leather interior, one of the guys remarks, "Smitty, how do you find yourself in an all black car?"

What Should You Do?

Option 1 – Ignore him.

Option 2 – Answer him with a rhetorical, "The same way you would in an all-white car."

Option 3 – Inform him that you consider that a redneck, and thus racist, remark.

A RACIAL SLUR

You participate in an office potluck. You bring cauliflower dip, however as people begin to leave, one of the women, an older woman, comes up to you and compliments you on the fried chicken dish.

What Should You Do?

Option 1 – Accept her compliment without reply.

Option 2 – Inform her that you did not bring the fried chicken.

Option 3 – Make no reply.

A RACIAL SLUR

Your son Donald is eleven years old. His nine-year-old brother Kenny has a much lighter skin color. One evening Donald tells you that white American kids at the school where he and Kenny attends often ask him, "How can you and Kenny be brothers and your skin is so much darker than his?"

What Should You Do?

Option 1 – Tell him to ignore the students because they're just little bigots.

Option 2 – Explain the details of how skin color variations occur among black Americans in much the same manner as hair and eye colors varies among white Americans.

Option 3 – Ignore your eleven-year-old's questions.

A RACIAL SLUR

You are a high school student. One day you as you go to open your locker, you notice that someone has scratched the word "nigger" into the paint on the locker door.

What Should You Do?

Option 1 – Just ignore it.

Option 2 – Report it to the principal or other school official.

Option 3 – Report it to the principal or other school official, and insist that the perpetrator(s) be expelled from school.

A RACIAL SLUR

You are a high school student. You are rather tall but you have no interest in sports. Mainly because of your height, other students—particularly white American students—joke or make innuendos about your not being a basketball player.

What Should You Do?

Option 1 – Ignore them.

Option 2 – Tease or joke back at them.

Option 3 – Treated it as normal humor since you do, after all, represent the stereotypical image of a basketball player.

A RACIAL SLUR

You are listening to the radio in you car as you drive alone the freeway. In a particular program you hear them report that black Americans and Mexican-Americans accounts for XX percent of the AIDS cases in the United States.

What Should You Do?

Option 1 – Simply accept the information as is stated on the radio.

Option 2 – Call or write the radio station and inform them that, by all indications, their reporting of the impact AIDS is having upon black Americans biased against black Americans. Inform them that the bias occurs not in the numbers themselves, but in the presentation of the data. Inform them that the XX percent figure should more appropriately be reported as the percentage of persons of a certain socioeconomic strata accounting for XX percent of the country's AIDS cases. Inform them that races don't get AIDS—people do. And people with certain specific types of behavior get it more than others. Explain that it is mostly those people—those with certain behavior patterns—no matter what their race, who are at the highest risk for getting the AIDS virus. Inform them that, generally speaking, similar data collected on any ethnic group in the same socioeconomic circumstances will tend to reflect similar rates of AIDS infection.

Option 3 – Simply turn the radio off, or change the stations.

A RACIAL SLUR

You are listening to the radio in you car as you drive alone the freeway. In a particular program you hear them report that black Americans account for XX percent of those on welfare.

What Should You Do?

Option 1 – Simply accept the information as factual.

Option 2 – Call or write the radio station and inform them that, by all indications, their reporting is misleading and biased against black Americans because it attributes the race of the welfare recipients as the causal factor, rather than their socioeconomic circumstances. Inform them that similar data collected on any ethnic group in the same socioeconomic circumstances will generally reflect a similar welfare-recipient percentage.

Option 3 – Turn the radio off or change the station.

A RACIAL SLUR

You are reading the newspaper. A particular article states that X percent of white American youths drop out of high school before graduating and that three times as many (X percent) black Americans youths will drop out of school before graduation.

What Should You Do?

Option 1 – Simply accept the information as factual.

Option 2 – Call or write the newspaper and inform them that, by all indications, their reporting is misleading and biased against black Americans because it attributes the race of the high school student as the causal factor for their dropping out of school, rather than their socioeconomic circumstances. Inform them that similar data collected on any ethnic group in the same socioeconomic circumstances would generally reflect a similar dropout rate. For the sake of simplicity, envision a socioeconomic environment in which all affluent and well-educated people are referred to as "informed" and all poor and undereducated people are referred to as "uninformed." Now, with these different labels in mind, let's revisit that same setting. You are reading the newspaper and in a particular article you read that X percent of the "informed" American youths drop out of high school before graduating and that three times as many, or X percent, of all "uninformed" Americans youths will drop out before they graduate. Similarly, the newspaper article should convey only the information communicated and not the biases of the research or reporting team members.

Option 3 – Cancel your subscription.

A RACIAL SLUR

You are in the company of black Americans when the discussion turns to the condition of our inner cities. Someone says that "black-on-black" crime is clear evidence that black Americans do not respect each other.

What Should You Do?

Option 1 – Ignore the person who said it.

Option 2 – Agree with the person who said it.

Option 3 – Inform that person that people who commit crimes commit them against people they see and not against those they don't see. The logic of this rather inane assertion is that black Americans who commit crimes do so against the people who live within their crime area. Since the crimes referred to occur generally within the inner city, then it is logical that the victims of these crimes would be other black Americans who also live in the inner city. In this socioeconomic activity, there is parity among the different ethnic groups. White American criminals commit crimes against white Americans, Vietnamese criminals commit crimes against Vietnamese people, and Korean criminals commit crimes against Koreans. Even family members commit more crimes against one another than against people outside of the home.

A RACIAL SLUR

You are reading your local newspaper when you come upon the following in an article: "The net financial worth of black Americans in the state averages $9,359, compared with $44,980 for white Americans. More than a third of black American men in California grow up in poverty, the study found. About thirty-one percent of black American families in California make less than $15,000 a year, compared to sixteen percent of white Americans and a quarter of Latino families. Conversely, white American and Asian families are three times more likely than black Americans to earn more than $100,000 a year." The slur implied in this report is that these data reflect from some socio economically factor that is uniquely limiting to black Americans as a result simply of they were black Americans, rather than that they were unskilled and under educated. As we did earlier, let us again envision the same report where the ethnic labels have been replaced by socioeconomic labels. And, as we did before, let us now revisit a rewrite of that same news report:

<u>Example #1</u>: You are reading your local newspaper when you come upon the following: "The net financial worth of poor and undereducated Americans in the state averages $9,359 compared with $44,980 for affluent and educated Americans. More than a third of poor and undereducated Americans in the state of California grow up in poverty, the study found. About fifty-six percent of the poor and undereducated American families in the state make less than $15,000 a year compared to sixteen percent of affluent and educated Americans families. Conversely, affluent and educated families are three times more likely than poor and undereducated families to earn more than $100,000 a year."

<u>Example #2</u>: You are reading your local newspaper when you come upon the following article: "The net financial worth of Poor Richard's children averages $9,359 compared with $44,980 for John Q. Well-Educated's children. More than a third of Poor Richard's children in the state of California grow up in poverty, the study found. About fifty-six percent of Poor Richard's children in the state make less than $15,000 a year compared to sixteen percent of the children of John Q. Well-Educated. Conversely, John Q. Well-Educated's children are three times more likely than Poor Richard's children to earn more than $100,000 a year."

These revisions remove race or ethnicity from the report and allow the under girding data upon which the misinformation is founded to surface. The second example of the revised versions also permits the reader to see that the statement disregards the obvious to assault the less obvious. Of course the children of the affluent and educated families will have a greater earning potential than the children of poor and undereducated families. That's what the news report should have said. However, the report could have gone on to cite the percentages of the different groups considered to be undereducated.

What Should You Do?

Option 1 – Simply accept the information in the article as it was published.

Option 2 – Call or write the newspaper and inform them that a more correct and unbiased article would not rest solely upon its racial indictment and would have more than likely been written along these lines: "The net financial worth of persons in the state with less than XX years of education averages $9,359 compared with $44,980 for persons with XXXX years of education. More than a third of the persons in California with less than XX years of education grow up in poverty, the study found. About thirty-one percent of the families in California with less than XX years of education make less than $15,000 a year, compared to sixteen percent of the families with XXXX years of education and a quarter of those families with XXX years of education. Conversely, those families with XXXX years of education and those families with XXX years of education are three times more likely than those persons with XX education to earn more than $100,000 a year. (Note: Because more black Americans fall into these Xs levels of education, they are affected by these disproportions as represented by these percentages)."

Option 3 – Explain to your children why such articles are so skewed, and teach them to disregard such racially biased materials.

A RACIAL SLUR

You are with a group of members from your church, all black Americans. Some of the men are discussing the recent success of the local high school football team. Someone in the assembly says, "Now you know that team wasn't going to beat our boys." Another adds, "Weren't all the boys on the other team white Americans? I don't think I saw a single black American player. Now how do you think they were going to win against all those black guys on our team?"

What Should You Do?

Option 1 – Ignore the conversation.

Option 2 – Inform the speakers that they are engaging in racial stereotypes.

Option 3 – Agree with them.

A RACIAL SLUR

Your study of African history convinces you that the African people in and around North Africa were more industrious and civilized than the African people south of the equator.

What Should You Do?

Option 1 – Should you just accept the argument that the Africans who lived farther south were not smart enough to establish great civilizations like those of the North?

Option 2 – Accept the premise that the southern Africans were not civilized enough to achieve such accomplishments.

Option 3 – Consider this perspective: Does the fact that the Empire State Building is not in De Moines, Iowa, mean that the people of Iowa are not as smart or as civilized as the people in New York? Or does it mean that since there is no New York-style Madison Avenue in Nashville, Tennessee, the people of Tennessee are less advanced than the people of New York?

Consistent with the apparent tendency of most historians of African history to set the achievements of the people in North Africa apart from the achievements of those in the South, it should be equally reasonable that discussions regarding American history should focus not upon the United States of America, but upon New York, Pittsburgh; or perhaps Detroit. Fair is fair. If historians who write about African history do not see Egypt as Africa, than why should other historians consider New York and California when appraising the industrial growth of America?

A RACIAL SLUR

You are overwhelmed by the news media's coverage of street gang violence. You see all too many young black American men, their hands cuffed behind them, being taken from police cars, held in jails, sentenced in courtrooms, and marched off to prisons. You may not ponder the question, but their high visibility does constitute a slur against black Americans.

What Should You Do?

Option 1 – Ignore the news media's saturation coverage?

Option 2 – Accept the prevailing notion that civilizing morality has broken down within the ranks and families of the gang members.

Option 3 – Perhaps you would like to consider this perspective: Inner-city street gangs are not engaged in a social or cultural activity. Rather, they are engaged in an economic activity. By that, I mean that their efforts are not aimed at enlightening the rest of the nation—or anyone else for that matter—regarding issues of morality, culture, or social values. As far as the evidence supports, they are engaged in these activities solely for the profit. Recognizably, there are kids who join these gangs for more esoteric reasons, but the modus operandi of the gang vehicle is to collect money. Reportedly they accomplish their money-raising objective by selling drugs, engaging in prostitution, robberies, shoplifting, and extortion. Since we've established their activities as having an economic goal, what differentiates their activities from that of the Wall Street tycoon who swindled people out of hundreds of millions of dollars? Or from those in the savings and loan fiasco that cost the nation's taxpayers billions of dollars? To contend that these two events are functionally different would be like contending that the aborigine's eating of a plant root dug from the ground is functionally different from the five-course meal from one of Beverly Hills finest restaurants. Of course, we all realize that the horrific component of street gang deaths outweighs by far the loss assets or revenues from stock investments. But beyond those differences, if one represents a breakdown in civil morality, then so does the other.

A RACIAL SLUR

You are with some of your office buddies at break time having coffee, donuts, and conversation. One of the guys, normally a well-intentioned person, is recounting events from one of his previous jobs. However, in the course of his recollections, he begins talking about incidents involving black Americans employees from that previous job having to do with some of their antics—incidents like the humorous, if embarrassing, comments made by a black American who was found asleep in the bathroom; another involving the equally-humorous and equally embarrassing comments made by the black American employee who came to work drunk; and others dealing with a variety of events including the one about two employees, a man and women, who were found having sex in a broom closet.

What Should You Do?

Option 1 – Get up and leave the table.

Option 2 – Remain at the table and laugh along with the other guys.

Option 3 – Tell him that you would rather he talk about something else.

A RACIAL SLUR

You inadvertently put your pen back into your shirt pocket without replacing its cap. The leaking pen produces a large stain of black ink onto your shirt. Upon seeing the stain, several of your co-workers jokingly ask if you are bleeding, the rude suggestion being that your blood is black like the ink stain, rather than red.

What Should You Do?

Option 1 – Just ignore the person's ignorance.

Option 2 – Inform the co-worker that you consider such a remark racially offensive and perhaps report it to the management.

Option 3 – Join in with your white American co-worker's sense of humor.

A RACIAL SLUR

You are a student in high school. Your parents have taught you the merits of a good education, so you really apply yourself to your studies. You generally get good or exceptional grades; however, when you attempt to be around or associate with the other black American students, they frequently accuse you of trying to be or act "white American."

What Should You Do?

Option 1 – Exaggerate your black Americanism in rhetoric and dress.

Option 2 – Stop or cut back on your studying so that your grades will fall a little.

Option 3 – Just ignore them. If they continue the practice of getting poor grades and you continue to get good or exceptional grades, realizing you'll be better able to explain the merits of studying hard to them in the years to come when they come to you looking a job.

A RACIAL SLUR

You are watching a movie. The setting of the story is an inner-city high school. The story line revolves around problems that the school is having educating its students. Some of the problems are truancy, drugs, dropouts, and teenage pregnancy. As you watch the movie, it suddenly occurs to you that while the black American students who are engaged in drug dealing are cast as violent, streetwise and vulgar, those of other ethnic groups are shown as slick, polished, and mannerly.

On another occasion, you are watching a movie in which a dozen prisoners are being transferred from one prison to another. Among them, three are black Americans and the remainders are either white Americans, or other ethnic minorities. Seated in the police department bus, all the prisoners, although obviously dangerous, are depicted as being generally disciplined except when the camera focuses on one of the black American prisoners, who is depicted as base, extremely dangerous, and threatening.

What Should You Do?

Option 1 – Get up and leave the theater or turn off the television.

Option 2 – Ignore them because they portray what real life is like.

Option 3 – Write, FAX, call, or e-mail your concern to the studio that released the movie saying. that it is your impression the media, both television and the movies, appears to go out of its way to communicate a negative image of black Americans to its viewers. Say that, although the movies do cast some very positive images of black Americans, when the number of positive images is weighed against the number and intensity of negative images, the net result, more often then not, is a demeaning racial slur.

9

MYTHS & MISINFORMATION

*"The great enemy of the truth is very often not a lie—
deliberate contrived and dishonest—but the myth...
persistent, persuasive."*

John F. Kennedy

MYTHS, MISINFORMATION AND THE BLACK AMERICAN COMMUNITY

The black American community is desperately in need of affirming myths. Currently, the wind sock of black American motivation is blowing in the wrong direction due to an assortment of socioeconomic forces which provide a continuous barrage of socioeconomically disarming, negative, denigrating, and demeaning legends, folkloric rhetoric, and undermining myths. Having lost confidence in the myth of the American Dream, or perhaps having never really having developed confidence in it, black Americans have taken a series of paths in search of an effective mythology of their own. In the course of that effort, the black American community has alternately hitched the wagon of its discontent to the mainstream American Dream, to Marcus Garvey's back-to-Africa movement, to professional sports contracts, to the music and entertainment industry, to notions of black supremacy, and to other separatist or black power-type applications. With only limited success resulting from any of these approaches, the black American community subsequently bought into the theme of Dr. Martin Luther King's stimulating and mobilizing "I Have a Dream" speech.

All—including the promises of Dr. King's dream—having failed, black American youths now hang out on various street corners emulating the music and dance routines of Michael Jackson. Or they gather in back-alley lots and shoot hoops, hoping that perhaps one day they will become another Magic Johnson or Michael Jordan. And when they realize that the chance to become another Jackson, Johnson, or Jordan is beyond their grasp, they rally in support of charismatic leaders of social or religious movements. Or perhaps become gang members. Between the 1920s and the 1960s, it was believed that success for black Americans lay in "going up North." By the 1970s, however, it was apparent to most black Americans that "up North" was no promised land either, and that, for the most part, opportunities in the northern cities were as empty of promise as "down South" had been. In the end, none of these efforts has satisfied black America's need for a self-validating belief system. And so the black American community remains in a holding pattern, awaiting the emergence of an affirming or motivating myth or belief system.

AFFIRMING MYTHS

Affirming myths have served as motivation for an assortment of national movements and events. Myths have long been recognized for the influence they have the potential to render. Both myths and legends have also long been acknowledged as vast reservoirs of potential cultural and social motivation. In this regards, author R. W. B. Lewis in *The American Adam* wrote, "A century ago, the image that contrived to embody the most fruitful contemporary ideas was that of the authentic American as a figure of heroic innocence and vast potentialities, poised at the start of a new history." Here Lewis is expressing *The American Adam*'s view that reflects the early American settler's sense of self-esteem and purpose. Freed, as was his perception, by a benevolent providence from the confining drudgery of European traditions, a new American Adam was a new man—in today's vernacular, a brand new model.

Having been given a second chance, the new Adam now sported a shiny new finish, a slick-looking design, with an aerodynamically sculptured form, and he was empowered by the same providential benevolence to castigate the old world—one that had become too consumed by its own ineffectiveness to be relevant to a brand new American Adam. And almost with the effect of putting the concept of this new American Adam into words, the back of the Great Seal of the United States of America contains a Latin phrase commemorating the sentiment of the founding of America, "*annuit coeptis*," meaning "God has smiled on our undertaking." The American Adam is by no means the only myth tapped for its potential energy. Any number of other nations, modern and historical have also drawn upon mythological figures or legends to affect the course of their national agendas. Another American myth, one that perhaps also flowed out of the myth of the American Adam or was certainly enhanced by its presence, was that of Manifest Destiny.

Manifest Destiny surfaced in America during the middle of the nineteenth century and resulted from a mixture of European noblesse oblige and New World's concept of the "noble savage." Adherents to the concept of Manifest Destiny advocated that America had a benevolent obligation to spread its city-of-God imagery throughout the less-developed nations and peoples of the world. The burden of the myth levied upon the young nation an imperialist-like thirst for growth and expansion. With its banners of Manifest Destiny flying high, in the spirit of nationalism if not in fact, America launched an operation of east-to-west expansion. During that period, the U.S. engaged Mexico in a war that resulted in the acquisition of Texas and purchased the Alaskan territory from the Russians. It acquired Oregon from the English and fought the Spanish over western territories that would eventually extend the United States from the Atlantic Ocean all the way to the Pacific Ocean.

The expansion westward served as an impetus for an entirely new genre of American myths. Capping the flavor of this new genre were such published favorites *as The Last of the Mohicans, How the West Was Won,* etc. Whereas the American Manifest Destiny was founded, however tenuously, upon a sense of morality, the potentials of such myths do not necessarily engage morality at all and have the potential to motivate for evil purposes just as easily as for good or moral purposes. Such was the mythical allusion to Aryan supremacy unleashed in Germany when the Nazi came to power. Drawing upon the notion that persons of Aryan stock were somehow superior to other races—and in particularly to the Jews—the Nazis, from 1932 until the war, took control of Germany, a nation that would have been, in today's jargon, classified as a third-world nation. In the course of about ten short years they built it into one of the world's most productive and militarily powerful nations of the 1930s and 1940s. The result of the initiative inspired in the German people by the myth of Aryan supremacy was the modern era's first national program of planned genocide. The propagation of the notion of Aryan supremacy among the German people ultimately resulted in the deaths of millions of innocent people.

Another myth that resulted in a devastating consequence for the holders of the myth was the fifteenth-century empire of the Aztecs in what today is Mexico. Accordingly, the presence of a particular myth or belief among the Aztecs accounts, at least in part, for the Spanish conquistador Hernando Cortez's successes in defeating the Aztec empire with comparatively few military troops. The Aztec god Quetzalcoatl, as the myth contends, upon departing the earth prophesied that he would return one day as a person with white skin. Montezuma, emperor of the Aztec empire, believed that because Cortez and his men had white skin, they were the returning god Quetzalcoatl and not only opened the city up to them but even lauded them with gifts and special entertainment. And so in this instance, the potential of the myth was exploited to diminish rather than enhance. Montezuma's failure to engage Cortez and his troops as military conquerors rather than as *gods* probably cost not only his empire, but also his life.

Finally, on a more practical level, a number of Americans have become familiar over the past few years with the television ads featuring a mythical lonely appliance repairman. Vested in the image of his loneliness is the contention that this particular appliance never, or almost never, needs repairing.

MYTH/MISINFORMATION

It is okay for black Americans to use racial slurs against other black Americans so long as they used only in the presence of other black Americans.

Response

This is an absolute untruth. The use of racial slurs within the black American community is ten times more damaging than its use by persons outside the black American community. The harmful effect of the use of such negative stereotypes undermines the motivation of black American children. It can further be argued that their frequent use within the black American community has had the net effect of building a self-defeating barrier to the aspirations of black Americans over the years. Also, there is reason to believe that the socioeconomic mobility of the black American community has been directly and adversely affected by the undermining properties of such negativism. In much the same manner as the use of street language during a job interview can prevent one from becoming employed, negative language can prevent one from moving from a mind-set of low self-esteem to one of high self-esteem. The sociological paradigm of negativism works on the same principal as the adage that "misery loves company." In the same manner that those in misery will seek to surround themselves with persons of similar circumstances, so do the discouraged and downtrodden love company. The seeds of their discouragement and discontent are sown daily into the hearts and minds of increasing numbers of young black Americans. Over the last generation alone, the parent-to-children conversations of too many black American families have had an injurious effect upon the way black Americans view themselves. And if we are to succeed at attaining socioeconomic parity, the black American community must work ceaselessly to disengage itself from practices that cause injury and to develop appropriate remedies to assuage the damage already done.

Myths or belief systems, as noted previously, are neutral in the application of their potentials. That is, they may be used as effectively to serve as motivational stimuli, to promote positive achievements well as negative results. Regarding the manner in which black Americans are using racial slurs against one another, the application is decidedly in the negative mode. In this application, the offensive components of these racial slurs are diminishing much-needed social momentum within the black American community. They deprive black Americans of personal self-esteem, and thus initiative. From the moment a black American child is old enough to relate to "Sesame Street," he is already conditioned, via intrafamily conversations alone, to believe success for black Americans is aberrational. These conversations introduce such a barrage of negativist impressions into the minds of black American children that by the time the average black American child reaches high school age he is already effectively discouraged. This is because, by that time, he has spent his formative years in a virtual brainwashing of racial negativism. Also by that time, the child is firmly convinced that he is essentially cannon fodder to the socioeconomic environment.

On the other hand, and in an entirely opposite flavor of dinner table conversation, Alex Portnoy says of his Jewish parents that, "The outrage, the disgust inspired in my parents by the gentiles, was beginning to make some sense: the goyim pretended to be something special, while we were actually their moral superiors. And what made us superior was precisely the hatred and the disrespect they lavished so willingly upon us!" The dinner table conversations in the Alex Portnoy's household as portrayed here are obviously much more likely to inspire a sense of motivational self-esteem in Jewish children than would a dinner table conversation of negativism or denigration. In a very similar light then, the dinner table conversations in the average black American home must not reflect a posture of offensive characterization and initiate one of promotional characterization instead.

MYTH/MISINFORMATION

Black Americans are like crayfish, or crawfish, in a bucket, forever pulling down those who would succeed.

Response

Beyond black Americans' liberal use of racial slurs, there are also large numbers of jokes and other race-demeaning metaphors. One such metaphor that has been around for a long time defines black Americans as being like crayfish, or crawfish in a bucket. As the analogy goes, the crayfish, or crawfish are unable to escape because each time one of them gets near the top of the bucket, another one reaches up and pulls it back down. The application argument of the analogy contends that black Americans have not escaped, indeed cannot escape, from poverty because each time a black American is on the verge of climbing out of poverty, another less successful black American will reach up and pull him or her back to the bottom of the socioeconomic bucket. I think a more appropriate interpretation of this phenomenon, to the extent that it applies to the black American community at all, is that unsuccessful black Americans are so desperate to succeed that they, lacking effective tools for their success, do grab onto whatever, or whomever, appears able to aid them.

MYTH/MISINFORMATION

The idea of black Americans competing with white Americans would be like having two runners, one with weights strapped to his ankles and the other without, compete in a foot race.

Response

Another and similarly equally misguiding metaphor depicts the black American community paired in a foot race with the white American community. This image is often used to characterize the disparity between the socioeconomic achievements of white Americans and those of black Americans. The analogy features two runners. One competitor, symbolic of the black American community, runs the race with weights affixed to his ankles. The other, symbolizing the white American community, runs unencumbered. The unencumbered (i.e., white American) runner runs free and without penalty while the weighted runner (i.e., black American) must compete virtually handicapped. This same analogy has been used on occasion to validate the need for affirmative action programs. The contention was that since black Americans were held back by slavery and other racial discrimination, affirmative action or some other compensatory approach was indispensable if black Americans were to achieve socioeconomic parity. The analogy, although reasonable on its face, is fundamentally a sophistry; that is, its conclusions are logically arrived at, but its initial premise is erroneous.

The "weighted ankles" characterization is flawed in at least two of its assumptions: First, it presumes that the foot race is either timed, or that the race will continue forever. Second, in either of the above scenarios, the analogy constitutes a negating racial image because it implies that the black American community, without state-sponsored affirmative action programs, is doomed to lag behind forever. A truer portrayal of the alleged foot race is that it is fundamentally not "a race" at all but rather merely a dash to see who arrives at the finish line, or socioeconomically speaking, at middle-class status, first. In this scenario, the argument being, that if the black American community puts forth a concerted effort, parity is achievable.

MYTH/MISINFORMATION

Black Americans do not stick together.

Response

Another myth in this series of denigrating and disparaging dialogues within the black American community is that black Americans do not stick together. Unlike a number of other immigrant groups in America, the black American community is not distinguished by language, cuisine, religion, or other "old-world" customs or traditions. Therefore, black Americans are not prompted by esoteric considerations to confine themselves to communal enclaves. Those ethnic groups or races that maintain such ties to their native heritage do tend to gravitate toward one another in more of a provincial fashion than black Americans do. As the result of their shared provincialism, those racial or ethnic groups characterized by these features frequently live in environments that are considerably more parochial than those of black Americans. A positive feature of such communities is that they tend to grow their own local economies. For instance, because people living in the community may prefer certain foods items that may not be readily available in regular supermarkets, neighborhood markets will be started to service their food needs. Also, other businesses will open to service other needs, such as native musical instruments and recordings, materials for dance and the arts, and for religious requirements. Also, if the community residents speak a native language, an assortment of social clubs or associations will also be included among the enterprises that will arise to service the community.

Upon observing the unit cohesiveness that apparently exists within these other racial or ethnic groups, it is easy to see why, in comparison, one would draw the conclusion that black Americans do not stick together as other ethnic groups do. But to compare the cohesiveness of the black American community to that of those ethnic groups that, within their Americanism, maintain distinct subsets of native religions, cuisine, languages, traditions, and customs would be like comparing the proverbial apples and oranges. True, a number of black Americans do live in community enclaves similar to those of other ethnic groups; but a difference exists in that residents in these communities are under no restrictions regarding their shopping preferences. They have few, if any, specific ethnic preferences and tend to shop more in concert with market forces than with ethnic preferences. Therefore, to draw the conclusion that, based upon the apparent unity of these other ethnic groups, there is no apparent unity among black Americans constitutes a negativism, or denigrating mythical notion. Had black Americans maintained their native African languages, continued to eat a uniquely African cuisine, lived and taught their children to live in accordance with West African customs and traditions, and maintained former native religious beliefs, then it would be reasonable to expect a normal comparison between black Americans and those races or ethnic groups that do maintain engagement with their native homeland and peoples. But black Americans do not have such ties to their native African homeland. The social and cultural materials used by some ethnic communities to build sub cultural fences are simply not present within the black American community. Consequently, unity among black Americans must be measured by sources other than by comparison to those racial or ethnic groups that have, at the core of their ethnicity, significant cultural and social features that differentiate from the black American community. Black Americans do not speak a native language other than English. For the most part they adhere to religious beliefs consistent with the religious character of America and do not engage in unique religious beliefs peculiar to their native Africa. The diet and cuisine of black Americans are not African but the same as that of other Americans. And other than the subset of customs and traditions that have grown out of the treatment of the black Americans in America, the customs and traditions of black Americans are fundamentally the same as those of all America. It is not esoteric interdependency that prompts black Americans to live in social enclaves; rather, it results from socioeconomic disparity. Generally speaking, there are few ghetto residents who would not immediately trade their ghetto addresses for an address in suburbia. The food that black Americans traditionally refer to as "soul food" was not necessarily developed out of a preference for chitterlings, ham-hocks, and black-eyed peas, but more specifically, because, in the southern states, these were the foods of impoverished people, no matter the skin color. And black Americans who have spent an inordinate amount of their American history at the lower socioeconomic rungs of society have integrated those foods into their traditions in much the same manner as the use of Indian corn and roasted turkey have become the traditional foods for Thanksgiving dinners.

Consequently, if one is to appraise the unity of black Americans, one must first observe the unity of the whole rather than seeking the unity of a subset. The habits and sociological demographic of black Americans do not lend themselves to the subset but rather to the whole. To the degree that features of a subset are present can easily be traced to the role that poverty plays in the habits and behavior of black Americans. Remove socioeconomic impoverishment from the affairs of the black American community and their sociological demography would render their habits and behaviors indistinguishable from that of the national character of America. Fortunately, or unfortunately, whichever is to your choosing, the behavior of black Americans is not prompted by any sufficient residue of any African values, habits, customs, or traditions.

MYTH/MISINFORMATION

A great black American debate exists over who has the darkest skin color and who has the lightest skin color.

Response

The thirty five million people of the black American community consist
of a wide dispersion and assortment of varying skin colors and other features. In fact, skin color variations among people of the black American
community range from people whose skin color is decidedly black on the
one hand to people whose skin is as pale as that of Snow White. Within
the spectrum of skin colors from black to white, those within the black
American community encompass the hues of all the earth's races of people. While black Americans should resist all tendencies to allow skin color
to influence their relationship to one another, it is unlikely that this effort
will be completely successful. Different skin colors are a fact of life. As
such, it will not simply go away. Even if black Americans were still living
in Africa, they would still have to deal with the issue of varying skin colors
or complexions.

Even Europeans have had to entertain the notion of skin color. During the
fifteenth century, a German mapmaker named Martin Benhaim invented
one of the world's first globes. In the area of the globe we now know as
Northern Europe, Benhaim identified the residents of that region of
Europe as "white people." On his globe, Benhaim designated the region as
"Here White People Live." Thus the people we now know as the English,
the French, and the Germans who emerged from such diverse groups as the
Anglo-Saxons, Gauls, and Jutes looked upon the much lighter
Scandinavians as "white people." So it is not just black Americans, but any
group having discernable differences, who must characterize those differences. Consequently, the whole issue regarding skin color is relative.
Consider a white American living and working alongside Kenyans in
Nairobi or alongside Brazilians in Rio de Janeiro. Just being exposed to
what is accepted in those locations as the predominant order of reference, it
would not take very long before the white American would become overly
conscious of just how very white his skin is when compared to that of his
friends and co-workers. The eventual consequence of such awareness might

not necessarily prompt him to darken his skin, but one can be sure that it would certainly prompt him to favor the beach over an environment that offered no sun-tanning possibilities.

And of course, the issue is not simply the fact that the skin color of some black Americans is different than that of other black Americans. The problem does not lie in the differences per se, but resides in the fact that those simple color differences tend to evoke a persistent reaction among the black American community. Thus the issue is not just the distinctions that accompany the differing skin colors, but rather the implications of those distinctions. The stage for managing the differences in skin color, both within the black American community and between black and white Americans, was set during the 1960s when Students for Nonviolence Youth Coordinating Committee (SNYCC), first engaged the, "look at me, I'm black and I'm beautiful" approach to understanding how to be a black American in a nation where people with white skin predominate. If black Americans are successfully to manage the issue of varying skin colors within their own ranks and the presence of white Americans all around them, they must hold onto the essential premise espoused by those students. That is, they must establish themselves as their own point of reference and build their self-esteem from that point onward.

The idea here is that people routinely establish reference points by which they assess their own perspective about different things. Since the skin color of the most prominent and most visibly successful ethnic group in America is predominantly white, there is, of course, a normal tendency for all nonwhite ethnic groups to view white Americans as the basic referent group. And even though such a practice may appear to favor the European appearance over others, such an assertion would be erroneous. Essentially, such behavior on the part of nonwhite ethnic groups would not differ much from similar behavior on the part of white Americans themselves. While they do not engage in this behavior regarding to skin color, with the possible exception of "tall dark and handsome," they very definitely do so regarding hair and eye color. Most white Americans do not naturally have blond hair and blue eyes. Yet they have created a billion-dollar industry for companies that manufacture and market and hair-coloring products and eye-color-altering contact lens. Allowing then, that the issue of skin color among the black American community is a relatively normal phenomenon, the task for the black American community is to not become entangled in the issue of skin color, but to better anchor itself in the heritage and historical legacy of its black American and African ancestry—and to realize that the black American community's schismatic relationship with skin color is fundamentally similar to white American's passion for blond hair and blue eyes.

However, to augment the notion of self-awareness and self-appreciation, particularly among black American youths, the black American community must work aggressively to promote the use of black American models in local, state, and national marketing media. The print, broadcast, and film media must be lobbied to showcase the beauty of black American and African women. I specify women because it is readily apparent that notions of beauty and of things that are beautiful originate with, and are an estate owned by the woman. Thus increased emphasis and exhibition of the beauty of the black-skinned woman will translate into a great commentary upon the image black Americans have of themselves. More and more African and black American women should be encouraged to pursue careers in which their beauty and poise are emphasized. Finally, after all is said and done, the different skin colors that exist within the black American community, and between the black and white American communities, must be seen in their proper context. And in that context it will be readily apparent that differences in skin color are just that—simple differences—having no hierarchical properties, nor otherwise providing a basis for preference.

MYTH/MISINFORMATION

That black American children should not be adopted by white Americans.

Response

Since the increasing numbers of petitions to adopt black American children is largely characterized by improvements in the relation between black and white Americans, it should be deemed a good thing. Had the petitions been made prior to the change in the relationship between the races (of course, the nature of the circumstances would not have allowed that to happen), I would also be inclined to think such adoptions would not have been beneficial. But under the current approach of racial integration, I see the adoption of black American children by white American parents as positive, both for the children and for the black and white Americans.

MYTH/MISINFORMATION

Black American-owned businesses tend to do shoddy work and, more often than not, operate in a less-than-businesslike manner.

Response

Management of a business is nonracial. Shoppers must utilize market forces to influence the quality of service or goods that they purchase from a business. Small neighborhood businesses where there is little competition sometime will tend to take advantage of its unique, noncompetitive market. However, the consumers still have the last word as to whether they will shop at such a business or to look elsewhere. The business acumen of an establishment is generally more influenced by their level of education and their professional training than it is their ethnicity.

MYTH/MISINFORMATION

Black American people are not as attractive as white American people.

Response

It is fitting to invoke the standard maxim, "beauty is only skin deep." However, while beauty may indeed be only skin deep, it is the fault or credit of perception that assigns its merit. More appropriately stated, "Beauty is in the eyes of the beholder." That black Americans tend to accept the European characterization of beauty as a standard makes no statement against the black American community. America, as the pre-eminent world power, has essentially affected all nations' and all peoples' concept of what is acceptable and what is beautiful. People the world over seek to dress and groom themselves to reflect what can only be referred to as the American or European look. The only meaningful difference between the impressions that affect black Americans and those which affect the peoples of other nations is simply that black Americans live, work, and play right in America's midst and are, therefore, more directly affected by its precepts. Nevertheless, it is the natural order of things that the most visibly successful people or nation will be the one other people attempt, more often than not, to emulate. People around the world, from China to Africa, will imitate things American. Some of them will go to extremes, such as surgically altering their eyes to achieve a European look, altering their manner of dress, bleaching or dying their hair, using skin-bleaching products or makeup to modify their complexions, etc.

That black Americans are affected by European notions of beauty is understandable , but that such notions should render them less apprecia-tive of their own beauty makes it offensive to the black American commu-nity. Only a heightened sense of one's own self-esteem can counter the influence of the western ideas of beauty.

MYTH/MISINFORMATION

There is enough racism in America to preclude the success of the black American community.

Response

There are no indicators to suggest there is sufficient racism is America to prevent the black American community from attaining socioeconomic parity. All the elements of legal access for the black American community to achieve socioeconomic parity are already in place. For example, when the flight controls of an airplane have been properly set for takeoff, the airplane has no choice but to go airborne at the appropriate airspeed. I think the same can be said of the black American community. In my opinion, all the proper controls for the black American community to take off have already been set in place. In the same manner that the ailerons, the rudder, the flaps, the slats, and the elevator of the airplane would have been properly set for takeoff, so also Thirteenth, Fourteenth, Fifteenth, and Twenty-fourth Amendments; Executive Orders 8802 and 9981; the 1965 Voting Rights Act; the 1960, and 1964, and 1968 Civil Rights Acts; the 1954 *Brown v. Board of Education* ruling; the substantial reduction in white supremacist terrorist attacks; and the easing of racial tensions have all been properly set to assure the black American community sufficient access for takeoff to socioeconomic parity. All that remains is for the black American community to rally enough motivating self-esteem and educational preparedness to reach takeoff speed.

When I say that there isn't sufficient racism to prevent the black American community's success I am not suggesting that there isn't any more racists in America. Think of it this way, if you decided to drive across country to a family reunion, you would reasonably expect to see any number of traffic accidents along the way. Some of the accidents that you see may even have resulted in serious injuries or fatalities. Yet in spite the accidents that you see, it is extremely unlikely that you will consider the risk too great to continue your trip. Your logic would undoubtedly be that even though there is some risk associated with your journey it is not threatening enough for you to turn back. Racism in America is much the same. We can anticipate, and do readily concede, that in the course of your working life, or profession career, you will encounter racism. The point being though, that the racism you encounter is minute compared to the racism that the previous generations experienced, and thus is not sufficient to discourage you, or any black American, from pursuing the goal or career objective of their choice.

Racism does not necessarily apply to a person who is simply prejudiced. In this context, prejudice is defined as an internal assessment on the part of the beholder or prejudiced person. In that regard, prejudice is defined in much the same manner as one might define the act of lusting. That is, as long as one keeps one's prejudice or lust within oneself, it is tolerable and, to some extent, understandable. However, if one's prejudice or lust is permitted to affect or interfere with the rights and privileges of someone else, then it ceases to be a prejudice and becomes an act of racism. Whereas being prejudiced is not legally culpable, acting on it does constitute a legally culpable act.

MYTH/MISINFORMATION

Black American children do not really want to succeed.

Response

If this were so, how would one explain the presence of young black American children and youths hanging out, as it were, on a thousand different street corners, desperately trying to emulate the music and dance routines of a Michael Jackson in the hopes that they too might become successful? Or the thousands upon thousands of youngsters gathered around the school gyms, the vacant back alley lots, and backyard hoops, hoping against hope that they might become the next Magic Johnson or Michael Jordan. No, the question is not whether young black Americans really want to succeed or not. The real question is, when will black Americans affirm within themselves that the American dream works. That it will secure their success just as effectively as it does the success of young white Americans?

MYTH/MISINFORMATION

All children born of mixed parentage, particularly where one parent is a black American and the other is a white American, are automatically black Americans.

Response

This kind of thinking harks back to the days of antebellum racism and it has no current merit. There are essentially no unilaterally accepted criteria for distinguishing all the members of one racial group from those of some other racial group. Consequently, from a visual point of view, some people from the black American community can look like white Americans and some white Americans can look like black Americans. Establishing the race of a child is a cultural and social election not bounded by science. If a child has one white American parent and one black American parent, the child is whatever race he/she chooses to identify with (notwithstanding that some such children visibly favor one race over the other).

MYTH/MISINFORMATION

The "Man."

Response

The "Man" is a myth born out of the Jim Crow era. Black Americans should refrain from using such a designation. Its usage contains negative implications for the black American community and originally referred to the "law," which was synonymous with white American men. Over the years, changes in the racial and ethnic makeup of police departments are forcing a decline in the use of such terms as "the man" as a stereotype.

MYTH/MISINFORMATION

Racism is responsible for most of the problems of black America.

Response

The socioeconomic disparity that presently exists between the Americans of African ancestry and the Americans of European ancestry is directly attributable to the history of repressive environment imposed upon the Americans of African ancestry. Yes, American racism has been a significant contributor to the socioeconomic problems that now afflict the black American community. However, racism in America today is not sufficient to prevent the black American community from achieving socioeconomic parity.

MYTH/MISINFORMATION

If a black American man straightens, processes, perms, or otherwise chemically grooms his hair, he's rejecting his own race.

Response

The only fitting answer to that question is another question. If a black American woman straightens, processes, perms, or otherwise chemically grooms her hair, is she rejecting her race? Or for that matter, if any person, man or woman, of any race straightens, processes, perms, or otherwise chemically grooms his or her hair, is that person rejecting his or her race?

If the answer to either of these two questions is "no," then the answer to the first question if also "no."

MYTH/MISINFORMATION

Pre-slavery-era Africans were uncivilized and barbaric.

Response

This is of course, grossly untrue (read, Chapter 2, "Who Were The 1619 Africans?").

MYTH/MISINFORMATION

Being the descendents of an enslaved people is shameful, and black Americans should avoid addressing that portion of their history as much as possible.

Response

Hardly. We embrace the heritage all Africans, including those who were enslaved, as our own heritage. The legacy of the enslaved Africans is our own legacy. While detesting their enslavement, we nevertheless esteem their contributions in the founding and establishment of this great country. And we long for the day, in which all Americans will come together and establish a monument, or tribute, to acknowledge their wrongful denial of their civil rights and to honor their contributions. As descendents of the enslaved Africans, we are Americans, born and bred. We have withstood the political trauma of enslavement and emancipation, the civil pains of terrorism and bigotry. Yet, concerning our patriotism, we have served with distinction, both in bondage and free, in every military engagement in our country's history. Concerning our loyalty, it is unimpeachable. America belongs to black Americans. Or at least, there are no others who can make a greater claim upon her.

Furthermore, as stated elsewhere, Congress is called upon to issue a formal statement condemning the findings of the U.S. Supreme Court regarding the citizenship rights of Dred Scott. While we recognize that Thirteenth Amendment repudiated the substance of the Taney Supreme Court decision, we feel this additional step is appropriate. It is also called upon to establish a monument via a perpetual memorial scholarship program. The program could be fashioned along the same lines, academically, as the

Rhodes Scholarship. It should be dedicated to the African immigrants who gave of their substance and their lives in enslaved servitude, to the effect that a morally based constitution emerged in this nation—a nation, I might add, sufficiently tempered in strength and fortitude to have both built and sustained the most powerful civilization on earth—and to incorporate into that program a formal acknowledgment that the trade in the enslavement of the Africans people was both illegal and immoral. Additionally, the nation should submit through formal diplomatic channels copies of such an acknowledgment to the governments of all African nations directly affected by enslavement of the Africans and the trade thereof.

In spite of the near-cataclysmic disaster the institution of slavery had upon the African and the black American people, circumstances themselves dictate that the four hundred years of abject misery be viewed not simply as misery but as the birth canal through which the concept of human rights was born. In the years leading up to 1946, the white-supremacy terrorists' appetite for violence against black Americans went virtually unchecked by written law or by law enforcement authorities. Scores of black Americans were intimidated, brutalized, and murdered. Others were summarily arrested under fraudulent charges of rape and other similar crimes and sentenced to death or to long terms of incarceration. Scores of other black Americans were denied access to polling places. Devious and divisive tactics such as poll taxes and grandfather clauses were used to validate denial.

The nation's first lady, Mrs. Eleanor Roosevelt, frequently expressed her disdain for the way black Americans were summarily mistreated. Having arrived on the national scene in 1932 with the election of her husband, Franklin Delano Roosevelt, as President of the United States, Mrs. Roosevelt and a small cadre of other women called upon the moral authority of the American community to motivate the national conscience. They prompted the nation by holding it accountable for its behavior vis-a-vis its declared ideals as expressed by the nation's

Declaration of Independence. Her benevolent concerns for the plight of the black Americans was later to be reflected in her advocacy of a human rights platform in the charter of the newly formed United Nations. Mrs. Roosevelt was one of four U.S. delegates to attend the first session of the United Nations General Assembly held in London in 1946, and she subsequently served as the United States' member and chairman of the Human Rights Commission. Under her strong support, the United Nations, on December 10, 1946, implemented the Commission of Human Rights. In 1948, that commission drafted the United Nations and mankind's first Universal Declaration of Human Rights. And in that same year this declaration was approved by the full United Nations membership. The Universal Declaration of Human Rights condemned the exercise of slavery, racism, genocide, or any other act of nationally endorsed racism. It also required that the U.N.'s member nations respect the rights, privileges, and dignity of all men.

MYTH/MISINFORMATION

America does not belong to black Americans. It is not their home.

Response

At the risk of sounding a bit ethnocentric, black Americans are undoubtedly the most consistently American of all the immigrant groups, with the exception only of Native Americans. Of the thirty–five million black Americans living in America today, all but a very few are descendents of the original African immigrants.

It is unlikely that any other immigrant group can make such a boast. The black American community can do so because, for in the 135 years since the docking of the *Clothilde,* and its final cargo of enslaved Africans, the arrival of other African people into this country has been minimal. This cannot be said of any other immigrant group. Roughly speaking, it is probable that over ninety percent of black Americans in this country today are descendents of the original African immigrants. The black American community began more than 375 years ago and for the past 135 years has essentially remained intact. And so, restating the myth that "America does not belong to black Americans, it is not their home," is a severely flawed assertion. America *does* belong to black Americans, and it *is* their home. At least there are no others who can make a greater claim upon her.

MYTH/MISINFORMATION

Black Americans won't shop at black-American-owned businesses.

Response

Black Americans are, no matter what our feelings are to the contrary, first and foremost, Americans. They shop via the influence of market forces and not in accordance with ethnic parameters. See also the response on a preceding pages regarding the" Myth and Misinformation assertion that "black Americans do not stick together."

MYTH/MISINFORMATION

Black Americans do not like to work for black American bosses.

Response

Whether this is true or not is of little or no significance. It is reasonable to assume that at least some black Americans may have a problem working for other black Americans. And even if large numbers of black Americans do not like the idea of working for black American bosses, it doesn't matter. There are no negative implications. It is simply one's prerogative as to whom they like to, or not like to work with, or for.

MYTH/MISINFORMATION

Black Americans men do not want to work:

Response

The presence of black Americans in the occupations described in the U.S. Census occupation distribution data table of this commentary proves the fallacy of such contentions. In fact, the presence of such a large numbers of black Americans working in a disproportionate number of lower-paying occupations would suggest an overwhelming rebuttal of such notions. A possible concession to this argument can be found in the plight of many undereducated black Americans whose aspirations to succeed are frustrated by their neglect of academic preparation.

MYTH/MISINFORMATION

Black Americans should not have to work harder to get ahead.

Response

"Should not have to" is an appropriate conclusion. However, it fails to address the initial problem, which is that more often than not, no matter what they should or should not have to do, black Americans do have to work harder. A similarly ineffective conclusion would be that a person should not have to work to pay for their college education, especially when other college students not have to work. Perhaps noble thoughts both, but neither addresses the principal motivational argument. That is, unless black Americans do work harder, their socioeconomic parity will come even slower.

MYTH/MISINFORMATION

Black Americans are inferior to white Americans.

Response

Less educated and poorer, yes. Inferior, no.

MYTH/MISINFORMATION

Enslavement of the Africans proves they were inferior.

Response

Ultimately it is not possible to know all the intricacies that initially led to enslavement of the African people. However, it is known that the Portuguese, who were a world power and whose ships ruled the oceans of the time, were the first of the European nations to become involved in the slave trade. Initially Portugal established diplomatic and trade relationships with a number of Africans nations. In fact, the current Portuguese ethnicity contains thousands, perhaps millions, of Africans whose descendents have become assimilated and absorbed into the ethnicity of the present-day Portuguese people. When the New World was discovered, Portugal, Spain, and other nations drew upon the Africans as a source of cheap, and subsequently enslaved, labor.

MYTH/MISINFORMATION

President Abraham Lincoln was a racist.

Response

Whether President Lincoln was a racist is irrelevant speculation. Any number of indicators points away from this conclusion, the chief of which is his issuance of the Emancipation Proclamation. The Emancipation Proclamation speaks louder than any spurious speculations as to the president's personal motives or intents. President Lincoln is known to have been a very religious man, and it is said that he wrote the Emancipation Proclamation in direct response to the outcome of the battle between General George B. McClellan and General Robert E. Lee at Antietam. During the battle, Mr. Lincoln, like Gideon in the Bible, asked God to give him a sign as to the disposition of those Americans who were in enslaved. In his prayer, Mr. Lincoln reportedly asked God to let General

McClellan win the battle if he wanted the Americans freed from slavery; but if He did not, He was to let General Lee win. Of course, General McClellan won the battle of Antietam. Reportedly, President Lincoln, upon learning the outcome of the battle immediately proceeded to draft the terms of the Emancipation Proclamation. The following is quoted from the first two paragraphs of the Emancipation Proclamation:

> "Whereas, on the twenty-second day of September, in the year of our Lord one thousand eight hundred and sixty-two, a proclamation was issued by the President of the United States, containing, among other things, the following, to wit:

> 'That on the first day of January, in the year of our Lord one thousand eight hundred and sixty-three, all persons held as slaves within any State, or designated part of a State, the people whereof shall then be in rebellion against the United States, shall be then, thenceforward, and forever free; and the Executive Government of the United States, including the military and naval authority thereof, will recognize and maintain the freedom of such persons, and will do no act or acts to repress such persons, or any of them, in any efforts they may make for their actual freedom."

ABRAHAM LINCOLN.
L. S./ WILLIAM H. SEWARD,
Secretary of State.

MYTH/MISINFORMATION

Black Americans are more brawn than brain.

Response

Not true. No additional response is deemed necessary.

MYTH/MISINFORMATION

I.Q. tests results prove black Americans are intellectually inferior:

Response

I.Q. (intelligence quotient) tests do not prove that black Americans are inferior to anyone. The Stanford Binet test generally applied in I.Q. tests is fashioned from the concept of a certain ideal model. To the extent that the social and cultural environments of black Americans pattern themselves in a fashion consistent with the order of the model, their performance on the test is indistinguishable from that of anyone else of comparable social and cultural environments.

MYTH/MISINFORMATION

Black Americans have "bad" hair, whereas other races have "good" hair.

Response

The hair of black Americans, or of the African race for that matter, is not characteristically straight. Although often referred to as being nappy or kinky, it is more characteristically tightly curled. And since both the words "kinky" and "nappy" were terms traditionally applied to denigrate the hair of black Americans, both are considered offensive racial slurs. A more adequate and descriptive term for most black Americans' and most Africans' hair is simply "curly." Curly hair is not straight hair and therefore it will not behave like straight hair unless chemically treated. Conversely, straight hair is not curly hair, and therefore it will not behave like curly hair unless it is also chemically treated. Hair is neither "good" nor "bad" except as its owner's intentions might purport it to be. If the fashion designers of the western world suddenly elected the wearing of black and curly hair styles as those to emulate (as they tended to during the days of the "natural" look), white Americans beauty salons accustomed to straight, tangled hair would have to undergo major renovations in their styling practices. They would have to retrain and resupply in order to accommodate such a change in their customary hairstyles. White Americans would have to color their hair, not blond or brunette, but black. And instead of salons styling straight hair, they would utilize an assortment of processes to turn straight hairstyles into curly hairstyles. Thus, as stated earlier, hair is itself neither good nor bad, except as one's intentions purport it to be.

MYTH/MISINFORMATION

Black Americans should not have little children's hair pressed, permed, or otherwise processed by a beauty shop.

Response

To the degree that chemicals and other agents involved in the pressing, perming, or processing one's hair are not injurious to the child, then there should be no social or other reason not to process a child's hair in any fashion that pleases the parents and the child, particularly if such process makes it easier and more expedient to groom the child's hair.

MYTH/MISINFORMATION

"Black-on-black" crime.

Response

To assert the premise of "black-on-black" crime implies malevolence is not reflected in crime statistics. That is, it suggests that black Americans seek out other black Americans so that they may commit crimes against them. The very notion of such a practice is not only repugnant, it is blatantly erroneous. Black Americans are not out to exterminate other black Americans. Therefore, to attempt to characterize such crimes as black-on-black crimes is to denigrate the character of all black Americans. The fact is that people commit crimes against those they are around the most. Most crimes committed in America are committed against people the criminal knows, or in some way or another associates with. Since the crimes generally referred to as black-on-black crimes usually occurs within the inner city, it is only logical that the perpetrators and the victims of such crimes will be people who live in the inner city, which has a high population density of black

Americans. But whether in the inner city or not, people commit crimes against the people around them. White American criminals commit crimes against white American people, Vietnamese criminals commit crimes against Vietnamese people, Korean criminals commit crimes against Korean people. Even family members commit more crimes against other family members than they do against people outside the family.

MYTH/MISINFORMATION

Black Americans, or Africans, are omitted from the Christian Bible.

Response

The Christian Bible contains a substantial body of references either to Africans as a people or to individuals who were African or of African descent. In one particular instance, it cites a significant occasion in which an angel is sent to direct the evangelist Philip to go south to a road going from Jerusalem to Gaza. Once there, Philip ministered to what in today's vernacular, be referred to as the Secretary of the Treasury of an Ethiopian (a Greek word meaning people with black skin) province. The Bible tells how the Ethiopian had come to Jerusalem to worship and was returning home when Philip approached him. Philip preached Christianity to the Ethiopian who accepted the faith and was baptized by Philip in a stream or other water source alongside the road on which he was traveling.

MYTH/MISINFORMATION

Islam is the traditional religion of the African people.

Response

Since, as cited above, Christianity came to Africa during the first century A.D. and since Mohammed did not found Islam until some six hundred years later, such an assertion is inconsistent with the facts of history. Islam entered Africa and established itself as a prominent religion during the seventh century, when invading Arabs swept across Northern Africa as a contingent of the Islamic "holy war."

MYTH/MISINFORMATION

Black American men prefer white American women.

Response

The answer to this is more statistical than social or cultural, while is quite probable that there are other features present in the making of such relationships. But by and large, the facts are that people marry the individuals they are around most frequently. If you are a black American whose income is in the six figures, you will undoubtedly see and socialize with many more white Americans in the course of a business day than with black Americans. Consequently, since people marry those they see on a regular basis, those black Americans who, by virtue of their socioeconomic status, socialize with more white American women than black American women are much more likely to marry a white American woman. And one must also remember that an eligible bachelor is, after all, an eligible bachelor. The same phenomenon applies to black American women who marry white American men, albeit less frequently.

MYTH/MISINFORMATION

The color black is associated with evil. And black Americans, because their skin color is black, share in that association.

Response

To submit oneself to such thinking is offensive, not only to black Americans and other people whose skin is black, but also to the human intellect in general. Whereas societies generally tend to associate goodness with light and evil with darkness, this notion confines itself to the everyday experience of daytime and nighttime. All the colors ascribed to human beings—black, brown, red, white, and yellow—contain degrees of both positive and negative social or cultural imagery (black gold versus black heart; golden brown versus brownout; red communist versus red, white, and blue; pure as the driven snow versus white as a leper; yellow gold versus yellow jaundice).

MYTH/MISINFORMATION

Black Americans are disadvantaged in the conference and boardrooms of corporate America.

Response

There are many reasons why this contention could be true: The racial attitudes of management, the social segregation that usually occurs when black and white Americans workers leave the work place, the notions of some black Americans that they can be as "black" as they want to be and still deserve the promotional support of management, and perhaps most significantly, loyalty. Managers and management place high value on loyalty.

In the case of simple bigotry, the only recourse in such a situation would undoubtedly be legal. But of the remaining reasons, the solutions are much more palatable. The issue of social segregation will require that black American management aspirants make a concerted effort to overcome the effects of the social segregation usually associated with the fact that black Americans tend to congregate with other black Americans during non-working hours. Being as "black" as one wants to be has it's own reward, or lack thereof. Although nepotism in American industry has been absent for a long time, one of the principles behind it is still alive and well. In the conference and boardrooms of American industries, a relationship akin to nepotism continues to thrive. There were a number of reasons why companies used to be operated almost exclusively by family members. However, for the sake of this commentary, we will focus upon only one—loyalty.

The idea that a relative could be trusted whereas an outsider might not be as trustworthy was one of the ingredients that fed the practice of nepotism. Over the years, a number of things changed in the way businesses were owned and operated, and these changes ultimately brought about the demise of nepotism. But business management and managers still cling to the idea of a common bond. Until a few years ago, the application of a "good ol' boys" network supplanted the absence of nepotism. Even though the "good ol' boys" network has experienced scorn and, to some extent, legal challenges, it is still the school from which most middle and upper managers are drafted. The name of the network may have been abandoned, or gone underground, but its principles are still current. Therefore, black Americans who aspire to management positions must address the issue of management loyalty.

MYTH/MISINFORMATION

Black Americans have to use English surnames because their own surnames were lost during slavery. Additionally, Africans were not permitted to use their own African names.

Response

This assertion relies heavily upon the premise that Africans used surnames during the during the sixteenth and seventeenth centuries when the European slave trade in West Africa began. The use of surnames is a relatively recent innovation in the history of names. In Africa, as well as in Europe, surnames generally originated as a feature of one's occupation, the place where one lived, or were possibly attributable to a person's appearance. One example of a surname that can be attributed to the place where the person lived is the African name Mendis. Manis, Mendis, is identified as the home of the African Cinque. In historical reference however, Cinque is referred to as Cinque of Mendis in much the same way as an Englishman named Thomas Moore might be referred to as Thomas of the Moors.

The actual use of surnames among Europeans did not come into play until the latter part of the medieval period, or middle Ages, and even then their use was generally limited to aristocrats, or those owning property. In much the same manner that black Americans have adopted English surnames, people of the Philippines, for instance, have adopted Spanish surnames. In fact, the use of surnames among Filipinos did not begin until the middle of the nineteenth century. Prior to that time, only a small number of Filipino people utilized surnames. Also, surnames among the Vietnamese people were frequently the surnames of famous or popular rulers. This practice of the Vietnamese vary very little from the practice of post-Civil War black Americans who choose their surnames from the names of former presidents or other popular persons. While there is evidence that some African people used surnames, there is also evidence that many other Africans did not. The constant use and application of misinformation and stereotypical mythical notions of black American inferiority is injurious to the overall aspirations the black American community. They are injurious not only to black American adults, but most of all to black American children. The entire genre or media of misinformation serves to undermine the pride and self-esteem of the youths and children of the black America community.

MYTH/MISINFORMATION

White Americans are the principal users of negative stereotypes against black Americans.

Response

Could be true, but probably is not. It is much more likely that black American media; music, books, homes, conversations, churches, and black Americans colleges and college campuses are the principal sources of such denigrating negative stereotypes. Almost any random survey of books written about black Americans—a great number of which are being written by black Americans—will turn up examples that play host to this kind of negativism. Even though the general thrust of a book's theme pretends favor or at least benevolence, the arguments they make often hinge upon imageries that convey negativism.

Make no mistake, media examples abound through which these daunting images enter into the black American community. One medium of particular concern because it is so intimate to the black American community, is through the congregation of the average black American church. An incredible amount of ambivalent and unfavorable commentary emerges from these congregations and from the church pulpits every Sunday morning. There are fifty-two Sundays in each year, meaning that a church congregation can be exposed to a constant source of unflattering, and perhaps repressing, remarks. If such an impenetrable ceiling of negativism hangs over the aspirations of black American youths, what possible chance is there for their successful movement through the socioeconomic network?

This assertion should not come as a surprise to black Americans, especially since the negativistic ceiling is composed primarily of racial slurs. And these racial slurs are more often than not used by black Americans against other black Americans. Racial slurs, by their own design, exhibit dualistic properties. Its basis of opposites loosely incorporates the logic that a thing is itself because it is not something else. From that premise, then, racial slurs, stereotypes, and other denigrating tactics are often employed by a given ethnic group in an its effort to enhance its own self-esteem by suppressing or undermining the self-esteem of another—probably a competing ethnic group. Simply put, it says, "I'll look good if I can make you look bad." So, when black Americans utilize such slurs against themselves, it is tantamount to self-destruction. That is, black Americans become the objects of its suppressive or "make you look bad" properties. For since these slurs are self-inflicted—used by black Americans against other black Americans—only the suppressive features are being employed. With all of this working against them, is it any wonder that our inner-city children and youth are being driven out into the socioeconomically dead-end streets of our nation?

Since migrating into the social realm of the black American community, these negative stereotypes have effectively diminished the self-esteem, thus sabotaging the motivation of millions of black Americans. Like an infectious virus, once one becomes infected, the demeaning effects of negativist stereotypes are extremely destructive. Currently these negativisms exist among black Americans under the cover of parochial folklore and have become an integral component of the average black American's every-day conversations. It is meaningless to tell our children and young people, "If you want to succeed in life you must get an education," for as positive as these twelve words are, they are insufficient to overcome the twelve thousand words of negativism that these same young people have already experienced.

MYTH/MISINFORMATION

The black American community should set itself apart nationalistically from the white American community.

Response

Generally, my answer to such a question would be an enthusiastic no! However, when we consider the socioeconomic disparity that the black American community is obliged to contend with for the next twenty or so years, it would be prudent to consider some things. When we consider the problems the black American community presently faces as a result of the socioeconomic disparity, it is evident that we must do some things differently.

For instance, some values and behaviors that are "affordable" or at least "tolerable" by the white American community are harmful and thus intolerable for the black American community. These values or behaviors ought to be considered "unaffordable" by the people of the black American community. Truth be told, the black American community lacks sufficient accomplishments or achievements in areas such as education, social integration, political participation, and socioeconomic parity to afford the distractive influence of ideas or practices inconsistent with their efforts toward achieving socioeconomic parity.

Part Three

THE BLACK AMERICAN COMMUNITY, IN THE 21ST CENTURY

Brothers and sisters, my heart's desire and prayer to God for the black American community are that they might achieve social-economic parity. For I bear them witness that they have a zeal for achieving it, but not according to knowledge. For, lacking adequate education, they have gone about establishing their own ideas of "making it" and have not submitted themselves to the regimen of formal educations.

(A paraphrase of Romans Chapter 10:1-2, The King James Version Bible)

10

THE BLACK AMERICAN COMMUNITY AND THE AMERICAN DREAM

As the black American community recreates itself to take on the twenty-first century it is imperative for it to define an agenda sufficiently broad in scope and in depth so as to definitively characterize the accomplishments that black Americans must achieve as they advances into this *brave new* century. The black American community of the twenty-first century cannot afford, and must not permit, a repeat of the ills of previous centuries—centuries characterized by enslavement, by political and legal disenfranchisement and, later, by years of racial subordination under a threat sustained by vigilante terrorism.

Among the items that the black American community must, of necessity, have on their twenty-first-century agenda are; (a) a united and affirmative opposition to any attempts to suppress, from any quarter, the enfranchised rights granted under the U.S. Constitution; (b) a plan by which it will move beyond its own enigmatic approach to its legacy as Americans, (c) a commitment to formal education of its children, and (d) the insight to integrate themselves into the social and cultural fabric of American life. To arrive at such a social and cultural place, the black American community must align itself with, and establish, an integrated approach to American society. Specifically, it must come to terms with the legacy of its own birthright. While most people would acknowledge that the black American community has not always enjoyed a smooth and uneventful relationship with the country as a whole, the bottom line is that America is home, bought and paid for, to the black American community. It is where the community's historical, cultural, economic, and resources are vested. If, as the saying goes, home is where the heart is, then America is where the black American community's heart is. After all, why would one invest so much of one's life's time and effort into an enterprise as the black American community has done in America, and then turn against it? That sentiment clashes head-on with what appears to be an inclination on the part of black Americans to boycott their entrance to the socioeconomic strength of America. After more than three hundred years of laboring as conscripted and enslaved laborers in the building of this great nation, why should they then refuse to share in the dividends or benefits of their own enterprise?

Of all the nations throughout the history of mankind, America has established the most successful government. It is the most equitable, the most moral, the most just, the most representative, the most enlightened, and the most economically sound and technologically advanced nation that mortal man has yet produced. If the black American community is to succeed during the coming century, it must draw upon the resources of so great a nation. As previously noted, unlike many other immigrant groups in America, the black American community is not distinguished by language, cuisine, religion, or other "old-world" customs or traditions. Black Americans must, therefore, seek bonding agents from within their own heritage of African and American ancestry. By bonding, one simply means that black Americans must be able to coalesce around some distinct cultural or esoteric fundamentals possessing sufficient values to define the black American community's unique identity.

If, for example, the black American community still spoke African as a second language, then such a language could serve as a point of cultural reference. Its presence would be adequate to define parameters that could help describe a unique black American community. Or if black Americans held distinctive religious beliefs or were affiliated around such a belief system, the religion or belief system would serve as an agency of coalescence. Barring all that, even if black Americans were simply distinguished by a unique cuisine, they could be differentiated from mainstream Americans. But they are not, nor are they bounded by old-country folklore or traditional customs. Since none of these components is present within the black American community, sources of coalescence must be sought elsewhere. In the past, and particularly since the 1960s, a popular and perhaps fashionable approach has been to import the fundamental components of a cultural system from Africa. However, if such efforts have not already failed, they are assuredly destined to fail for the simple reason that importing cultural values from one country to another is impractical and considerably more difficult than, say, importing VCRs. Whereas VCRs can be purchased in one country, transported across the ocean, and plugged into an electrical outlet in another country, cultural values do not operate in that manner. One cannot simply load up on African cultural traits, ship them across the ocean, and plug them into the value systems of the black American community. Culture doesn't work that way. Importing a culture from Africa for utilization by the black American community would be equivalent to importing cars from the United Kingdom where they drive on the left side of the street and attempting to market the same cars for the streets of America. This is in no way an attempt the disassociate the black American community from the anchor of its generational heritage, but simply a recognition of the fact that the cultures of Africa, like those of any cultural group, emanate from, and are sustained by, the elements of their own construction and evolution.

Again, unlike some other immigrant groups, the black American community has been intrinsically American and thus disconnected from the cultures of Africa for nearly four hundred years. Utilizing our schedule of twenty-year generational intervals, those 375 years translate into more than nineteen generations during which the culture of the black American community has been distinct and separate from that of Africa. Black Americans are too far removed from the land, landscape, and language components from whence the African cultures evolved to have any effective kinship with them. In their attempt to cover themselves within the idioms of African cultures, black Americans place themselves at the great risk of applying a cultural mimicry that may profane the legitimate cultures of the very Africa they seek to embrace. As I see it, such external applications have about as much to do with getting in touch with one's African heritage as Al Jolson's singing jazz in black-face enabled him to relate to black American soul.

Instead of cultural mimicry, the black American community would do far better if, rather than attempting to connect with Africa by leapfrogging the 380 years of its American ancestry, it would embrace the past twenty generations. Whereas, black Americans have traditionally sought to distance themselves from the issue of slavery, the approach has been about as unsuccessful as the person who seeks to forget having been abused as a child. The enslaved African men and women labored on behalf of their country and have done nothing their black American descendents should be ashamed of or be reluctant to acknowledge. Neither their contributions to the country nor their moral stature as men and women of character should be diminished. In terms of service, can anyone contend that their contributions were any less meritorious, less ennobling, less American, or less sacrificial than the contributions of those who fell at Gettysburg, Pearl Harbor, Normandy, Iwo Jima, Heartbreak Ridge, those whose names now appear on the Viet Nam War Memorial, and yes, those brave souls who went down with Flight 585?

It is unfortunate that, to most black Americans, the period in which their American ancestry was defined by enslavement has become a vast and unmanageable cultural and historical wasteland. The net effect that this wasteland has had was the ten-to-eleven-generation breakdown in the historical linkage of family names and of regional heritage. Even though these same historical links were routinely lost or discarded as irrelevant by the descendents of other immigrant groups, black Americans still look upon the breakdown in their historical linkage as an act of American exploitation. If the black American community is to go beyond its current sense of self-denial, though, it must embrace those ten-to-eleven generations of Africans and the descendents of those Africans who contributed to the building of this country under its system of human enslavement. Black Americans must cease taking circuitous routes around the wasteland of their past and turn that wasteland into a fertile legacy as befitting a people who, paraphrasing Sir Winston Churchill, journeyed all the way across the oceans, across the mountains, across the prairies, and across the centuries, not because they were pliant as sugar candy, but because they were determined as their fathers had been, and as their legacy demands of their descendents.

As the black American community looks forward into the opportunities offered by a changing world, it can ill afford to look back in anger. Again to quote Sir Winston Churchill, "If we open a quarrel between the past and the present, we shall find that we have lost the future." Therefore, that bonding for black Americans community will begin to take effect when the America-to-Africa connection is established, not through excursion flights into Nairobi on a 747 jet, but through the personal and historical résumés of the men and women of those ten-to-eleven generations whose gnarled hands and lashed backs paid our fare. So, instead of outward manifestations of cultural mimicry to affirm its African connection, the black American community would do better to stop treating its American citizenship as an unwelcome gift and value it for the priceless gem it is. For the past four hundred years, and continuing to today, men and women from all over the world have risked life and limb to acquire American citizenship and illegal American residency.

As noted earlier, cultural maturity occurs generally within the first three generations an immigrant group spends in America. Even if one posed the argument that the black American community was enslaved and therefore not a participant in the melting pot, this logic would fail on the basis that, since the emancipation, black Americans have had more than six generations in which to develop an Americanized cultural base.

In previous chapters we attempted to show how the families, neighborhoods, communities, and even governments of Africa became dysfunctional as a result of the disappearance of so many Africans during the slavery trade, when three and a half million Africans family members, friends, and fellow citizens suffered those losses. We also showed how the people kidnapped from their homes were transplanted, with utter disregard for their humanity, up to ten thousand miles away. Additionally, we showed how they and their fellow Africans were deployed in a myriad of strange lands stretching up and down the Atlantic coastline some six thousand miles from Boston to Buenos Aires. We further showed that, after arriving in America, these unwilling immigrants withstood up to three hundred years of uninterrupted and dehumanizing enslavement and ethnic bigotry. And how, as an enslaved people, they labored with their hands and contemplated in their heads, as they worked with other immigrants to build the structure and infrastructure of the greatest nation on the earth. In spite of the heart-wrenching agony in the lives of the African immigrants, there is strong evidence that their passionate sense of nationalism remained intact. Any number of incidents in the history of this country's military engagements–from Crispus Attucks in the Revolutionary War to the blood-stained sands of – the Persian Gulf, and more recently America's war against terrorism,—illustrate the intensely passionate nationalism and loyalty of the descendents of the African immigrants. If Patrick Henry's words, "Give me liberty or give me death," are symbolic of the American passion for freedom, so are James Forten's words, "I am here a prisoner for the liberties of my country; I shall never, never prove to be a traitor to her interest" symbolic of that same passion for freedom.

Some might ask, what's the basis of my assertion that America deserves the unqualified loyalty of black Americans. After all, they would be apt to remind me, the black American community has suffered brutal, unmitigated horrors at America's hands. To such detractors one can reply that, in spite of all the atrocities suffered by the African immigrants and their descendents, America is still their home. And from another point of view, because of all their suffering, the descendents of the African immigrants have an even greater stake in America as their country. Fundamentally, America is, after all, as much a home to the descendents of the 1619 Africans as it is to the descendents of the 1620 Pilgrims. In fact, if the members of other immigrant groups think they have the "right" to call themselves Americans, we the more. We arrived here in 1619, on board a Dutch man-of-war battleship. Our ancestors, like those of no other immigrant group, served this country for two hundred years under a system of harsh enslavement, followed by century of a deadly terrorist campaign, and we embrace their legacy as our heritage. As to our nationality, we are Americans. Concerning our patriotism, we have served with distinction, both in bondage and free, in every military engagement in our country's history. Concerning our loyalty, it is unimpeachable.

With such distinguished credentials, why then are so many black Americans engaged in words and practices that help sustain a culture of denial and negativism regarding black Americans and their history in America? When black Americans, and particularly the children, hear American history discussed by other black Americans, they often hear only the negating aspects of the enslavement, Jim Crow segregation, and the violent acts committed by white-racist terrorists. Those periods did exist and are an integral part of American history, but there are more. Throughout the length and breadth of those painful years, there were also the imposing periods of their American heritage. It is that ennobling heritage that fashioned a people who, transported from Africa, labored under enslavement, yet found and took to heart the God of their deliverance. I think it well and good that black American children learn about the struggles of these Americans, and it is important that they be esteemed, even in their agony, as proud Americans.

One of the more particularly harmful and negative points of view that has seemingly stuck like the proverbial glue in the hearts and minds of the black American community is the contention that black Americans were not represented in the "men" of the, "we hold these truths to be self-evident, that all men are created equal" statement of the United States Declaration of Independence. The arguments for this point of view are as varied in their focus as are those articulating them. Some have drawn connecting lines of logical extensions, though conceptually sophomoric, between the statement in the Declaration of Independence and the three-fifths compromise legislation of twelve years later. They have extrapolated from these two sources the contention that the Declaration of Independence obviously did not intend to include black Americans as equals. If it had so intended, they argue, why did the Constitutional Congress legislate that a black American was only three-fifths of a citizen? They often follow up this argument with a summary statement befitting a French coup d'état, charging that one cannot be created equal and at the same time be considered only three-fifths of a citizen. Others argue that if black Americans had been considered equal in the words of the Declaration of Independence, America could not have kept them enslaved. Still others simply mouth the refrain that America is a racist country governed by racist rednecks, and therefore would obviously not have considered black Americans equal to white Americans.

To facilitate my argument as to the implications that the Declaration of Independence held for America and their application to the welfare of the black American community, I have incorporated the last and nineteenth article of the Declaration of Independence that serves as an indictment and protest against King George III of England, for his role in the initiation and perpetuation of slavery and the enslavement of Africans. It is to be noted that this paragraph was removed from the ratified version of the Declaration of Independence at the behest of the convention delegates from Georgia and North and South Carolina.

THE DECLARATION OF INDEPENDENCE

When in the Course of human events, it becomes necessary for one people to dissolve the political bands which have connected them with another, and assume, among the Powers of the earth, the separate and equal station to which the Law of Nature and of Nature's God entitles them, a decent respect to the opinions of mankind requires that they should declare the cause which impel them to the separation.

We hold these truths to be self-evident, that all men are created equal, that they are endowed by their Creator with certain unalienable Rights, that among these are Life, Liberty, and the pursuit of Happiness. That to secure these rights, Government are instituted among Men, deriving their just Powers from the consent of the governed. That whenever any form of Government become destructive to these ends, it is the Right of the People to alter or to abolish it, and to institute new Governments, laying the foundation on such Principles, and organizing its Powers in such form as to them shall seem most likely to effect their Safety and Happiness, Prudence, indeed will dictate that Government long established should not be changed for light and transient causes; and accordingly, all experience hath shown, that mankind are more disposed to suffer, while evils are sufferable, than to right themselves by abolishing the form to which they are accustomed. But, when a long train of abuses and usurpations pursuing invariable the same Object, evinces a design to reduce them under absolute Despotism, it is their right, it is their duty, to throw off such Government, and to provide new Guards for their future security. Such has been the patient sufferance of these Colonies and such is now the necessity which constrains them to alter their former Systems of Government. The history of the present King of Great

Britain is a history of repeated injuries and usurpation, all having in direct object the establishment of an absolute Tyranny over these States. To prove this let Facts be submitted to a candid world.

01. He has refused his Assent to Laws the most wholesome and necessary for the public good.

02. He has forbidden his Governors to pass Laws of immediate and pressing importance, unless suspended in their operation till his assent should be obtained; and when so suspended he has utterly neglected to attend to them.

03. He has refused to pass other Laws for the accommodation of large districts of People, unless those People would relinquish the right of Representation in the legislature; a right inestimable to them and formidable to tyrants only.

04. He has called together legislature bodies at places unusual, uncomfortable and distant from the depository of their Public Records, for the sole purpose of fatiguing them into compliance with his measures.

05. He has dissolved Representative Houses repeatedly for opposing with manly firmness, this invasion of the rights of the People.

06. He has refused for a long time, after such dissolutions, to cause others to be elected; whereby the Legislative Powers incapable of Annihilation, have returned to the People at large for their exercise; the State remaining in the mean time exposed to all the dangers of invasion from without and convulsions within.

07. He has endeavoured to prevent the Population of these States; for that purpose obstructing the Laws of Naturalization of Foreigners; refusing to pass other to encourage their migration hither, and raising the condition of new Appropriation of Lands.

08. He has obstructed the Administration of Justice by refusing his Assent to Laws for establishing Judiciary Powers.

09. He has made Judges dependent on his Will alone, for the tenure of their offices, and the amount and payment of their salaries.

10. He has erected a multitude of New Offices and sent higher swarms of Officers to harass our People and eat their substance.

11. He has kept among us, in times of Peace, Standing Armies without the Consent of our legislatures.

12. He has affected to render the Military independent of and superior to the Civil Power.

13. He has combined with others to subject us to a jurisdiction foreign to our constitution and unacknowledged by our law giving his Assent to their Acts of pretended Legislation;

 a. For quartering large bodies of armed troops among us;

 b. For protecting them by a mock trial from punishment for any Murder which they should commit on the Inhabitants of these States.

 c. For cutting off our Trade with all parts of the world.

 d. For imposing Taxes on us without our Consent

 e. For depriving us in many cases of the benefits of Trial by Jury.

 f. For transporting us beyond Seas to be tried for pretended offenses.

 g. For abolishing the free System of English Laws in a neighboring province, establishing therein an Arbitrary government, and enlarging it Boundaries so as to render it at once an example and fit instrument for introducing the same absolute rule into these Colonies.

 h. For taking away our Charters, abolishing our most valuable laws and altering fundamentally the Form of our Governments;

 i. For suspending our own Legislatures, and declaring themselves invested with Power to legislate for us in all cases whatsoever.

14. He has abdicated Government here, by declaring us out of his protection, and waging War against us.

15. He has plundered our seas, ravaged our Coasts, burnt our towns, and destroyed the Lives of our People.

16. He is at this time transporting large Armies of foreign Mercenaries to complete the works of death, desolation and tyranny, already begun with circumstances of Cruelty and perfidy scarcely paralleled in the most barbarous ages, and totally unworthy the Head of a civilized nation.

17. He has constrained our fellow Citizens, taken Captive on the high Seas, to bear Arms against their Country, to become the executioners of their friends and brethren, or to fall themselves by their Hands.

18. He has excited domestic insurrections amongst us, and has endeavoured to bring on the inhabitants of our frontiers, the merciless Indian Savages, whose known rule of warfare, is an undistinguished destruction of all ages, sexes, and conditions.

19. He has waged cruel war against human nature itself, violating its most sacred rights of life and liberty in the persons of distinct peoples, who never offended him; captivating and carrying them into slavery in another hemisphere to incur miserable death in their transport thither. This piratical warfare, the opprobrium of infidel powers, in the warfare of the Christian King of Great Britain. Determined to keep open market where MEN should be bought and sold, he has prostituted his negative for suppressing every legislative attempt to prohibit or to restrain this execrable commerce: and that this assemblage of horrors might want no fact of distinguished die, he is now exciting those very people to rise in arms among us, and to purchase that liberty of which he has deprived them, by murdering the people upon whom he also obtruded them: thus paying off the former crimes committed against the liberties of one people, with crimes which he urges them to commit against the lives of another.

In every stage of these Oppressions, We have Petitioned for Redress, in the most humble terms; Our repeated Petitions, have been answered only by repeated injury, A Prince, whose character is thus marked by every act which may define a Tyrant, is unfit to be the ruler of a free People.

Nor have We been wanting in attention to our British brethren. We have warned them from time to time of attempts by their legislature to extend an unwarrantable jurisdiction over us. We have reminded them of the circumstances of our emigration and settlement here. We have appealed to their native justice and magnanimity, and we have conjured them by the ties of our common kindred, to disavow these usurpations, which, would inevitably interrupt our connexions and correspondence. They too have been deaf to the voice of justice and consanguinity. We must. therefore acquiesce in the necessity, which denounces our Separation, and hole them, as we hold the rest of mankind, Enemies in war, in Peace, Friends.

WE, THEREFORE, the Representatives of the UNITED STATES OF AMERICA, IN GENERAL CONGRESS assembled, appealing to the Supreme Judge of the World for the rectitude of our intention, DO, in the Name, and by Authority of the good People of these Colonies, solemnly PUBLISH and DECLARE, That these United Colonies are, and of Right, ought to be FREE AND INDEPENDENT STATES; that they are absolved from all allegiance to the British Crown, and that all political connexion between them and the State of Great Britain, is and ought to be totally dissolved; and that, as FREE and INDEPENDENT STATES, they have full power to levy War, concluded Peace, contract Alliances, establish Commerce, and do all other Acts and Thing which INDEPENDENT STATES may of right do. AND for the support of this Declaration, with a firm reliance on the protection of divine Providence, we mutually pledge to each other our Lives, our Fortunes, and our sacred Honor.

In a way, it is ironic that the Declaration of Independence has come under such negative criticism by the black American community. For if the words of Thomas Jefferson are to be taken upon their merits—and we have taken his words on the basis of their merit for the past two hundred and twenty-six years—then a case can be made that the Declaration of Independence probably meant more, or at least as much, to the black American community as it did to the white American community. Its obvious that President Abraham Lincoln took Jefferson's words on the basis of their merit when he said in his Gettysburg Address that, "Four score and seven years ago our fathers brought forth, upon this continent, a new nation, conceived in liberty, and dedicated to the proposition that *all men are created equal.*"

It is unfortunate that one of Jefferson's most ennobling, most emotionally charged, protests was rejected by delegates from Georgia and South Carolina and thus not included in the final version. In that article, Jefferson not only charged the British king with keeping an open market where "enslaved people" were bought and sold, but also that he was, "determined to keep open market where MEN should be bought an sold." If, as some have contended, black Americans were not included in the "men" of the "we hold these truths to be self-evident, that all men are created equal" statement of the United States Declaration of Independence, then why would Jefferson specifically identify the enslaved Africans as "MEN" in his protest when the term "enslaved people" would, at least grammatically, have worked just as well?

From this vantage point it would appear that the dehumanizing perspective against the African immigrants came more from the politicians of Europe than from those of the newly formed United States of America. This accusation alone identifies the powers of Europe as the primary architects behind the initiation and maintenance of the slavery trade. Additionally, the English King had prohibited or resisted attempts by the colonies to bring their political practices in line with their political philosophies. Jefferson charged, "He has prostituted his negative for suppressing every legislative attempt to prohibit or restrain this execrable commerce." How else should such words be interpreted except to infer that most of the American colonies, and particularly Virginia, had initiated legislation to prohibit or restrain slavery and the trade in the enslavement of Africans, but were prohibited from doing so by King George III? Further, before the Declaration of Independence, the colonies were obviously still under the king's rule, they were obliged to operate under his laws, and at his pleasure. In England, it would be another fifty to sixty years before the British Parliament would abolish slavery, first in England and then in its many territories and colonies around the world.

Therefore, had the Declaration of Independence not signaled America's independence from England, it is possible that those black Americans living in Massachusetts, New Hampshire, Pennsylvania, Connecticut, Rhode Island, New York, and New Jersey would have had to wait another fifty to sixty years, or perhaps well into the nineteenth century, before receiving their freedom. On the other hand, almost as soon as the Declaration of Independence was ratified, those colonies and the independent commonwealth of Vermont began immediately to ban enslavement of the Africans and to abolish slavery within their respective borders. On July 2, 1777, exactly two years to the day after the signing of the Declaration of Independence, Vermont began a process of emancipation that would be followed by the states of New York in 1799, Pennsylvania in 1780, Massachusetts and New Hampshire in 1783, Connecticut and Rhode Island in 1784, and New Jersey in 1804.

The remaining six of the original thirteen colonies were situated in the agricultural regions of the south. As such, their interest in slavery and the trade in the enslavement of the Africans took on a considerably different perspective. Whereas the economies of the northern colonies were based on industry and had an abundant source of labor supplied by the steady influx of European immigrants, the economies of the southern colonies was based principally upon agriculture.

Consequently, where the northern colonies were able to view the question of slavery in its moral and philosophical context rather than its application, the southern colonies were obliged to view slavery from a much more practical application rather than from the context of moral implications. By the beginning of the nineteenth century, there were approximately 750,000 African Immigrants in the United States and the overwhelming majority was enslaved. Slavery and the trade in enslavement of Africans, had become an integral component of the southern economy. As it had been with the seventh and eighth century B.C. Greeks who had enslaved the frontier tribes of ancient Europe in order to meet the growing labor demands back in their Greek homeland, so it was, to some extent, with the southern colonies. And so, where the seven colonies of the industrialized northern regions began abolishing slavery almost immediately after the signing of the Declaration of Independence, the colonies of the agricultural Southern regions did not, even though during the thirteen years following its ratification, many southern and northern plantation owners, moved by Jefferson's Declaration, freed many of those enslaved. However, as a governmental act, the Southern colonies refused to follow their lead. Many of them, however, responded to the moral implication of the Declaration by enacting legislation to prevent further importation of Africans immigrants. As the years passed, the southern states found that the demand for African laborers rather than declining, rose sharply.

One of the reasons for this sudden rise was the introduction in 1793 of Eli Whitney's cotton gin, which increased a farm's productivity by substantially increasing its ability to separate the cottonseeds from the cotton fabric. This innovation undermined any thoughts that the southern states might have had that enslavement of the Africans would just gradually disappear. Instead, it became a seemingly fixed and indispensable component of the economic infrastructure of the South. Just as important, it also became an integral and socialized feature of the southern lifestyle. These two events sealed the southern states' collision course with the economically independent and ideologically different states of the North. Having delayed following in the footsteps of the northern states by nearly ninety years (1777 to 1865), the southern states finally conceded to emancipation only after being vanquished in a bloody civil war. It was then that the African immigrant community of 1776, particularly in those colonies where slavery was abolished, was clearly served well by the Declaration of Independence. Even the most ardent advocates of the negative approach should find it difficult to defend their arguments by contending that the legislative activities undertaken by the representatives at the Continental Congress did not represent, wholly and severally, the interests of the African immigrant community.

No one would contend that these representatives were unbiased, or that they, in the guise of their noble statesmanship were unmindful of the great tragedy of slavery, and yet permitted it to endure for the sake of economic and political expediency. Another of the negative views that has greatly harmed the self-concept and self-esteem of black Americans, and particularly the children, has been the much-touted assertion that the three-fifths compromise, made during the Constitutional Convention, was arrived at by white-supremacist-minded legislators who contended that the enslaved Africans were biologically inferior and should, therefore, be counted as only three-fifths of a white American. Considering the actual issues at stake during the convention's discussion of how each state should be represented, it is a genuine mystery to me as to how such a misinterpretation ever got started. There was nothing in the issues being discussed by the convention delegates to lend itself to such an interpretation unless, of course, the misinterpretation resulted from a deliberate intent to misinform.

The Constitutional Convention of 1787 met in Philadelphia, Pennsylvania, on May 25, 1787. For almost four months the delegates debated, contested, and cajoled until finally, on September 17, 1787, they adjourned. Their primary purpose was to draft a constitution that would assure a strong national government. Since winning its independence from England, the infant nation, consisting of thirteen colonies and Vermont, had been governed under the Articles of Confederation drafted by the First Continental Congress in 1774 as the prelude to their Declaration of Independence. In the following years their independence, the Articles of Confederation had functioned as the governing mechanism for federal government. However, as the states began encountering increasing problems, it was determined that a stronger national government was needed. It was in response to this need that fifty-five delegates from the states governments met in Philadelphia in May 1787. The three-fifths compromise resulted from issues dealing with state representation. When the convention began, the smaller states insisted upon each state having the same number of representatives, regardless of their respective populations.

The larger states, of course, insisted upon representation commensurate with their respective populations. A plan drafted by James Madison, a delegate from Virginia, offered that representation at the national level should be proportional to populations and that, such representatives should be elected by the American people, rather than being chosen at the state level. While Madison's proposal received prompt acknowledgement, its plan for proportional representation in both the upper house (Senate) and the lower house (House of Representatives) was rejected in favor of a constitution that would allow equal representation for each state in the upper house and proportional representation in the lower house.

The debate over this question probably produced some of the most peculiar arguments among convention delegates. Delegates from the southern states, whose operational practice had been to denigrate the humanity of the enslaved Africans, were now fighting for their right to full political representation as men, and citizens. On the other hand, delegates from the northern states were arguing that since the enslaved Africans were denied the franchise of citizenship, they also should have no representation in the government. "After all," the northern delegates might have told their southern counterparts, "if you do not wish the enslaved Africans to exercise the franchise of their own citizenship, then neither should you be permitted to exercise it for them." The argument being, that if the southern states truly wanted full representation for the enslaved Africans, then they would be obliged to manumit those Africans to enjoy the full benefit of their citizenship, otherwise, no freedom, no political representation. Just how anyone could read an account of the convention and draw the conclusion that the convention delegates' three-fifths compromise was an act of stark racism is beyond me. Not only was the compromise decidedly not for the purpose of relegating black Americans to a less than whole person status, it really never directly addressed race at all. Recognizably, that when the compromise refer to free persons and persons under slavery, it was, generally speaking, referring to white Americans and to enslaved black Americans.

The formula for establishing a state's congressional representation was that five enslaved persons equaled three free persons. Note that the formula made no distinction as to whether the *free* persons were free white Americans, or free ex-slaves. The ruling simply established the equation whereas five enslaved Africans would have counted as the equivalent of three free persons, no matter whether the skin color of three persons were black or white. As a matter of fact, a number of black Americans lived out their lives as free men and women and continued to live in the southern states during that time. While it is not possible, nor is it the intent of this chapter, to speak on behalf of or against the particular racial views of the delegates, it is possible to determine some of the implications of their legislation. Like the question of the "men" in the "we hold these truths to be self-evident, that all men are created equal" statement of the Declaration of Independence, the three-fifths ruling of the 1787 Constitutional Convention has enjoyed a similar assault upon the moral character of the nation. Flowing from that indictment, it has had a dysfunctional effect upon the relationship the black American community has toward itself and toward the nation.

The Declaration of Independence said–and meant–that all men were created equal. And, despite slavery and despite the three-fifths compromise, the hopes and aspiration of the founding fathers was that the ideals inherent in the Declaration of Independence would one day be realized. Because it is necessary that black Americans of this century ultimately undertake a restructuring of the elements of their American heritage, an unabridged copy of the United States Declaration of Independence has been included in this chapter. Additionally, Article 19, that infamous article that accused King George III of being the authority behind the trade in the enslaving the African people has been reinserted. While the article failed to win the support of the Continental Congress delegates from the southern states and was thus was excised from the original, it should nevertheless always be included, as an addendum, in any and all publications of the Declaration of Independence issued from, or published by and within the black American community. This particular article, more than any other, validates the inclusion of the plight of the black Americans community in the Declaration lodged against King George III and the English government.

If Thomas Jefferson and the other authors of the Declaration of Independence did not intend to acknowledge black Americans as men in the "we hold these truths to be self-evident, that all men are created equal" statement, then it would be inconsistent to assume they would have used "men," with such emphasis, in the "determined to keep open market where MEN…" statement of Article 19. Additionally, it should be noted that this article contained the only underlined passages in the entire Declaration of Independence document. The question is, has the relationship between the white American community and the black America community been the kind that would foster the level of potent and passionate nationalism being espoused in this chapter? The answer of almost thirty-five million black Americans is a resounding *no*. On the surface, such a response can easily be reconciled with the afflictions endured throughout history by the black American community. After all, thirty-five million people must never be permitted to forget the abuses of slavery and Jim Crow segregation.

But in the greater context, to reject or to boycott any of the opportunities available to black Americans would be worse as it would be like, as the expression goes, putting salt on an open wound. America is, after all, a very rich and deserving country. In the course of its history, it has had a more profound impact upon world morality than any nation before it. And without any other evidence to the contrary, the black American community is obliged to function on the premise that Antony and Isabella of the original 1619 Africans considered America a deserving country. When their son, who may have been the 1619 Africans' first American-born child, was born in 1624, Antony and Isabella named the child William, an American name.

If in their perception of the way things were in 1624, Antony and Isabella were moved to give their first American born child an Americanized rather than an African one, as other immigrant parents were undoubtedly doing, it seems reasonable that the black American community of today should make a similar commitment to its heritage. If not, are we then not left with the question of whether the effects of slavery and the Jim Crowism that followed it have had such a devastating pathological affect upon the black American community that it is consigned to wander about in the desert of socioeconomic disparity for another six generations? An example of the black American community's disassociation with its American heritage can be seen in a sampling of some of the names that parents in the black American community often gives to their children. When other immigrant groups arrive in America, they often immediately begin changing their foreign-sounding names to more American-sounding ones.

Black American parents of nineteenth (1966–1995) and twentieth (1986–2015) generation children have begun to give their children African or African-sounding names. This may simply be a legitimate effort to give tribute to their African ancestry. Or it may be an effort on the part of these parents to ignore or leap-frog the eighteen generations of their American ancestry and cut a straight ancestral path back to Africa. If the latter is their intent, then such a divisive approach to their ancestry would argue that they obviously do not hold those eighteen generations of their American ancestry in very high esteem. All of this is occurring in the very presence of the traditional mode of Americanization. That the melting pot phenomenon is still occurring is evident among the people of other ethnic groups, who, while black Americans are changing names like Johnny Lee Brown, Joseph Williams, Timothy Smith, and Elmer Jones to Muhammed, Kareem, Abdul, and Imamu, are changing names like Poh-leng Nguyen, Cheng Lin Chung, Vladimir Keldysh, and Sung Yung Pak into names like Billy, Josephine, Timothy, and Eleanor. Since such action is a radical departure from a pursuit of the American dream, I am obliged to inquire of my black American community, why did we do this?

11

THE BLACK AMERICAN COMMUNITY'S WORLD VIEW

"The colored [black American] population of the United States has no destiny separate from that of the nation in which they form an integral part. Our destiny is bound up with that of America. Her ship is ours; her pilot is ours; her storms are ours; her calms are ours. If she breaks upon a rock, we break with her. If we, born in America, cannot live upon the same soil upon terms of equality with the descendents of Scotsmen, Englishmen, Irishmen, Frenchmen, Germans, Hungarians, Greeks and Poles, then the fundamental theory of America fails and falls to the ground."

The Soul of Black Folk,
W. E. B. DuBois

Members of the twentieth generation (1986–2015) must understand that, as the theme quotation attests, the destiny of the black American community and that of America are irrevocably linked by the common ties of a wedded ancestry of cultural values, national heritage, and fervent patriotic nationality. Or perhaps more succinctly put, as America goes, so goes black America. Understanding and believing this concept is paramount to the approach of this chapter regarding the worldview of the black American community.

Thus, having no destiny separate from that of the United States obliges the black American community to take steps to assure its ability, and the

371

continuity of that ability to meet existing challenges and those that will be encountered as its fair share of the role the United States has been chartered by fate to play, both at home and abroad. One of the steps required to secure that continuity is for each black American to be familiar with the history and current events active on the world scene.

Furthermore, the youths of the twentieth generation (1986–2015), more than any of their predecessor generations, must be educated, whether in the school system, church, or home and be equipped with an effective understanding of world history and American's current political and economic world strategies. The level of education must be such as to enable these young black Americans to develop a mature and comprehensive understanding of the geopolitical and economic relationships existing between the United States and the other nations and peoples of the world. Each black American youth of the twentieth generation (1986–2015) is under an obligation, a mandate from the black American community to become proficient in his understanding of the nature and merits of America's geopolitical strategies as it might impact the next generation of black Americans.

In the 135 years since the ship *Clothilde*, the last of the ships used to transport Africans docked at an American port, the world has undergone dramatic restructuring. Empires and kingdoms are no longer the national motivation of each government. Smaller nations with more effective and efficient governments are the order of the modern day. The emperors and kings of the old political order have given way to presidents and premiers of the modern order. Concepts such as the chain of beings and the divine right of kings have long ago succumbed to the modern concepts of human rights and the sovereign rights of the individual. Instead of new-world nations and old-world nations, there are now first-world, second-world and third-world nations. In the years since the end of the enslavement of the Africans, which meant an end to an epoch in which millions of African immigrants died, humanity has continued to suffer massive tragedies. In at least four episodes in the past hundred years, mankind has been obliged to witness historical scenes in which millions of people have, under the guise of political expediency, been officially and systematically exterminated.

Although the enslavement of the Africans ended with the arrival of the *Clothilde*, the suffering and exploitation of the nations and peoples of Africa continued for another hundred years. As if the millions abducted during enslavement of the Africans were not injury enough, European governments moved and colonized the entire Africa continent when the enslavement of the Africans ended. As a result, the African nations and their peoples had their cultures, industries. socioeconomic affairs, and political boundaries dismantled and confounded by European colonization. From the latter part of the nineteenth century, the governments of Europe invaded the African continents en masse. The traditional cottage industries of Africa were destroyed or disappeared in favor of the more productive industries of western Europe. Political and national boundaries that had operated for thousands of years of African history were routinely dismantled in favor of artificially erected boundaries as dictated by European practitioners. European Christianity replaced traditional beliefs, and European languages supplanted indigenous languages. Natural resources mined, sawed, drilled and harvested in Africa were hauled off to European factories, and the proceeds, rather than being paid back to the Africans, were distributed among European shareholders. This exploitation of Africa on a global scale continued for almost a hundred years. However, the Africans were persistent in their opposition to colonization, and in 1956, they succeeded in gaining independence for the nation of Ghana. In the almost fifty years since then, the African people have succeeded in reasserting themselves culturally, industrially, socially, and economically, throughout Africa and are well on their way toward reaffirming Africa's political and national boundaries. All these events have occurred since the arrival of the *Clothilde*.

The world is now in the beginning years of the twentieth-first century. After having endured two generations under the threat of nuclear annihilation, black Americans and the world has for the past few years be able to breath a sigh of relief. In 1986, the political and socioeconomic structure of the USSR collapsing under the burden of its own hypocrisy dismembered itself in a crescendo of confederated pieces falling into place. With its demise, America stands as the pre-eminent power in the world as we enter the twenty-first century. From this perspective, black Americans are encouraged to think of the United States of America as the key player in the management of the technological and economical resources of the world. Over the past hundred years, the United States has become the principal broker of the world's resources. Consequently, black Americans must fulfill their roles as constituent players in the management of the technological and economic resources of the world.

To aid young black Americans in understanding the historical events that led up to the United States to become the principal power broker of the world's technology and resources, I shall attempt in as brief a manner as possible to provide an historical analysis of how, when, and why America came to occupy the seat at the head of the world's table of technology. Technology, as it appears on the surface, currently consists mainly of sophisticated space-age electronics that animate an assortment of mechanical devices varying from children's toys to space shuttles. However, farther back in the picture, what is now referred to as space-age technology emerged from what was once called the industrial revolution, which has unquestionably been the most productive innovation in the history of humanity. From a single trigger event that occurred in the Nile Delta of Africa over four thousand years ago, the industrial revolution has altered the behavior and perspectives of virtually every man, woman, and child on the face of the globe. Throughout the world, wherever it has spread, it has either served the needs of mankind by improving the quality of life or has supported its temporal vengeance by becoming an agent of destruction.

Now, as the twenty-first century positions itself, the industrial revolution, which fundamentally began as a crude wooden plough used to harvest grain in the alluvial soils of the Nile Delta, returns in a poetic sort of way via a circuitous journey around the world to the fertile soils of its origin. Returning, as it began, simply as an innovative approach to improving the quality of life of mankind. Only it arrives, not just as a crude wooden plough, but also as its metal-finished luminescence and light-blinking descendant technology. In the historical perspective, the industrial revolution should probably be more aptly classified as an industrial evolution rather than an industrial revolution. Although, from a retrospective point of view, I suppose if one were to consider some of the more disruptive features demonstrated during its emergence, it could be seen as revolutionary. In its own time frame, though, it evolved in minute stages along four thousand years of protracted history. As such, it exhibited considerably less tumult than is usually associated with a revolutionary event. In trying to present the industrial revolution as simply and succinctly as possible, I shall chronologue its emergence as the origin of a river slowing winding its way through varied terrain, collecting and redistributing deposits from its many tributaries along its way to the ocean. In this analogy, as the figurative river progresses along its way, it more or less reflects how the industrial revolution moved from an erstwhile insignificant event to world impact. For the industrial revolution also wound its way through an assortment of different lands, collecting and redistributing technological ideas as deposits from the innovations of many different peoples along its historical path to the world of the twenty-first century. From the model for our figurative river of the industrial revolution, we shall turn to America's pre-eminent river, the Mississippi. Often referred to as "Big Muddy" the Mississippi River is a great example of the phenomenon of a river that winds its way through varied terrain collecting and redistributing deposits along its way to the Gulf of Mexico and the ocean.

The Mississippi River begins its journey in northern Minnesota and gathers runoffs from approximately twenty to twenty-five states in the area. As it flows, it collects water and fertile topsoil deposits from the Missouri River, the Ohio River, the Red River, and many other tributaries that feed into it. The flow from these sources considerably increases the size, substance, and volume of the Mississippi. Meanwhile, the river continues on its journey south passing through different terrain and states, their borders lines up against the river's opposite shores as if attending a great aquatic spectacle. Then, having completed its long journey, the river finally empties into the great basin of the Gulf of Mexico. In a manner similar to the Mississippi River, the industrial revolution began. As can best be determined, this occurred sometimes during the second millennium B.C. in the fertile crescent of the Nile River Valley. For the purpose of this analogy, the area around this Nile River Valley should be envisioned as a great basin, for indeed the area does consist of the Mediterranean Basin.

Again, for the purpose of this approach, think of the Mediterranean Basin as the mouth or origin of the river of the industrial revolution, or for purposes of this commentary let's call it the Flowing-River-of-the-Industrial-Revolution. The basin lake is fed by at least six principal tributary rivers, and its overflow drains off, as mentioned, into the Flowing-River-of-the-Industrial-Revolution. In this analogy, the tributaries represent the technical innovations and inventions that came from an assortment of historical times and geographic regions of those two landmasses. From the African landmass flowed the first of the tributary stream. Emerging as though from an underground source, the Flowing-River-of-the-Industrial-Revolution metaphorically began as this trickling stream. It began in the form of a wooden plough being drawn by animals recently domesticated. The plough, prompted by the invention of agriculture, is symbolic of the industrial revolution. Simply put, it is the story of mechanization—tools and equipment, powered by an energy source external of mankind and used to reduce its (mankind's) labor and enhance its quality of life. The plough, though crude by today's standards and simplistic in design, was the principal implement that contributed to the establishment of urban or city dwelling. Before agriculture, before the plough, people were nomadic and followed the wild animals herds that represented the bulk of their food supply.

With the development of agriculture, made feasible by the use of the plough and irrigation another Nile Valley innovation—it was no longer necessary for families to migrate long distances to follow the herds. Now, with agriculture and domesticated animals, a constant food supply was assured without annual migrations. With a stable food supply, people began to witness their first sustainable food abundance. With this abundance came the need for a variety of other services such as central control over the abundance. Out of that need came what we now call civil governments and out of the need to regulate irrigation canals, planting seasons and food surpluses, other activities such as meteorology, record keeping, metrology, and taxes evolved. Flowing into this basin of accumulated knowledge was another stream, which flowed from the ancient land of Lydia. In its sediment of technical innovation, it held knowledge on the use of the schist stone. The schist stone was a portable device capable of assessing to gold content of coins. It was discovered that when gold coins were rubbed across the smooth flat surface of the stone, the color of the residual mark would indicate whether the coin was pure gold or alloyed with silver or copper. This procedure validated the merits of gold coinage, and its use spread quickly throughout the region and beyond.

The use of the touchstone, which is how the schist stone became known, was as important to the business of merchandizing as the Rosetta Stone would become to the study of Egyptian hieroglyphs. Another tributary of valuable knowledge flowing into the Mediterranean basin of industrial knowledge came from Greece during the golden age of Greek philosophy. Within its cultural sediments, it carried ideas regarding the application of pneumatics and hydraulics in the development of tooling and industrial equipment. From still farther away, another tributary flowing into the mouth of the Flowing-River-of-the-Industrial-Revolution came from the territories occupied by the Roman Empire. As the waters of the Roman tributary cut its way across the Latin soil, it carried with it silt and sediments particles containing designs for the manufacture and use of running water to power heavy equipment an intracontinental network of highly developed roads, use of a widespread communications systems, and sophisticated legal systems and governmental bureaucracies.

The fifth tributary river began in China and flowed into the basin lake from cities and towns thousands of miles away. Across the lofty peaks of the great Himalayan mountains, inventions and techniques discovered by the Chinese flowed many miles to the knowledge basin of the Mediterranean site. The ideas and inventions these waters carried included the composition and use of gun powder, a system for setting printing type, and methods for making paper. Finally, around the twelfth century, the last of these tributaries of dispersed knowledge flowed into our metaphorical basin. Its flow raised the level of knowledge high enough to cause it to overflow into the tributary of the Arabs whose scholars had made great strides in translating ancient Greek writings. It became the primary conduit through which the knowledge from our fictional basin flowed into a Western Europe that was just waking up from a thousand years of Medieval Dark Ages. Since the fall of Rome in 476 A.D., Western Europe had essentially lain dormant.

However, as the thirteenth century approached, Western Europe became to the Flowing-River-of-the-Industrial-Revolution, what the Gulf of Mexico is to the Mississippi River. All the knowledge that had flowed into the Mediterranean basin from its many tributaries now flowed directly into an awakening Western Europe. The results would make Western Europe appear as the seedbed of the Industrial Revolution. That it played a significant role is not subject to question. The facts are, however, that Europe became the Flowing-River-of-the-Industrial-Revolution's fertile delta where almost any crop planted would grow bountifully. But as the Mississippi River empties into the Gulf of Mexico, the Gulf flows into the Atlantic Ocean.

In this perspective, the United States became the ocean of the Industrial Revolution, distributing its resources, techniques and benefits throughout the rest of the world. If Western Europe's successful application of the thousands of inventions and technical ideas fed by a bounty of other sources, made it appear as the seed bed of the Industrial Revolution, the United States surely did Western Europe one better. Utilizing a similar knowledge transfer that tagged Western Europe as the birthplace of the industrial revolution, the United States has become the pre-eminent technological superpower among all nations of the earth. Even though the Flowing-River-of-the-Industrial-Revolution began by drawing upon the innovations and techniques of an assortment of the world's peoples and flowed through many lands and peoples, its oceanic destination was Western Europe. In Europe the natural flow of the river was absorbed much as the Mississippi River's flow is absorbed in the Gulf of Mexico. From Europe, the technology of the Flowing-River-of-the-Industrial-Revolution no longer flowed via natural drought but was carried by the currents of political and ethnic affiliation. Evidence to support that contention is apparent when one notes the current distribution of the more industrialized nations. For instance, six to seven hundred years following the Flowing-River-of-the-Industrial-Revolution's flow into the Western European basin, only selected nations with political affiliation with Western Europe have had free access to Europe's industrialization resources. If one were to take a map of the world and mark off all the traditionally industrialized nations, one would soon find that all the first-world nations, which are considered to be the more technologically advanced, were dominated by descendents of Western European immigrants.

Although some of the United States' power and prestige is based on the morality of its political system (as is articulated in its Declaration of Independence and in the U.S. Constitution), its enormous growth in power and world influence is more properly attributable to its advanced technological advantage, and of course, its free-enterprise economic system. These combined two features have accounted for the country's unprecedented economic and political growth, both at home and throughout the rest of the world.

For the black American community is fulfill its destiny in the world community, members of the twentieth generation (1986–2015) will have to become familiar with the components of the free enterprise and technological features of the United States. They should understand the edge or strength the United States has in the areas of political, technological, and free enterprise entrepreneurialism, which are fundamentally as effective as a currency of power in the world. And enable the United States to reach objectives with other nations and governments that would otherwise not be possible, were it not for its dominant role in technology and its free-enterprise economy. In the past hundred years, other nations have begun developing highly sophisticated technological systems. All things being equal, this trend is expected to continue, and with considerably more speed than in the past hundred years.

Also, the black American community should be mindful of the probability that the socializing properties of America, which have often been attributed to a melting pot phenomenon, are probably no longer as active as they once were. As a result of the slowdown in the melting-pot process, cultural idioms like the American character, the American mind, or the American Adam—much-publicized products of the melting pot—are becoming more and more anachronistic. In a way it is ironic that the main reasons for the disappearance of these unique American components can, for the most part, be ascribed to the same reason that the country became a world leader in technological growth in the first place. In the golden days of the past when immigrant groups arrived in America, the country was virtually shutoff from the rest of the world. This is not meant to suggest that the country was under some kind of legal, political, or medical quarantine. It was not. It was shutoff from the rest of the world by the sheer distance between North America and Europe. And if the distance between the continents was not sufficient—after all, the distance between the continents is the same as it has always been—there was the problem of transportation. With industrial technology being what it was in the sixteenth century and the time and cost of transportation to travel between continents, most immigrants were landlocked, never to visit their home again. Reference to being virtually landlocked from the rest of the world does not intend to suggest that it was impossible for the immigrants to visit their homes again but rather it refers to the thousands of miles of ocean that stood between America and the landmasses of the Old World.

Just the fact that it took a very long time and cost a lot of money for people to travel on ocean voyages in those days, made traveling to and from America, a once-in-a-life time venture. As a reference, consider that a family migrating from Africa or Europe to America was taking on a journey that today would be comparable to a family migrating from Earth to Mars. In fact, the Mars migration might be less demanding because the migrating family would most likely maintain ongoing radio contact with Earth and with their family and friends on Earth. On the other hand, in the seventeenth and eighteenth centuries, when a group said goodbye to their family, friends, and loved ones when moving to America, it was quite probably the last time they would ever see those family members and friends. Consequently, those immigrants who came to America developed a value system, habits, and behavior unique to their new home. In a way, the original immigrants to America, including the African immigrants, became subject to forces that Charles Darwin, in an entirely different context, referred to as "descent modification."

In *The Origin of Species* Charles Darwin identified this phenomenon as operating among the endemic birds of the Galapagos Archipelago. In his treatise, Darwin noted that during his visit to the Galapagos Islands, he found that because of its distance from the South American continent and any other substantial land masses, the island's bird species were virtually shutoff from similar species of any of the island's continental land masses. As a result of this isolation, Darwin noted that 21–23 of the island's twenty-six land birds could not fly far enough to leave the island and had developed features unique to their island habitat. Darwin's discoveries regarding the island's local bird population are comparable in its application to the situation that confronted this nation's original immigrant populations. In the same fashion that the land birds of the Galapagos Islands developed peculiarities commensurate with their environment, the immigrant groups developed habits, values, and behaviors peculiar to their American surroundings. So unique was the new American character that it was referred to variously as the American Mind, or the American Adam, as distinct from a European mind, etc.

The concept of the melting pot is also founded upon the very premise that the isolation would produce a unique American character. But it appears that twentieth-century technology has already begun to put an end to the cultural isolationism that turned foreign immigrants into Americans. Immigrant groups who currently migrate to America do not have to bid final good-byes to their families, friends, and loved ones as their predecessors once did. Now, a family group, or individual can pack their bags in Nairobi, London, or Tokyo and in only a few hours, they are walking the streets of New York, Atlanta, or Los Angeles. And when they become homesick, they can just pick up the telephone and call their former home, and chat with all their family members. This kind of freedom sustains cultural ties and identity. With such access to their former homelands, immigrants are no longer cutoff from their cultural identity.

Thanks to the benefit of air travel and low transoceanic fares, newly arriving immigrants will be able to return home often enough to maintain social and cultural ties with their native homelands. These return visits will further re-enforce their values and customs, reducing the impact the melting pot had upon earlier American immigrants. In that sense—they come to America, but then they fly off home again for home visits—they are very comparable in behavior to what Charles Darwin observed in the island's marine bird population. Darwin defined the marine birds as those that could fly long enough and far enough to visit other major landmasses. He noted that of the island's eleven species of marine birds, only two of the eleven had developed features that he classified as peculiar to the Galapagos Islands. Darwin also noted that even on islands where the indigenous bird population was not as likely to leave the island, incoming birds of the same species tended to counter the forces of descent modification.

In our analysis, those incoming birds would be comparable to the visits to America by members of the immigrants family's relatives and friends. The frequency of those visits, like the frequency of the incoming birds, would also tend to counter the isolationist forces necessary to drive the melting pot that has historically played such a role in turning the various immigrants groups into a greater whole that would be identifiably American. Therefore, black Americans will have to develop a greater sense of international awareness and tolerance.

12

RATING THE SOCIO ECONOMIC PROGRESS
OF THE
BLACK AMERICAN COMMUNITY

In this chapter we shall attempt to provide a summary report on the progress that black Americans have achieved during the past nineteen generations (1619 through 1955), and the additional progress succeeding generations (1936–2015) are obliged to make and sustain the momentum necessary to accomplish socioeconomic parity. To assess the progress achieved and to rate the work that remains to be done, we will be utilizing a letter-grade format. The reason for this particular grading format is to take advantage of the popular familiarity associated with the school report card to communicate the notions of a passing versus failing grade.

The black American community has been in America since 1619, and yet after almost four hundred years, and nineteen generations of American residency, the black American community continues to lag behind its white American counterpart in socio economic accomplishments. While it is true that in this post-civil rights era the disparity has been substantially narrowed by members of the seventeenth (1926–1955) and eighteenth (1946–1975) generations, much more remains to be accomplished. This chapter sets forth the remaining obligations of the seventeenth (1926–1955) generation's third tripartite (1946–1955), and the continuing obligations of the eighteenth (1946–1975) and nineteenth

(1966–1995) generations. To emphasize the educational mandate, this chapter will present a wide assortment of facts and figures taken from data curried from U. S. Census Bureau and the U.S. Bureau of Labor Statistics reports. The specific data offered herein is presented as corroborative evidence, or supportive background for the argument that if the socioeconomic estate of the black American community is to be improved, black Americans of the nineteenth (1966–1995) and twentieth generation (1986–2015), the two post civil rights era generations, must carry out an intense program of internal and self-serving affirmative action.

Based on data from the U.S. Census Bureau and the U.S. Bureau of Labor Statistics, in March of 2000, the U. S. population was 274,087,847. The black American population, which is 13.0% of the total population, was 35,631,420. Summarily, that means that if one were to conduct a survey, they should justly expect to find an average of 13% of all occupational positions in the nation, held by black Americans. Such a survey should show, for instance, that 13% of members of the U. S. Senate and 13% of the members of the entire U.S. House of Representatives should, statistically, be black Americans. Not only that, but 13% of all of the nation's CEOs and an equal percentage of all U. S. Military and military generals should also be black Americans. And yes, all things being equal, it means that 13% of all the nation's presidents should also be black Americans.

That being said, it also mean on the converse, that 13% of the nation's college students, Bachelor Degree graduates, and 13% of the nation's advanced degree graduates should also be black Americans. And, by this token, no more than 13% of black Americans should be categorized as school dropouts nor should the percentages of black American inmates in the nation's jails and prisons be greater than the same 13%. In this scenario, if reality is to prevail, you can't have parity in the former without parity in the latter.

Table II in chapter 7, on *Socioeconomic Parity* list 134 of the occupational categories shown in the U. S. Census Bureau's listing of U. S. Employment in occupational sub-categories. Statistically, black Americans should occupy 13.0% of each of the occupational categories shown. However, in reality the distribution of black Americans in the various occupational categories is anything but statistically proportioned.

The table is sorted by the column labeled, *BAC's(black American Community) Percentage of Total Employment*. As can be seen in the table, there are 21 occupational categories in which black Americans make up less 30%(see the last column) of the 13 percent necessary for socioeconomic parity. Most of these 21 occupations such as; *financial managers, architects, civil engineers, nuclear engineers, aerospace engineers, mechanical engineers, natural scientists, dentists, real estate sales, lawyers and judges*, are coincidently among the nation's higher paying salaried positions. And in one particular category of occupations, that of, *managers, marketing, advertisement and public relation*, the percentage of black Americans employed is only 0.9%, or less than 1%. In that category alone there are a total of 419,000 Americans employed as *managers, marketing, advertisement and public relation* positions. By the numbers, 13 percent, or 54,470 of those 419,000 persons should be black Americans. The fact that only 0.9%, or 3,771 black Americans are actually employed in that occupation, means that there are 50,699 (54,470 – 3,771) high paying positions in the *managers, marketing, advertisement and public relation* occupation that statistically belong to the black American community that black Americans are failing to take advantage of. Notwithstanding the lack of parity in education and socio cultural integration, the fact remain that there are 50,699 jobs, the difference between the number of black Americans that statistically should be employed in this occupation, and those that actually are, that are paying high salaries to someone other than the black American Community. If we allow that these 21 occupational categories pay and average annual salary of over $75,000.00, the 50,699 lost jobs translates into more than $3.8 billion additional dollars that would be going into the socioeconomic estate of the black American community just for this category alone.

In all 21 of the occupational categories shown in this grouping, there are a total of 11,352,602 Americans employed in these various occupations. 13 percent, or 1,475,838 of those employees should be black Americans. The actual percentage of black Americans in these occupations range from the very low 0.9% referred to earlier to 3.9%. If we just take the highest figure of 3.9%, you can see that less than 442,751 black Americans are currently taking advantage of these high paying jobs. Since black Americans are at only 31% to 60% of parity in this grouping, that means that they are bringing only 31% to 60% of the more than 13 billion dollars they are due. The next time a black American tells you how expensive an education is, refer to this paragraph to show them how expensive the lack of an education has become. The salaries in these 21 occupations are very high, but the percentage of black American participating in these jobs is very low, less than 30% of that required for parity. Therefore, the black American community gets a "D" grade for their low percentage participation in these 21 occupational categories.

In the next grouping of categories in the table, line items 22 through 57, there are 35 occupations in which the percentage of black American participation is well below the 13 percent required for socioeconomic parity. The total number of Americans employed in these occupations is 67,622,777. Of this figure, 8,790,961 of those employed in these occupations should be black Americans. But if we use just the average of 6.25%, we can see that less than 4,226,423 black Americans are indeed so employed. Data from the U. S. Census Bureau's Current Population Survey for March 2000 shows that, although substantial progress has been made in education, black Americans continue to lag white Americans by a rate 62%. Whereas 18.4% of white Americans graduate from college with Bachelor Degrees, the percentage of black Americans with Bachelor

Degrees is down to 11.4%. And in the area of advanced degrees 5.1% of black Americans graduate from college with degrees higher than a Bachelors compared to 9.3% of white Americans who do. Thus the disparity in occupational distribution is practically mirrored in the disparity in education achievement. The salaries in these 35 occupations are also among the higher paying jobs, and even though the percentage of black American participating in these jobs is higher than those above, it is still 60% or less of that required for parity. Therefore, the black American community gets a "C" grade for their participation in these 35 occupational categories.

There are 25 occupational categories shown on lines 58 through 83. The percentage of black American participation in these 25 occupations, while not as low as the percentage seen in the previous two groups, is nevertheless below the 13 percent necessary for parity. There are a total of 32,634,713 Americans employed in these occupations. Of this figure there should be 4,242,690 black Americans employed, but there are only 3,818,261. The percentages of black Americans in these occupations varies from 8.1% to 11.7%. While these percentages are considerably higher than those cited in the first group, line items 1 through 21, these occupations also pay lower salaries than those in line items 1 through 21. And, as we are beginning to see, the percentage of black American employed in these categories tend to be inversely proportional to the amount of education that is required by that particular group of occupations. The salaries in these 25 occupations are not necessarily among the higher paying jobs, and even though the percentage of black American participating in these jobs is higher than those above, it is still only 61% to 90% of that required for parity. Therefore, the black American community also gets a "C" grade for their participation in these 35 occupational categories.

The participation of the black Americans in the following group of occupations is commendable. In these 21 occupations, line items 84-105, the number of black Americans participating is between 11.9% and 14.1% percentage. These percentages equates to 91% to 110% of parity. Parity is considered achieved in those occupations in which black American partic- ipation equates to 91% to 110% of the 13% necessary for national parity. Even though the black American community has attained parity in these 21 occupations, a quick visual survey of the following list of occupations easily suggest that parity here is a mixed blessing. Some of the jobs could pay well, while others would undoubtedly not pay very well *(Pre-kinder- garten and kindergarten, General office clerks, Agricultural and related occu- pations, Administrators and official public administration, Cashiers, Waiters' and waitresses' assistants, Supervisors, Production inspectors, testers, samplers and weighers, School, recreation, religious workers, Barbers, Trucks, heavy and light, Public transportation attendants, Computer equipment operators, Computer operators, Police and detectives, Health technologists and techni- cians, Transportation and material moving occupations, Chief executives and General Administrators, Material moving equipment operators, Records- process occupation, except finances and Motor vehicle operators).*

Parity in this sense then is not the parity that we have been stressing, but rather it is simple the level in which the education skills of the black American community reconciled themselves with the existing market place. Since parity in these 21 occupations do not favor the initial objec- tive set out for achieving socioeconomic parity, nationally, the black American community still gets only a "B" grade in these occupational categories.

Lastly, line items 106 through 131 of the occupational categories' table represent the core of the disparity that exists between the descendents of the African immigrants and that of the descendents of the European immigrants. There are 34,790,950 Americans employed in these 26 occu- pations. These are all low-paying occupations in which extremely large numbers of black Americans, due to their extremely low skills, are concen- trated. These highly concentrated numbers of black Americans depletes the socioeconomic strength of the black American community to be more effective in the professions and other high paying positions. The percentages of black American employed in these 26 occupations varies from the 14.7% employed in the *Operators, fabricators, and laborers* occupation through the 30.8% of black Americans employed as maids and housemen. These percentages translate into 113 to 237 percent of the black Americans necessary for parity. With black Americans making up 30.8% of the people working as maids and housemen nationally, means that 13 percent of the population is performing almost one-third of the maid and housemen work in the country. We would be quite happy and content to hold down 13% of these positions, but 30.8% mean that thousands of black Americans that should be employed as; *financial managers, architects, civil engineers, nuclear engineers, aerospace engineers, mechanical engineers, natural scientists, dentists, real estate sales, lawyers and judges* are severely under utilized. These extremely high percentages of black Americans employed in these very low paying jobs reflect, unfortunately, the meager levels of education present particularly among the second tripartite (1936–1945) and third tripartite (1946–1955) of the seventeenth generation (1936–1955), and to a lesser extent, similar educational shortcomings among members of the first tripartite (1946–1955) and the second tripartite (1956–1965) of the eighteenth (1946–1975) generation. The continued presence of this disproportion of educational skill will haunt the black American community's quest for socioeconomic parity as long as it exist.

The salaries in these 26 occupations are among the lowest paying jobs and the percentage of black American participating in these jobs is considerably higher than parity requirements therefore, the black American community also gets a "D" grade for their participation in these 26 occupational categories.

Line item 133 shows that there are 1,452,000 black Americans that are currently unemployed. The total U. S. unemployment is 8,142,000. If black Americans made up only 13% of that figure, the total black American unemployment would be 1,058,460. That there are 1,452,000 unemployed black Americans means that their portion of the this category is unacceptably high. Is in fact 137 percent of the parity figure of 1,058,460 unemployed black Americans. This excess qualifies this category for the letter grade of "F." As stated in Table IV, a letter grade of "F" means that that the number of black Americans in this category are non productive and exceeds by a good degree the 13.0% allowed for parity.

And finally, the black American community gets a well-earned "F" letter grade the category of *prison and jail inmates*. According to the U. S. Department of Justice's Bureau of Justice Statistics, the number of prison and jail inmates in the nation is approximately 1,600,000. Of that number 39.07 %, or 625,000 are black Americans. Using the 13% parity figure, there should be no more than about 200,000 black Americans in the nations jails and prisons. Painfully this category more than qualifies for the letter grade of "F." As stated in Table IV, a letter grade of "F" means that that the number of black Americans incarcerated in our nations jails and prisons far exceeds the 13.0% that we allow for parity. And in this instance, even allowing for the 13% parity of the black Americans to be in jail or prison, or otherwise outside of an occupational category is extremely offensive to the black American community's quest for socioeconomic competency. These 625,000 men and women should rather be in enrolled in, and receiving degrees from the nation's colleges and universities. This could then be moved into the higher paying occupational categories to assist in offsetting the socioeconomic deficits present there.

PASS-POSITIVE LETTER GRADE "B"	FAIL-POSITIVE LETTER GRADE "C"	PASS-NEGATIVE LETTER GRADE "D"	FAIL-NEGATIVE LETTER GRADE "F"
A letter grade of "B" means that the number of black Americans employed in that occupational category meet or exceed the 13.0% necessary to achieve socioeconomic parity, and that the particular occupational category pays a favorable salary, or income.	A letter grade of "C" means that the number of black Americans employed in that occupational category does not yet meet nor exceed the 13.0% necessary to achieve socioeconomic parity, and that the particular occupational category pays a favorable salary, or income.	A letter grade of "C" means that the number of black Americans employed in that occupational category meet or exceed the 13.0% necessary to achieve socioeconomic parity, but that the particular occupational category pays less than a favorable salary, or income.	A letter grade of "F" means that that the number of black Americans employed in that occupational category far exceeds the 13.0% necessary for socioeconomic parity and that the particular occupational category is viewed as an unfavorable to the parity objective.

Table VII

The inordinate distribution of black Americans among the lower-paying occupations in the preceding tables represents the core of the socioeconomic disparity that afflicts the black American community. However, the distribution figures themselves are only symptomatic of the real technical problems that are the dramatic lack of skills and educational preparedness among members of the black American community.

The figures also represent a statistical analysis of the socioeconomic disparity that exists between the fortunes of the descendents of the African immigrants and those of the descendents of the European immigrants. And although the core of the disparity issue is not the only reason that black Americans lag behind white Americans, that fact alone ought be sufficient to keep the issue near the top of the black American socioeconomic agenda. Keep in mind that the issue is not just one of race. It goes much deeper than the differences in the fortunes of the black Americans and the white Americans. It revolves around the fact that the black American community has been in America for such a long, long time. Black Americans, though forcibly drafted and enslaved, arrived in America hundreds of years before the country was open to general or popular immigration through which other immigrant groups arrived.

Currently, black Americans make up at least one-eighth of the national population yet their statistical share of the nation's fortunes lags considerably behind that one-eighth proportion of the population. Admittedly, enslavement and the hundred years of Jim Crow terrorism played a significant role in delaying the black American's access to the nation's resources. However, notwithstanding the rough estimate of a seven-to-twelve percent adversity factor attributable to latent racism, the national market place is now accessible to all black Americans. And by applying a seven to twelve percent compensatory effort, we can overcome that negative adversity factor and still succeed in the market place, the spurious acts of modern day racists, terrorists, kooks and nuts notwithstanding.

An added issue that drives the subject of parity to the top of the agenda is the painful consequences that black Americans have suffered and continues to suffer as a result of social and economic deprivation and the ills associated with them. Achieving socioeconomic parity would rectify these two conditions, which in themselves ought, to be sufficient argument that parity should become a non-negotiable component of the aspiration of every black American.

Historical speaking, socioeconomic parity can be validated as being a statistical right of black American heritage. On the basis of the increased access available to black Americans of the nineteenth (1966–1995) and twentieth (1986–2015) generations, it is inherent that socioeconomic parity be their generational legacy to the children of future generations.

It is the purpose and quest of this commentary that every black American be challenged to act in the corporate interest of all black Americans and that each pledge his support in promoting the education of all black American children, particularly the children of the third tripartite (1986–1995) of the nineteenth generation (1966–1995), and children in the first tripartite (1986–1995) of the twentieth generation (1986–2015). Black American children from the third tripartite of the twentieth generation, nor those born after the twentieth generation should have to be born into the realm of poverty that currently so evident in the socioeconomic environment of so many black Americans.

And on a generational and personalized basis, how do we, as members of the nineteenth generation riding the crest of a 383-year residency, propose to explain to the children of the twentieth and twenty-first generations what we have been doing to benefit their lives? Having been residents and citizens of the most affluent and equitable nation on earth for all those years, enslavement and Jim Crow terrorists, notwithstanding, how do we look them in the face and explain why we, among the nation's longest and most consistent residents, continue to share a disproportion of the national resources?

It will be beyond our ability to explain this to our children if black Americans do not rid themselves of this socioeconomic affliction now since its aberrational properties will continue to haunt the self-esteem of all future generations of black Americans. These properties will also continue to be used as collaborative support for the bigoted ideas and spurious arguments of the distorted and small minds of those who, perennially claims that people with black skin are not as smart as people with white skin. There is no reason why future generations of black American children should have to contend with, be exposed to, or ponder the demerits of such trivial contentions. The reality is that we really should not have to face the children of those generations with such a paltry report card. As previously offered, we contend that applying classic models of upward mobility can solve the black American community's problems of poverty and ignorance. Understandably, those models did not work and indeed could not have worked—except in limited circumstances—during the periods of enslavement or the era of Jim Crow terrorism. For during those periods, the principal component of any classic approach—that of access—was not legally available to black Americans. However, the black American community now has access, and the principles of such classic approaches can be applied. One proposed solution is that the disparity noted in the occupational distribution tables be addressed, using the simple but classic approach of educating black American children. And even allowing the seven-to-twelve percent adversity factor referred to earlier, an affirmative program of educating black American children will, as is illustrated in the herd of cattle metaphor, finally enable them to take their place around the middle-class watering hole.

BLACK AMERICAN-OWNED BUSINESSES IN MAJOR, KEY MARKET AREAS

PLACES, OR CITY AND STATE WHERE FIRM (BUSINESSES) ARE LOCATED	UNIVERSE ALL FIRMS (BUSINESS) OPERATING IN THE CITY NOTED	NUMBER OF FIRMS (BUSINESSES) THAT ARE OWNED BY BLACK AMERICANS	PERCENTAGE [1] OF BLACK AMERICAN FIRMS (BUSINESSES) OPERATING IN THIS CITY (Parity = 13%)	PERCENTAGE [2] OF SALES, RECEIPTS FROM BUSINESSES OWNED BY BLACK AMERICAN BUSINESSES (parity=13%) [2]	GRADE [1]	GRADE [2]
Atlanta, GA.	38,412	7,853	20%	.71%	A+	F
Birmingham, AL	15,265	3,477	23%	.5%	A+	F
Charleston, S.C.	9,493	863	9%	.6%	B	F
Charlotte, N.C.	43,854	4,803	11%	.49%	B	F
Chicago, IL	176,605	23,576	13%	11.5%	A	B
Dallas, TX.	107,337	7,661	7%	10.5%	C	B
Denver, CO.	56,961	2,178	4%	.34%	F	F
Detroit, MI	26,085	11,282	43%	21.7%	A+	A+
Houston, TX.	17,3651	16,855	10%	.46%	B	F
Jackson, MS.	14,762	3,117	21%	11.9%	A+	B
Los Angeles, CA.	341,117	17,593	5%	.35%	F	F
Memphis, TN.	36,334	8,080	22%	.9%	A	F
Miami, FL.	52,327	2,954	6%	.56%	F	F
New Orleans, LA.	30,262	6,425	21%	24.3%	A+	A+
New York, NY.	649,717	63,327	10%	.44%	B	F
St. Louis, MO.	202,761	3,431	17%	.5%	A	F
Washington, DC	45,297	10,909	24%	25.2%	A+	A+

Table VIII

Date from the U. S. Census Bureau was used to compile this report. Source: U. S. Census Bureau, 1997 Economic Census Minority-and Women-Owned Businesses

In a figurative sense, too many black Americans are attempting to get to the middle class watering hole through the career path doors marked sports and music. These and the chance paths doors marked win the lotto, or hit it big at the casino are extremely high-odd career paths and much more often than not, they don't pan out. Yet these are some of the traditional and haphazard paths that black Americans have resorted to in their effort to become successful. As a result, there are in this figurative example long lines of black Americans, particularly young black Americans practicing their hoop shots, dancing in the streets, or practicing their music in the long shot hope that they'll be the next one drafted, or discovered. While they figuratively stand in long lines waiting for their big chance, there are no long lines at the entrances to the career path doors marked medical doctors, lawyers, nursing, business managers, engineers and law enforcement officers.

Visually, think of it this way. There are a large number of these career path doors that lead into the room of success. Inside this room is the career success that everyone is seeking. There are a large number of people of all ethnic groups standing in front of career path doors labeled medical doctors, lawyers, nursing, business managers, engineers, law enforcement officers, scientists, accountants, mathematicians, etc. However, that an inordinate number of the young black Americans are lined up in front of the three career path doors labeled sports, music and entertainment. This commentary seeks to challenge the practice by offering a better way. There is a particular career path door that leads to the middle class watering hole that black Americans need to focus on especially over the next two or three generations. That career path door is the one-labeled business manager, or more specifically business owner. While black Americans have a good and lengthy history of participating in business ownership their participation has traditionally been in ownership in smaller business enterprises located well within the black American communities, or neighborhoods.

Also, since the great migration to the northern cities in the early part of the last century, most black Americans were obliged to focused on occupational positions which offered a secure regular, or weekly paycheck and not so much on the risks associated with business ownership. Since being successful in a business obviously required market environment receptive to your business, black Americans were substantially handicapped by an environment that here-to-fore has not been receptive to black owned businesses. And so, the only business opportunities that available to members of the fourteenth generation through the eighteenth generation have were businesses that operated well within black American neighborhoods, or communities. Such businesses consisted mainly of restaurants, barbershops, and beauty shops and of course funeral homes, or undertaking.

It is now time for members of the nineteenth generation and twentieth generation to take the black American community to the next level in business ownership. Table VI is a listing the business activity in 17 of the nation's major markets. In three of these markets (Detroit, MA. the District of Columbia, and New Orleans, LA.) black Americans owns (as defined by the U. S. Census Bureau) businesses in numbers that far exceed the 13.0% parity requirement and have sales and receipt that are also above the parity figure. Two other markets areas (Chicago, IL. and Jackson, MS.) in which the number of businesses, or firms, owned by black Americans are also above parity, but the sales and receipts from these businesses falls slightly below parity. Then there are the remaining 12 market areas, or cities in which neither the number of businesses owned by black Americans, nor the sales and receipts from these businesses comes anywhere close to matching the parity figure. This is the area where the nineteenth generation and the twentieth generation must focus their entrepreneurial resources over the terms of their generations.

In the preceding pages of this chapter on the report card of the black American community, we have identified that black Americans do indeed lag behind in their efforts to acquire what can be defined as their statistical share of America's socioeconomic resources. The statistical share of resources is defined as that which would ordinarily be credited to black Americans, based upon their proportion of the general population and their comparable distribution within the areas of skills development, education, and social integration.

In the following pages we shall define the objective, approach, and method recommended to successfully overcome the present socioeconomic inequity. Perhaps in another idyllic state of naivete, I have targeted the years 1995–2006 for the implementation of programs to accomplish these objectives. The year 2006 represents the beginning of the twenty-first generation (2006–2035) of black Americans in since the arrival of Antony and Isabella.

In prior illustrations and examples, we have demonstrated how, when other peoples and nations faced similar and seemingly overwhelming odds, they were able to overcome them by using formally defined strategies and applying classic models. We previously explained how the Japanese government, when confronted with the awesome task of moving its people from a state of feudalism into the industrial age, succeeded by enlisting the assistance of the British government to provide equipment and training for the Japanese people. Prior to that, the disparity between the industrialization of Japan and that of the West was greater even than the disparity now faced by the black American community. During the 1850s, Japan was still faced with warring and sparring warlords. Its citizenry had essentially no rights, or access to any rights. Worst, they lived in a state akin to enslaved servitude. Though the emperor officially ran the country, the fate of its citizens, more often than not, rested in the hands of its warlords. Often competing and feuding over various issues, the warlords, or Samurai, practically ran the country in their own manner and for their own interest.

After the arrival of Admiral Perry's steamships in the 1850s and his demonstration of industrial power, the feuding warlords realized it was time for a change. Following that, the Japanese government commissioned the assistance of the British government to develop its own industrialization program. In just about forty-nine years after they began the project, the Japanese government could boast of an industrial base comparable to that of its teacher and mentor, the British. The black American community has even greater access to the sources of training and of skills development.

Also, we related how that the Germans of post-World War I, notwithstanding their reprehensible political and social agendas, girded themselves about their own resources in their quest to improve their dilapidated post-war economy. Additionally the Germans were also tasked with repairing a self-esteem that had been wrecked by the military, social, and political devastation suffered at the hands of the Axis Powers during Germany's defeat. In its wake, the German people had essentially lost the will to mount any kind of an aggressive program to pull themselves out of the socioeconomic pit they had fallen into upon the collapse of their economy. And with virtual chaos all about them, a simple though perverted call to self-esteem was able to not only elevate this self-esteem but to also motivate them to build one of the world's more powerful economies and expedient military regimes in a period of less than ten years.

Again, discounting the horrendous acts perpetrated upon its own people, the Germans nevertheless were able to pull themselves together and build an effective economic power base. Still more examples can be found to illustrate that when a people organizes itself about a task, it can often be accomplished. Even today, many nations and peoples—some remnants of the former Soviet Union: Hungary, Poland, the Czech republic, the Republic of Slovakia, and all CIS states, including present-day Russia, are busy marshaling plans to improve their socioeconomic systems which would afford them a greater share of the world's resources.

Perhaps the country of the former Soviet Union that is most visible to Americans is what was formerly known as East Germany. Now fully politically unified into Germany itself, the citizens of the former East Germany are still plagued by the remnants of that country's depressed sociotechnological development. Yet, in spite of such depression, the German government has implemented a plan by which it intends to elevate the sociotechnological status of the former East Germans to that of the rest of Germany within ten to fifteen years after its re-unification.

If the former East Germany is most visible to most Americans, then South Africa, and President Mandela are certainly the most visible examples for the black Americans.

When I began work on this book, Mr. Nelson Mandela had just been released from prison in South Africa. And now although he has indeed been elected and served his term as president of South Africa, he presided over a nation whose socioeconomic structure has been wrecked by sources, both internal and external. Internally, the nation's infrastructure has been damaged as a result of years of sociopolitical unrest and paramilitary activities. Externally, for a period of almost twenty years, outside governments and multi-national businesses either divested themselves of their interests in the South African economy or boycotted its enterprises altogether. The net results of the paramilitary attacks the actions taken by the various governments and the multi-national corporations were, of course, a major success. The other side of the coin is that for them to have been as successful as they were, these actions were counter-productive to the South African economy. Their success against apartheid proves that they were successful in damaging the South African socioeconomic infrastructure. It is precisely this damaged infrastructure that South Africa's new president, Nelson Mandela, has to improve. Of course being the prudent, savvy politician that he has shown himself to be, one can be assured he will succeed and that the means he will enlist to achieve such a socioeconomic recovery, will closely follows the patterns of formal and classic economic development. Moreover, one can be doubly sure that education will be one of the keynote features of a South African recovery program.

In a manner similar to that illustrated in the foregoing examples, the black American community must recognize that all roads to socioeconomic improvement pass through the nation's educational system. All the paradigmatic illustrations offered above are meant to emphasize the point that changes or socioeconomic improvement efforts needed in the black American community require programs modeled upon formal theories and precepts, such as those required in a national quest for socioeconomic improvement. They also emphasize the point that random approaches, individually applied solutions, lotto's, haphazard catch-as-catch-can hustles, working in the lower-paying occupations, criminal enterprises, barbeque stands, and gang violence, will not resolve the socioeconomic inequity that currently exist—only more education will. I repeat, all roads to socioeconomic equity pass through formal education. After all is said and done, it should be repeated again. The objective of any program for improving the socioeconomic plight of the black American community must include strategies that align themselves along classic lines.

From a certain point of view, though, I suppose that one could look upon this situation and apply the optimist-pessimist test as to whether the glass is half-full, or half-empty. Are black Americans on the way up, continuing to fill higher and higher-salaried positions, or is the glass half-empty and they, black Americans that is, are thus stagnant? This predicament is essentially the equivalence of owing a great debt. The whole "debt" can be paid off by simply taking the excess number of black Americans currently employed in the low-salaried occupations and moving them to fill the deficits occupations in the higher-salaried professions. Following this line of thinking, let's proceed with the debt-to-pay metaphor. In such a scenario, the black American community is the manager of two separate accounts. As manager, it has borrowed from one account, the high-salaried occupations account—and has transferred, say because of the lack of education, the presence of racism, or because of the Jim Crow terrorists, those resources into the lower-salaried occupations account. Now that Jim Crow terrorism is no longer a threat, those resources now can be transferred from those lower-salary paying occupations into the higher salary occupations account. In one account—that of the lower-wage occupations—a surplus of roughly three million employees exist, and in the other—the high-salaried account occupations—there is an equally large shortage.

To resolve such an awesome obligation or debt would be nearly impossible if, as debtor, the black American community had no collateral assets. But in effect, it does. As indicated there are statistically more than enough employees in the lower-salaried occupations to pay off its debt to the high-salaried occupations account.

However, and continuing on with the metaphor, although numerically there are enough black Americans in the low-salaried occupations to satisfy the three-million-employee debt, those black Americans have not had sufficient education and training. In order to satisfy the qualifying requirements of the higher-salaried occupations, they would have to be reeducated and retrained. And so, even though the numbers are there, the three-million-employee debt still cannot be paid with undereducated and thus unqualified employees.

The only solution available is that the millions of undereducated and unskilled black Americans be educated and trained to meet the qualifying requirements of the high-salaried occupations. One way this can be accomplished is through a giant "get out the vote" type of call-to-education campaign. Perhaps through such an effort, the black American community may be prompted to return to school and be re-educated. Theoretically speaking, this is, of course, possible. If every black American over twenty-five rushed out and completed his education, the problem would simply go away and equity could be within the community's grasp within the amount of time it would take to complete all the qualifying education. But alas, this is not likely to happen. Black Americans are not going to rush out in huge numbers to complete their education and totally alter their lives, which, of course is understandable.

However, in the absence of an educational revival, if the black American community is to pay off its deficit of millions of employee's debt, it will have to think more in the long rather than in the short term. Under short-term thinking, all black Americans would rush out, earn their new sheepskins and begin earning salaries as doctors, lawyers, and managers. Again, whereas this is theoretically possible it is not very probable.

Under the long term approach, the black American community needs to implement a program by which it can successfully motivate at least the approximately five million one-to nine-year-olds of the twentieth generation (1986–2015) to become educated and qualified employees. The results of this effort will begin to pay off its three million-employee debt by 2026 and have full and unquestioned parity by the year 2035.

13

A MEMORIAL DAY TRIBUTE TO THE AFRICAN IMMIGRANTS

On Memorial Day each year black Americans are requested offer the following tribute to the Africans Immigrants that were conscripted into slavery in the service of the nation. The tribute is to be made in deference to all black Americans of the past, but specifically to the first generation(those 21 Africans who landed at Jamestown in 1619) through to the thirteenth generation(1846–1875). Those generations of Americans were denied the benefits of their rights as citizens, and were systematically compelled, under the color of authority, to serve their nation under a system of enslaved servitude. In tribute to those generations, we black Americans of today, or the fifteenth (1886–1915), sixteenth (1906–1935), seventeenth (1926–1955), eighteenth (1946–1975), nineteenth (1966–1995), and twentieth (1986–2015) generations initiate this annual, on-going Memorial Day tribute in their honor.

The memorial observance proposed by this commentary is organized much like a Jewish Seder, or Passover meal. It should open with the reading of Thomas Jefferson's accusation against King George III and the British Parliament's participation in the enslavement of the peoples of Africa.

After that reading biblical passages may also be read.

Just before the memorial meal, each participant is to symbolically experience the distaste that our ancestors held toward their enslavement. This symbolic act is accomplished by tasting the oil of the *ricanus communis* plant. The principal main symbolism of tasting the oil is its distastefulness; the collateral symbolism calls for renewal. It prompts black Americans to expunge their lives of old habits and ways that would obstruct or inhibit their progress.

The *ricanus communis* tree grows throughout the countries of West Africa. The oil is processed from the seeds of the plant, is marketed in American as castor oil. It is sold under an assortment of labels.

After that comes the eating of the traditional meal. The current practice within the black American community of eating a "traditional" meal on New Years Day is very appropriate for this occasion. That meal, routinely served on New Year's Day should be re-dedicated as the memorial meal. The preparation of its traditional dishes of corn bread, ham hocks, chitterlings, yams, okra, black-eyed peas, greens, etc., should be continued as these dishes are representative of the basic foods available to our ancestors during their enslavement.

The recommended day for this event is the first day of January of each year. It is selected for two reasons. First, we wish to acknowledge the first day in January as the effective date of the Emancipation Proclamation. Secondly, we acknowledge that the first day of January because it has become something of a New Year's tradition for black American families to eat a traditional meal on this day. At the end of the commemorative observance, the first two paragraphs of the Emancipation Proclamation should be read before all.

Therefore, the suggested order and details are as follows.

Act One

The program is to be opened by singing, or reading the lyrics from the song by James Weldon Johnson, Lift Every Voice And Sing, known as the "anthem" of the black American community:

Lift Every Voice And Sing
James Weldon Johnson

Lift ev'-ry voice and sing, till earth and heav-en ring,
Ring with the har-mo-nies of lib-er-ty;
Let our re-joic-ing rise, high as the lis-tening skies,
Let it re-sound loud as the roll-ing sea.

Sing a song full of the faith that the dark past has taught us,
Sing a song full of the hope that the pres-ent has brought us;
Fac-ing the ris-ing sun of our new day be-gun,
Let use march on till vic-to-ry is won.

Ston-y the road we trod, bit-ter the chast-ning rod,
Felt in the days when hope un-born had died,
Yet with a stead-y beat, have not our wea-ry feet,

Come to the place for which our fa-thers sighed?
We have come o-ver a way that with tears has been wa-tered,
We have come, tread-ing our path thro' the blood of the slaugh-tered,
Out from the gloom-y past, till now we stand at last
Where the white gleam of our bright star is cast.

God of our wea-ry years, God of our si-lent tears,
Thou who hast brought us thus far on the way;
Thou who hast by Thy might, Led us in-to the light,
Keep us for-ev-er in the path, we pray.

Lest our feet stray from the places, our God, where we met Thee,
Lest our hearts, drunk with the wine of the world, we for-get Thee;
Shadowed be-neath Thy hand, may we for-ev-er stand,
True to our God, true to our na-tive land.

Act Two

The next item—to be read from Thomas Jefferson's article implicating King George III and Great Britain in the abduction and enslavement of the Africans in the North American colonies:

"He has waged cruel war against human nature itself, violating its most sacred rights of life and liberty in the persons of distinct peoples, who never offended him; captivating and carrying them into slavery in another hemisphere to incur miserable death in their transport thither. This piratical warfare, the opprobrium of infidel powers, in the warfare of the Christian King of Great Britain. Determined to keep open market where MEN should be bought and sold, he has prostituted his negative for suppressing every legislative attempt to prohibit or to restrain this execrable commerce.

In every stage of these Oppressions, We have Petitioned for Redress, in the most humble terms; Our repeated Petitions, have been answered only by repeated injury, A Prince, whose character is thus marked by every act which may define a Tyrant, is unfit to be the ruler of a free People."

Act Three

Next, the reading of this passage from the Emancipation Proclamation"

"That on the first day of January, in the year of our Lord one thousand eight hundred and sixty-three, all persons held as slaves within any State, or designated part of a State, the people whereof shall then be in rebellion against the United States, shall be then, thenceforward, and forever free; and the Executive Government of the United States, including the military and naval authority thereof, will recognize and maintain the freedom of such persons, and will do no act or acts to repress such persons, or any of them, in any efforts they may make for their actual freedom.

ABRAHAM LINCOLN   L. S./ WILLIAM H. SEWARD, Secretary of State."

Act Four

Next, tasting of the *ricanus communis* seed oil. Tasting of the oil is to be administered by the most senior woman, or women present during the ceremony. It is suggested that the oil be removed from the commercially labeled bottle and placed into a ceremonial dish or container. It is further suggested that each participant taste the *ricanus communis* oil issued onto their tongue with a silver spoon.

Act Five

Eating of the traditional meal of ham hocks, chitterlings, yams, okra, black eyed peas, greens, corn bread, sweet potato pie, etc.

Act Six

The memorial is to be closed by the most senior male present with the reading of these words from W. E. B. DuBois' *The Gift of Black Folk*:

"Who made America?

"Who made this land that swings its empire from the Atlantic to the Sea of Peace and from Snow to Fire—this realm of New Freedom, with Opportunity and Ideal unlimited?

"Now that its foundations are laid, deep but bare, there are those as always who would forget the humble builders, toiling wan mornings and blazing noons, and picture America as the last reasoned blossom of mighty ancestors; of those great and glorious world builders and rulers who know and see and do all things forever and ever, amen! How singular and blind! For the glory of the world is the possibilities of the common place and America is America even because it shows, as never before, the power of the common ordinary, unlovely man. This is real democracy and not that vain and eternal striving to regard the world as the abiding place of exceptional genius with great black

waste of hereditary idiots. We who know may not forget but must forever spread the splendid sordid truth that out of the most lowly and persecuted of men, Man made America. And that what Man has here begun with all its want and imperfection, with all its magnificent promise and grotesque failure will some day blossom in the souls of the Lowly."

ABOUT THE AUTHOR

Les Washington attended college at the California State University in Fullerton, California where he studied Comparative Literature. He later switched majors and received a BA Degree in English.

He spent an additional two years at the California University in Fullerton doing Post-Graduate work majoring in American Studies. Writing has always been Les's aspirations, and "Generations" is a fulfillment of that aspiration. Les began working on "Generations" in September of 1991. It was substantially completed in 1994.

Generation, as a commentary, is the result of the author's intense passion for the black American Community. The book represents the course, or growth path, that Les envisions for the American people and in particular for the black American Community.

While Generations is not put forth as an academic work of professorial scholarship, the author does feel strongly that it is a work of sound social and cultural merit and one that warrants the attention of every American.

Les has two daughters and two granddaughters. He has lived in Costa Mesa, California, for the past 20 years.

BIBLIOGRAPHY

Allen, Robert L., *Black Awakening in Capitalist America*. Garden City, New York, Anchor Books, 1970.

Ardrey, Robert, *African Genesis*. New York, Dell Publishing Co. Inc., 1972.

Atkinson, Carolyn, et al., *Black Psychology*. New York, Harper & Row, Publishers, 1972

Bennett, Lerone, Jr., *Before the Mayflower* (revised ed.). Baltimore, Penguin Books, 1966.

Blum, John M., Catton, Bruce, Morgan, Edmund S., Schlesinger, Jr., Stampp, Kenneth, Woodward, C. Vann, *The National Experience*. Harcourt, Brace & World, Inc., Chicago, Ill.,1968.

Burke, James, *Connections*. Boston, Little Brown and Company, 1978.

Campbell, Fleming, & Grote, *Discipline Without Punishment at Last*. Harvard Business Review, July-August, 1985.

Catton, Bruce, *This Hallowed Ground*. New York, Pocket Books, 1967.

Darwin, Charles, *The Origin of Species*. New York, The New American Library of World Literature, 1964.

Davidson, Basil, *A History of Central Africa*. Garden City, New York, Anchor Books, 1969.

Davidson, Basil, *A History of East Africa*. Garden City, New York, Anchor Books, 1966.

Davidson, Basil, *A History of West Africa*. Garden City, New York, Anchor Books, 1966.

Douglass, Frederick, *Narrative of the Life of Frederick Douglass*. An American Slave, New York, New American Library, 1968.

Dougherty, James, and Yoseloff, Thomas, *The Magna Carta*. New York, Random House, 1957.

Drotning, Phillip T., *Black Heroes in Our Nation's History*. New York, Washington Square Press, 1970.

Du Bois, W. E. Burghardt, *The Gift of Black Folk: Negroes in the Making of America*. New York, Washington Square Press, 1970.

Du Bois, W. E. Burghardt, *The Souls of Black Folk*. Greenwich, Connecticut, Fawcett Publications, Inc., 1961.

Fage, J. D., *Africa Discovers Her Past*. London, Oxford University Press, 1971.

Fanon, Frantz, *The Wretched of the Earth*. New York, Grove Press, 1968.

Franklin, John Hope, *From Slavery to Freedom*. New York, Alfred A. Knopf, 1974.

Fromm, Erich, *The Anatomy of Human Destructiveness*. Greenwich, Connecticut, A Fawcett Crest Book, 1973.

Haley, Alex, Roots, *The Saga of an American Family*. New York, Dell Publishing, 1977.

Harris, Joseph E., *Africans and Their History*. New York, New American Library, 1972.

Huchton, Laura M., *Protect Your Child*. Pennington, N.J. Princeton-Hall, Inc., 1985

Lifton, Robert Jay, *Boundaries*. New York, Vintage Books, 1969.

Lewis, R. W. B., *The American Adam*, Chicago, The University of Chicago Press, 1975.

Maslow, Abraham, *Toward a Psychology of Being*. New York, D. Van Nostrand Company, 1968.

Moliere, *Le Misanthrope*. 1666, Act III, sc. vii.

Mondlane, Eduardo, *The Struggle for Mozambique*. Middlesex, England, Penguin Books, 1970.

Moore, Clark D. & Dunbar, Ann, Ed., New York, Bantam Pathfinder, 1972.

Oliver, Roland, and Fage, J. D., *A Short History of Africa*. Middlesex, England, Penguin Books, 1970.

Oliver, Roland, *The Dawn of African History*. New York, Oxford University Press, 1968.

Plato, *Five Great Dialogues*. Roslyn, New York, Walter J. Black, Inc., 1942.

Robinson, James Harvey, and Brested, James Henry, *Outlines of European History*, Part I. Ginn and Company, New York, 1914.

Robinson, James Harvey, *Medieval and Modern Times*. Ginn and Company, New York, 1919.

Roth, Phillip, *Portnoy's Complaint*. Bantam Books, New York, 1970.

Schachner, Nathan, *Thomas Jefferson*. Random House, New York, 1956.

Staples, Robert, *The Black Family*. Belmont, California, Wadsworth Publishing Company, 1971.

Tate, Cecil F., *The Search for a Method in American Studies*. Minneapolis, University of Minnesota Press, 1973.

——, *The New National Baptist Hymnal*. Nashville, Tennessee, National Baptist Publishing Board, 1980.

Twombly, Robert C., *Blacks in White America Since 1865.* New York, David McKay Company, Inc., 1971.

Unger, Merrill F., *Unger's Bible Handbook.* Chicago, Moody Press, 1967.

U. S. Census Bureau, Current Population Survey, March 2000, Racial Statistics Population Division

U. S. Census Bureau, Public Information Office

U. S. Department of Justice, Bureau of Justice Statistics

Van Doren, Carl, *The Great Rehearsal.* New York, Viking Press, 1967.

Vansina, Jan, *Kingdoms of the Savanna.* Madison, University of Wisconsin Press, 1970.

Washington, Booker T., *Up From Slavery.* New York, Bantam Pathfinder, 1970.

Webster, Staten, *The Education of Black Americans.* New York, Intext Educational Publishers, 1974.

Woodson, Carter G., *Mis-education of the Negro.* Washington, DC, The Associated Publishers, Inc., 1969.

Wells, H.G. *The Outline of History. Vol. II*, Garden City, Garden City Books, 1961.

Willie, Charles V., Kramer, Bernard M., and Brown, Bertram S., ed., *Racism and Mental Health.* Pittsburgh, Pennsylvania: University of Pittsburgh Press, 1973.

——, Tuesday Magazine, *Black Heroes in World History.* Bantam Books, New York, 1969.

Zaide, Gregorio F. and Sonia, *Philippine History & Government.*------------
----

0-595-25386-5

Made in the USA
San Bernardino, CA
24 August 2018